Millennial Munros

A Postman's Round

Charlie Campbell

Ringwood Publishing
Glasgow

First published in Great Britain in 2017 by
Ringwood Publishing
Glasgow
www.ringwoodpublishing.com
e-mail mail@ringwoodpublishing.com

ISBN 978-1 901514-33-9

British Library Cataloguing-in Publication Data
A catalogue record for this book is available from the British Library

Typeset in Times New Roman 11
Printed and bound in the UK
by
Lonsdale Direct Solutions

This Book is dedicated to Charlie's Angel – my mother Madge, whose unending love and support over the years has been immeasurable.

Contents

Prologue

Long ago in a faraway place, lived a little boy. Avid pursuits like mini-rugby, fishing, and messing about on his bike occupied the boy's spare time but that didn't stop him from having athletic dreams. Top class sprinting was forlorn, middle and long distance running as much a pipe dream. However, the flame of athletic endeavour wasn't totally extinguished, it was only turned down to that of a little pilot light, burning in the background in the hope that one day something would come along to fully ignite it and let it burn bright…

Part I: The Background

1 – The School Years

Like any journey, we must start at the very beginning. Like most people, my first introduction to the countryside came through my parents. Going for a 'run in the country' in the car at weekends was fun and exciting. A picnic out at Mugdock or Carbeth was far enough for me, being about a twenty minute drive from Glasgow's West End.

During my primary school years I did nothing athletic apart from weekly gym classes and the annual sports day each June. It's fair to say that at this time I was average at anything sporting but I did harbour a competitive eagerness. So much so that in Primary 6, about a week before the sports day, I went to the local school playing field to practice some short sprints and a couple of four hundred metre runs. I was disappointed to find a week later I couldn't win an event outright, only second or third place at best.

This theme followed me into secondary school for the first three years. A trip to the school's holiday cottage in 1983 found me climbing a few of the Cairngorm giants and also Ben Nevis, but I must admit that they were just long slogs and I wasn't overly inspired. Around this time I also did my first fifty miler on the bike when a school friend and I had an argument about who was the better cyclist (I won). I quite liked cycling and especially watching the Tour de France on television. I didn't really go out on the bike that much though. In those days it was more for a purpose than a training stint, such as when I cycled along the busy A82 to the River Leven in my big wellies and fishing gear on my old lady's upright bike – what a sight I must have looked.

The change came in 1984. That year, I remember as a sunny summer, or maybe I just got lucky with the weather on my various trips. As a sprightly fourteen year old, I was very fortunate that Kelvinside Academy had lots of extracurricular activities including the Combined Cadet Force. Easter 1984 found a large group of us on Arran. I left knowing that there

3

was something about the high ruggedness of the mountains that I was attracted to.

Other events that summer led to what was going to be a metamorphosis for myself. At the end of June, after term ended, I was down at my first camp with the CCF at RAF Shawbury. Part of the training was an evening run, a race in full coveralls (basically a cotton overall) for five miles through the lanes and roads of rural Shropshire. I found the run difficult, finishing about eightieth out of one hundred and twenty. Maybe not immediately at the time but, in retrospect, I remember thinking that I would not allow myself to struggle so much during a run, or in any event for that matter. A few weeks later, I found myself, mother Madge, sister June and brother Colin, making our first attempt at the West Highland Way, ninety-five miles along Scotland's busiest long-distance path between Glasgow and Fort William. This went fine for the first two days to Cashel campsite, but my sister had caught a bug and was vomiting at four o'clock in the morning in the close confines of our tent – lovely. We returned to Glasgow. I was very disappointed at not completing the walk, so my mother asked her brother if he would take me along for a second attempt.

Uncle Brian had been one of the first people I had heard of to walk the West Highland Way, back in 1982, and he had also been one of the first participants in the running boom of the early eighties, so he was an inspiration to me. Walking with him was going to be a challenge and he showed no leniency to the young neophyte of long distance walking. Four days after starting from Glasgow, we found ourselves in Fort William and although I was blistered and had found it hard, the fourteen-year old was happy and the sense of achievement was high. This was enhanced on the bus journey home when I gazed in wonder at the mighty peaks of Glencoe.

That August, another holiday school trip found us climbing the most northerly Munro, Ben Hope in Sutherland, on yet another beautiful sunny day. I can vividly remember that, having climbed it, I started walking faster on the descent, passing school mates along the way, until about three quarters of the way down, there was only one friend a hundred yards ahead. I wanted to catch him before the finish but he was as competitive as I was and the final stretch down to the road saw us both sprinting flat out in our big army boots, all for the glory of being first back to the minibus.

4

Another school year started, and with it, my endeavour to get fit. The first few attempts were laughable, grinding to a halt after a mile with a stitch in the side and having to walk home. However, perseverance is the key and with just a few runs each week, my fitness gradually picked up and I managed to continue this right through the winter.

Into 1985 and as the number of runs increased each week, so did my fitness levels. All the running paid off when I went again to summer camp at RAF Locking and this time I won the cadets' road race. I could hardly believe it, but it had shown me the importance of training. The only other highlights of that summer were managing to pass all my 'O' grades and walking the West Highland Way twice: once with Mum and Colin in five and a half days, and then on my own in three days – all because I'd broken the camera on the first trip and had to do it again to take photos for my Higher Geography project the following year.

Gradually the running continued to improve, but my first double training day of five and a half miles in the morning and seven and a half miles in the evening was a bit over-zealous for a growing fifteen-year old. Still, if that's what the 'real' runners did, then I wanted to try it. Apart from running, I took part in a wide variety of other sports and in the following summer I managed to get my glider pilot's licence. It was also around this time that I became more aware of the sport of fell running. I had previously read a magazine article on Joss Naylor and the black and white photograph of this lean and weathered hard man of the hills looked intriguing to me. My interest increased when I saw a short television clip about Kenny Stuart, one of the best hill runners in Britain at the time, and thought it was amazing how he ran over the hill and away from the rest of the field and then skipped down the other side. It immediately struck me that this was freedom – you could almost fly in this sport.

My hill walking had continued with the school trip each Easter to Arran and after leaving Year 6 in June 1987, I walked the West Highland Way two further times that summer, making me a veteran of five West Highland Way walks by the age of seventeen. All this experience would be put to good use in the years to come. I'd read somewhere that there were people out there who could actually run the whole route continuously from start to finish – wow! Now that really did catch my attention.

2 – The Big Bad World

With the school years over, the next period in my life were grey years as far as training, running, hills and also life were concerned. I started a degree course but didn't like a couple of the subjects so after first year I dropped out; maths and physics were never really my forte. Not knowing what to do next, I started a Business Studies course, however,the same scenario resulted with me failing most of the exams the following year. Industrial relations and economics were just not me.

Thus the end of 1989 saw me unemployed and 'signing on', a process which would become familiar over the next few years. Employment Training at that time did have some worthwhile courses so I found myself enrolling on a Health and Fitness Instructor's course. The training venue was one of the best equipped health clubs in Glasgow and with only one day a week of formal teaching from Moray House PE lecturers, this left plenty of time for my own personal training. My brother had bought a basic barbell and dumbbell set a few years earlier and with his initial enthusiasm waning, he sold it to me. Delving into the rudimentaries of weight training, both in theory and practice, after a couple of years of training at home I'd managed to put on a little bit of muscle to my basically ectomorph (skinny) frame. Now with free rein in a huge gym, I made the most of it and although still doing some running, I got more into weight training.

This was more appropriate for my course anyway as I already had a good grounding in the principles of cardiovascular training, but had to build on the knowledge of strength and muscular systems. Build I did, both physically and mentally. By the spring of 1991, I was a fully-fledged fitness instructor with grand ideas of personal training. Being self-employed, the stark reality was that I was still unemployed and signing on. Another year later found me taking further fitness qualifications through a private company at a rather large price, and although I got work instructing and leading a few classes here and there, nothing much developed. During all this time, I'd only gone out on the odd hillwalk on my own, or with my friend Iain Barr from my school days.

The outdoor scene changed in many ways for me in 1993. Firstly, I still had an enthusiasm for long distance endurance events despite the fact that I didn't actually do any and wasn't that clued up about them either. I rose early one cold and bright Sunday morning in February, put on a lightweight pair of Hi-Tec trail boots and tracksuit bottoms, packed some basics into an old canvas rucksack, threw on a fleece top and got Mum to drop me at the start of the West Highland Way in Milngavie. Jogging slowly for about seven miles to where the route crosses the main road before Gartness, I then walked and jogged along the undulating A81 all the way to Callander to visit my gran. By the time I got there I was caked in salt and sweat, every moving area chaffed to bits, and virtually unable to walk with cramped and seized muscles. Taking several minutes to lower myself into a bath that she had kindly offered, and wincing as the water stung the raw skin, with about twenty-nine miles completed, I thought maybe I wasn't cut out for this long distance malarkey after all.

I had begun yet another course in the January of that year but this one was going to be the most influential. The Prince's Trust Course for volunteers lasted for twenty weeks and gave me a great taste of several areas I had not experienced before: conservation work, helping out with physically and mentally disabled groups, and so on. Best of all, it brought back my old love of the Great Outdoors. This was what I'd been missing since my school days and helping out for two weeks at the Glencoe Outdoor Centre with youth groups was a delight. Having finished my twenty week course, I continued to volunteer at the Maryhill base as assistant team leader, working with the next group of volunteers. I really enjoyed this and I decided that I should apply for an Outdoor Education Degree.

I applied in September 1993 and got a very good recommendation from my Prince's Trust team leader, Graeme. Despite this being a very competitive course, I was invited to interview in the February of 1994. By this time, however, I had started two part-time jobs, one with Alzheimer's Scotland and the other as a physiotherapist's assistant in the NHS. I have very few regrets in life; anything that doesn't work out as planned I just put down to experience and move on. But not doing that course is one decision I do regret, repeat for effect, I DO REGRET. I remember being totally objective and thinking things through. I decided to stick with my part-time jobs and to withdraw my application. I can't remember exactly how I justified it to myself at the time – probably the money – but despite getting a third part-time job, by the end of 1994 I was again unemployed and going nowhere fast. As Del Boy in *Only Fools and Horses* would say, 'What a plonker!'

In September 1993, however, I still believed that I was going for the Outdoor Education course. I knew that one of the requirements for the Summer Mountain Leader certificate was to keep a logbook of at least forty days hillwalking, preferably on big hills like the Munros. I therefore bought myself a blank notebook and decided to be a bit more dedicated and analytical in my hill exploits. This started very hesitantly, with one day of walking and one Munro logged in September and a whopping two days and four Munros in October.

In November, more influentially, I had been down at a party in Bedfordshire one Saturday and drove home on the Sunday to find my father had recorded some programme about 'two guys who had done the Munros in a one-er, or something like that.' I was reasonably interested and since I was doing nothing else, thought I'd give it a look. Over the course of the next hour, I watched how this duo beat the record for the quickest round of the two hundred and seventy-seven Munros. I was amazed that they had managed it in an incredible fifty-one days. Then and there I had this feeling that I had at last found a purpose. Here was something that I really believed, from the instant I saw it, that I could achieve. I knew that I was never going to break the one hundred metres record or marathon record, or any other record for that matter, but something about this was different and the fact that it was all played out in the beautiful and rugged hills of Scotland was perfect for me. Maybe, just maybe, this was finally it.

3 – The Learning Curve

With the spark of the dream ignited, I realised that this project would take years. I first wanted to walk all the Munros and build up my running distances.

Having always wanted to run a full marathon, in April 1994 I entered the Lochaber event with about three weeks' notice. Having not run any big distances, I went out and completed twenty odd miles for a training run and then rested up. My cousin's stag party the night before certainly didn't help and the following day I suffered but still managed to run three hours fifty-four minutes, which I felt was okay considering the circumstances.

During the previous few years I had completed one or two wee hill runs, mainly up and down Dumgoyne in the Campsie Fells. By chance I'd been browsing in one of the outdoor shops in Glasgow and came across a Scottish Hill Running calendar for the year. I glanced through it and there before me were the details of the West Highland Way race. Having heard about this race since my late teens, I'd always thought it would be amazing to actually attempt it and now here was my chance. I couldn't resist and I managed to get a late entry.

Two months later on the nearest Saturday to midsummer, we kicked off at three o'clock in the morning from Milngavie with light rain and, in typical Scottish style, the rain just got heavier all day. I had been going steady, walking/jogging for about forty miles, but then the rot set in and I slowly started grinding to a halt. At Tyndrum, I got some warm clothes and food, and my brother, Colin, joined me on the stretch to Bridge of Orchy. By this time I just couldn't run, so after a slow walk, the race marshal informed me that I was in last place and the race was being stopped at the next stage, Kingshouse Hotel, due to the unrelenting conditions – runners were being pulled out with hypothermia and exposure. Knowing the condition I was in and not wanting a slow plod over Rannoch Moor in the darkness, I decided to call it a day and head for home. Thus ended my first taste of ultra-distance and I was quite happy with my total of sixty miles.

The Munros really started for me when I teamed up with two friends to go for a hillwalk in April 1994.We arranged for a jaunt up Ben Vorlich at Loch Earn and that was the start of what was to become a most adventurous journey for this trio. Personally speaking, I had only logged a handful of Munros up to that point, but I have to admit I got bitten by the bug big-style in May 1994 and became a dedicated bagger. Nothing magic had happened, no great turning point, just something that made me want to go out every weekend and see how many Munros I could climb.

Once a week I did an overnight shift as a carer and it gave me time to read. For hours, I would ponder my guidebook on the Munros, enjoying the photos of these beautiful hills in far away places that I was going to visit and taking in all the routes and stats as best I could. Reading *Hamish's Mountain Walk* was inspirational too. In 1974, he had completed a continuous round of the Munros, the first person to do so. Thus started my Munro campaign.

A few part-time jobs kept me going through 1994 but at year's end I had nothing. A full-time sales job I thought I had didn't pan out. This theme continued into 1995 with various driving jobs providing enough money to keep me and fund my weekend sorties and a few beers along the way. That was all I really wanted at that point. Our Munro tally together certainly grew quite quickly and by the year end I was sitting on one hundred and seventy-one. I also had another go at the West Highland Way race that year but I jogged at too fast a pace and this time I was totally seized-up by Tyndrum; I hadn't yet learned the secret of pacing and electrolytes.

Along came 1996 and a bit of a brewer's droop hit my Munro score. Needless to say a woman was involved, this lady having quite a pronounced effect on myself and my lifestyle. The result of our intense relationship was that I didn't get out to the hills as often as I wished and my hill fitness suffered. However, in the June of the year I managed a personal victory.

I entered the race again and totally revamped my whole race strategy. My plan was to start much slower and do longer stretches of walking, and since I'd been devouring information on the importance of salts in ultra events, I drank loads of fluid and electrolyte replacement. This worked nicely and with Mum joining me for the last fourteen miles, I was over the moon as I jogged into Fort William on a sunny Sunday morning. Ninety-five miles and over eleven thousand feet of climbing in just under thirty hours was good enough for me. I'd also learned the importance of psychology in this race, as I had been looking forward from the start to meeting my girlfriend, who was coming up to support me in the second half of the race, and also one of my best friends, Mark Pacitti. I was determined to keep going until I saw them and then when I did, it gave me the boost I needed to keep me going to the end. This type of psychological boost also turned out to be an important factor when the Munro run came around.

The shackles of what had become a doomed relationship were broken in the first few days of the New Year. I returned to my training and hills with vigour but at twenty-seven, I was feeling like the days of youth were rapidly disappearing. I decided I'd better knuckle down and sort out my life. I had by this point become self-employed, and once I'd fulfilled my daily duties of administration, I had ample time to think about things. I was sure that I still wanted to have a go at the Munro record and I made this my primary goal; everything else in my life was going to be planned around it. The first thing to do was to actually finish walking my first round, so I looked at the hills we had left and I made out a schedule for the rest of the year for Ian, Iain, and I. The three of us had a rekindled zest and most weekends saw us out hitting the hills with some of our biggest walks to date.

A little incident in March, however, brought home to me the frailty of the game – not the hill game – the whole big game!

It was Ian MacPherson's turn to drive and he collected Iain and myself. We headed up the A82 early on a cold and crisp morning. Cresting the high point of the road, going round a corner, I felt the back end of the car gradually swing out and it just kept going. Instantly, the three of us knew we were in for a sore one and I'll always remember the sound of our slight wails as we left the side of the road at around forty miles per hour. The car left the embankment slightly airborne, then hurtled across the top of the heather and stones for a good distance before a huge thud saw us come to an immediate halt. I was in the back seat and not wearing the seat belt. I slammed into the back of the passenger seat, eating the headrest for breakfast. We were all okay, however, and upon seeing large plumes

11

of steam and smoke coming from the engine, we evacuated the car like Olympic sprinters.

We watched the car for a few minutes. Realising it was not going to explode, we tentatively made our way back, shaken and definitely stirred. Inspecting the scene, we saw how lucky we had been. The car's marks could be seen through the heather. It had miraculously jumped a large concrete drainage ditch that had been in our path. Maybe not wearing my seat belt had been a blessing in disguise, as looking inside the car, I could see that the rear seats had split and been pushed forward with the momentum, and all our gear in the boot had partly forced it's way into the rear seating compartments. The engine was sitting about eight inches higher than normal, and at the bottom was a huge boulder which the car had hit and which had smashed the sump, splitting the lower engine in two. I can truly say that the car was a write-off, but the story doesn't end there.

Having calmed down, we walked back up to the roadside. Upon reaching the tarmac, the three of us flew off in different directions doing Torvill & Dean impersonations and we knew immediately what had caused the accident – black ice everywhere. The plan was that Ian and Iain would walk the half-mile back to the top of the road to try and get reception on the mobile phone, and I would stay with the car and look after all our expensive gear. I walked back down to the car and poured myself a large cup of coffee from my Thermos flask, adding an equally large measure from my 'emergency' hip flask of whisky. I sipped my coffee and enjoyed the strong taste of the whisky whilst gazing out at the view: beautiful snow-capped hills were glinting in the early morning sunshine and looking down the length of Loch Loyne, they were perfectly reflected on the flat blue waters, matched by our smashed blue Ford Escort in the foreground – a truly glorious morning to have a crash.

As I stood by the car, I noticed several other motorists slow down and look but no-one stopped to offer help. After a while, however, a car passed then turned around and came back and stopped. Two young ladies got out and offered their assistance. They were French exchange teachers based in England and up for a couple of week's holiday in Scotland. After nearly an hour chatting they said they had to be on their way. Just as we were exchanging hugs and kisses goodbye, Ian and Iain arrived back in a police car. I remember the look on their faces as I explained how I had innocently come to be in their embrace. Iain and myself were at the roadside waving goodbye when suddenly there was a loud whack and cracking noise. We looked at each other and said, 'Surely not,' but found they had got too close to the police car and smashed the wing mirror on the way past. One of them ran back, had a quick word with the police driver and then went back to her car and was off like a shot.

With the statements and formalities done, the recovery truck duly arrived and somehow managed to pull the wreck from its semi-entombment in the moorside. We were then taken to Fort Augustus and the car was deposited at the local garage where we made our phone calls home. Our lift, coming from Airdrie, was not going to arrive for several hours so there was only one thing to do – hit the pub. The slight problem was at eleven on a cold Sunday morning, there wouldn't be many pubs open in Fort Augustus. A dishevelled trio, we wandered around looking like we had been dragged across a hillside backward. Since that was basically the truth it helped us get a sympathetic response from the barman at The Loch Inn. The doors were locked and we were just turning away when he came by; although he wasn't officially opening until midday, he opened the backdoor to the pub and let us in. A pint and a whisky each, and as we watched the barman start a warming fire for us, we toasted our own survival. Four hours later and thoroughly warmed, Ian's brother, David, found us and took us home.

That night whilst getting ready for bed and still running high on emotion and alcohol, I started crying and found it difficult to control myself. Okay, so it hadn't been a major accident, but it hit home to me how easily it could all have been so different. All my cares and wants and my daft little life could have been over and that would have been it, no second chance, no second nothing. My favourite motto of *carpe diem* would certainly have much more significance from this time on.

4 – Joining the Clubs

A couple of weeks later, I was driving through Glen Shiel when some deer ran out from the side of the road. Despite screeching tyres, I hit one side-on, the poor beast landing on the bonnet, rolling up onto the roof then shooting back off the front again when the car skidded to a halt. It hit the road with quite a thump. Miraculously the tough brute got up and ran off to join the herd, but the front wing of the car and the headlight didn't have such a lucky escape. The real damage was psychological, however, after years of trouble free journeys north, two accidents in two weeks left me a nervous wreck and I was a very wary driver for the next few months. Despite these little distractions, our hillwalking exploits were progressing nicely for an end-of-1997 Munro finish. Around April, I'd decided I'd better improve my hill running skills, so I entered the Ben Lomond hill race.

Alisdair Campbell (no relation) replied and, noticing that I lived locally, invited me to come along and run with Westerlands Cross Country Club, who met at Anniesland, less than a mile from my house. Having always read the race results in the paper, I already knew the club name. This was mainly due to one runner in particular, a certain Mark Rigby, who for years had been winning hill races and was also associated with ultra-distance hill events. I figured that if this guy was in the club, then it was the one for me: you only learn from the best. On my first Wednesday club night I was made very welcome and I could hardly believe how genuinely pleasant and down to earth everyone was. Keen to get really fit and start doing interval training again, my second week found me at the old Westerlands track and on this Tuesday evening there was only the two of us, Mark and myself. Doing four hundred metre repetitions, Mark was allowing me a large head start and during one rep, as he was catching up, it hit me that here I was having the privilege to train with a British Internationalist – this was great stuff.

My fitness levels built up nicely with steady weeks of Tuesday intervals, Wednesday club runs, Thursday hill reps, and big Munro days at the weekends, when the West Highland Way race came around again, the training paid off and I managed to take four hours from my previous year's time and clock twenty-five hours fifty-three minutes; certainly a good improvement, but still outside the magical one day barrier. Another notable point of the summer was when my uncle Brian informed me that they had just added another few Munros to the list – 'Yeah, very funny,' I said. That was until I read the paper the next day which had the story that there were indeed new Munros. But how? The Scottish Mountaineering Club had made a revision of Munro's Tables so that eight summits had now been granted Munro status and one deleted, giving a new total of two hundred and eighty-four. Luckily Ian, Iain, and I had already covered three of these and could add in the additional five in upcoming walks, so it wasn't a problem for us.

The theme for me for the rest of the year was basically hill races one weekend and big Munro days on the next weekend, and as we approached winter, the excitement began to build for the three of us. Our tally crept into the high two-hundreds. We had already decided our last Munro would be Stob Dearg on Buachaille Etive Mor on Sunday 21st December. We invited friends and family and when the day arrived, we went for it. I was thankful that the weather was relatively mild for the time of year and that there was no snow, as my mother and father were joining us for the top. Plodding along steadily, the group made their way up the corrie, turning left onto the ridge. As the summit came into view, Iain, Ian and I held back. We certainly savoured the moment as we strolled up together, with our ensemble cheering. Our final Munro, the end of a long and enjoyable campaign, and as we sipped our champagne there was a shared mutual respect for what we had been through, an appreciation all 'Compleatists' will be familiar with. There were no views that day but it didn't matter, we were all just glad to be there and to make it back down in one piece despite being a little tipsy. Thus 1997 ended, and there were no more Munros.

5 – What To Do Now?

I found out that there was indeed life after death, or more exactly, life after the Munros, and I decided that it was time to start drawing up more serious battle plans for a continuous round and record attempt. Being self-employed had a distinct advantage and I made full use of Mum's huge cloth-cutting table in our unit. It was ideal for getting all the maps out, usually four or five OS Landrangers at a time, and trying to plan the perfect route. I had already done some rough route planning by looking at an overall Scotland Munro map and dividing it down into what I thought were achievable days. I decided to use a similar overall route to that of Gibson and Johnston but I was going to make some refinements. This was dictated primarily by the number of days that I was going to aim for; since the record stood at just over fifty-one days, trying to get under the fifty-day barrier was a good start.

My reasoning at this time was also dictated by some psychology that I was going to use on myself. Since being a wee boy, my mother has always drilled into me that, 'If you are going to do a job, then do it well.' Coupled with the fact that I've always thought the saying 'Aim for the stars and you're sure to hit the moon' to be pretty sound, I decided to aim high – very high in fact. Forty days was going to be the target and although I felt comfortable with this myself, I was aware that there might be a few people who would scoff. So I kept my ambitious target to myself. Of course I would lose days to bad weather, drop time with injuries, slow up with fatigue, but surely budgeting with a ten day leeway would be enough to dip below fifty.

The route planning and logistics were going to be absolutely crucial. Having originally started with just a few lines mentioning what hills I would be attempting for a day, I realised that this wasn't good enough, especially if I was needing back-up in desolate places or, heaven forbid, a bad accident occurred. Starting again, I wrote up an A4 sheet per day of the exact route I would be attempting, with all grid references and rendezvous points, and calculating distance covered and height climbed. This was a time-consuming and laborious process but to keep me motivated, all I had to do was play 'Book of Days' by Enya, the theme tune from the Gibson & Johnston documentary, and it brought the magic of running the Munros right back to me.

The early months of 1998 passed quickly as I was absorbed in maps and trying to gain fitness again for another season. Fortunately for me, another chance happening occurred that would help out two years later. Brian Bonnyman from Westies and I were of a similar running ability and we had decided to go in for the Scottish Islands Peak Race. This involves a pair of runners, together with a yacht and a crew of three, starting from Oban, running the highest points on Mull, Jura and Arran, while sailing between the islands, finishing at Troon in Ayrshire. Hard for the sailors trying to keep awake day and night, but not exactly easy for the runners with about sixty miles and eleven thousand feet of climbing involved.

Brian and I, having safely entered as runners, now only had to find a boat to get paired up with. The organiser phoned Brian and gave him the choice of two boats: a fast trimaran, which was looking for a couple of fast runners, or a mono-hull that was looking for a couple of decent runners. Having heard some nightmare stories from runners who had been on fast boats before and not wanting to overestimate our athletic ability, we decided to go for the safer and easier option of the mono-hull, especially since this was going to be our first attempt at the race. Brian got the details and rang me back – 'You're not going to believe whose boat we are on,' and immediately carried onto tell me: 'Mr Boyd Tunnock' of biscuit fame. We met up with Boyd and crew for the race mid-May, and after an eventful weekend on wave and hill, were glad to finish, saying we'd keep in touch.

For the previous few months I'd been toying with the idea of making an attempt at a Ramsay round, a challenge of twenty-four Munros, including Ben Nevis, in twenty-four hours. Training had been going well and with a steady boat race behind me, I thought I was ready. In the intervening two weeks, however, I also completed the Isle of Jura fell race and in hindsight this did not help with recovery. Pacers organised, on the last weekend of May I set off at midnight up the Ben. I was bang on schedule at the top but it was already mild and humid and I was sweating heavily. Stevie Bell, pacing on this stage, was starting to lag behind a bit, maybe due to his heavy rucksack with four litres of fluid and gear for me.

Time had been dropped by Aonach Mor and Beag and on the stretch out to the Grey Corries, I knew things weren't going to plan. On the summit of Sgurr Choinnich Mor, about an hour down on schedule, I decided to call it quits and told Stevie, who I think was slightly relieved. We wandered along the rest of the Grey Corries and then cut through to our next meeting point at Fersit beside Loch Treig. At least I'd learned from this that, although I'd been taking electrolyte fluids, the concentration of salts in it were just not adequate for fast paced ultra-events. More worrying still was the dent in my psychology, that if I couldn't even get a quarter way through a Ramsay without blowing up, how was I going to manage a continuous Munro attempt?

The West Highland Way race was to be next, but watching the opening game of the 1998 World Cup between Scotland and Brazil in the pub put paid to that. Over-indulging that evening, I slipped down a flight of stairs and landed at the bottom with my left ankle folded at a rather interesting angle with my full weight on top of it. At least it wasn't broken, the physio told me, but it was badly swollen with some ligament damage. The race was out the window, but my club mate Manuel Gorman was attempting another big run, to celebrate our club's twenty-first anniversary. This involved going from Ben Hope to Ben Lomond with over a hundred other Munros in between. I therefore decided to help him out on a few stages and walk in with a tent and gear to some of his more remote stop-overs. I joined Manny three weeks later as he finally made it to Ben Lomond and after hearing about his trials and tribulations, I wondered if I'd be able to go through the same except on more than twice the scale. At this stage the task seemed daunting but I knew I still wanted to give it a go.

Trying to resurrect something for the later season, my final big event was the English Ironman Triathlon, to be staged down in Wolverhampton that August. At the start of July I was still only managing two or three miles easy jogging on grass, due to the ankle injury, so I was leaving myself only six weeks to get fit for a marathon and all the rest. During this time I also did as much background research as I could about ultra events and salts, and bought some electrolyte capsules from America. The ankle managed to hold up and I put in some of my best training ever for a month. Although I finished at the back of the field, I'd managed to get through nearly two and a half miles of swimming, one hundred and

18

twelve miles of cycling and twenty-six miles of running, off the back of one month's quality training. I was pleased.

Following a few smaller races, the season drew to a close with my usual lay-off in December. At this point I asked Boyd Tunnock if he would be able to help towards my Munro plan and he kindly offered some cash to put towards my costs and as many biscuits as I wanted. I'd managed to finish detailed route-planning for the run and this was a weight off my mind. At year's end, Mum and I decided to finish up with our business and self-employment. I therefore needed a job, pronto. I went down and asked at my local Royal Mail sorting office. Luckily they were looking to start people, so I was taken on as a part-time postman. The hours were quarter to six to nine thirty-five, Monday to Saturday and, apart from not earning much money, this was going to be perfect as it meant I would be up early six days a week and pounding the pavements with a heavy mail bag – good training in its own right. It also meant that I finished early and could then spend the rest of the day training and working on the logistics.

It had certainly been an interesting year and I had learned a few more lessons that would be vital for the Munro run.

6 – Party like it's 1999!

So 1999 was finally here and this was the year that I'd always planned to go for the Munro run. I started off extremely keen, getting in the training and settling into the postie job. The organisational front wasn't going too well, however. The main object was to obtain a motorhome, which was necessary for backup. In my naivety I thought this would be no problem; just state that you are doing a record-breaking attempt for a worthwhile charity, good publicity for any sponsors, and *voilà*! – a motorhome will land on your doorstep. I wrote letters to the big motorhome rental firms in Scotland and got a range of responses from none to polite refusals. I asked through friends about obtaining one and even spoke to a local guy about the possibility of hiring his but all to no avail. I felt I had tried every avenue and option and by now it was March. I knew I was pushed for time to make the decision to go ahead or not. One final incident swayed my decision.

In March, a trivial argument with my brother somehow managed to blow up into a fight and fall-out, with the result that he told me to 'Shove my bloody Munros up my arse.' This was a serious problem. All along, I had hoped to have a back-up vehicle, which would have a driver and also a co-pilot/navigator. This would mean my mother, who said she'd do the driving for the whole trip, wouldn't have someone to help her navigate. I had originally pencilled in Colin to act as navigator for about half of the planned journey, or about three weeks. Now that he had bailed out, I was left with a big headache.

I thought long and hard about the predicament I was now in and realised that too many things were not falling into place. I would have to postpone the whole thing. With the decision made, I swore to myself that I would definitely be going for it in 2000 and I would make sure that everything was sorted and in place. There would be no muck-ups next time round.

With this in mind, rather than relax for a few months, I kept working

20

away on preparation. Mum and I had come to the conclusion that we'd have to work on obtaining a motorhome. We kept an eye on the market to see if there were any up for sale at an affordable price but we just couldn't find anything suitable in our price range. In the meantime, I went on several trips up north for some reconnaissance of routes I'd planned.

What has swimming got to do with running the Munros? Well I didn't just want to do another continuous quick round. If possible I wanted to try and make it different or novel. It struck me that no-one had yet completed a one hundred percent self-propelled journey; boats in some shape or form had always been used to get to the Munros on Mull and Skye.

I therefore came up with the grand idea of swimming between the island sections, thus making my Munro round more novel and pure, – all in one fell swoop. Great idea if you are a good strong swimmer, not so great if swimming is one of your weaker disciplines, where a few dozen lengths in the local pool feels hard, never mind the sea.

I figured it made most sense to make only one island trip which would be to or from Mull to save maximum time, so I either had to start or finish on Mull. Now that swimming was part of the plan, it was obvious I would have to start on Mull so that I hit the swim on day one whilst at my strongest, with maximum upper body strength.

Consulting the map, the shortest sea crossing from Mull looked like Fishnish to Lochaline, across the Sound of Mull. When I checked the crossing in May 1999, I was a bit daunted by it. It looked a long way across, and would certainly be a very difficult swim; if there was bad weather then I could forget it as it was too exposed. Still, I heard of one or two local folk who had swum it before for charity, so at least I knew it was possible. I then met up with Philip Robertson who ran the diving school in Lochaline and made arrangements for a back-up boat the following year. I left him feeling much happier.

My route turned out in the end to be very similar to Gibson and Johnston's record round in 1992. In a nutshell, starting from Mull, my proposed journey was to complete all the more western and southern Munros, around Glen Coe, Glen Lyon, etc., head north-east to the Cairngorms, sweep back west through the Central Highlands to Skye and then the final push north to finish on Ben Hope. A nice easy few lines on paper but a world away in reality.

My other recce that summer was for my planned second sea swim of the journey. In July 1999 I went up to Glenelg to look at the short crossing to Kylerhea on Skye. What this lacked in size, it certainly made up for in quality. By my estimate, it's only five hundred metres across the channel but the water absolutely whizzes through here. Still, if this was what was written in my plan then it was going to be done.

Speaking to the ferry owner, Roddy McLeod, I told him my aim and he just looked at me with an inane grin, as if waiting for the punchline, and then appeared genuinely surprised when I told him I was serious. He was going to organise a back-up boat with crew and would work out exact times and tides and let me know; all I had to do was call him the following year, nearer the event – great!

At this time, basically a year in advance, I thought I'd better start booking up people and getting their commitment for back-up in the motorhome driven by Mum. June, my sister, was keen to lend a hand and she offered four weeks of her time and holidays and Big Iain Barr said he'd give me one week of his holidays. With these promises, I felt that some solid meat was being put on the bones of the plan and things were already starting to look more positive for doing it in 2000 despite still having no motorhome.

On the fitness front, I'd started the year well but with the run postponement, tailed off a bit after March. Brian and I participated in the Scottish Islands Peaks race again and I also started the West Highland Way race in June, but I wasn't going well and decided to call it quits at Bridge of Orchy. My main aim for the summer, however, was to have a go at the Scottish Ironman, held at Aberfeldy in the September. Just thirty of us started and a long slow swim in Loch Tay saw me emerge last by almost fifteen minutes. A gruelling bike course made me want to quit the whole thing, but passing two competitors helped with the mental battle and then a tough hilly marathon to finish saw three more survivors drop behind me. I don't think I have ever been so glad for a race to end, and my engraved finishers' glass has a proud place in my collection.

At the end of the year, with my main aims for the season under my belt, I completed a few smaller races and wound things down, allowing myself, both physically and mentally, a complete rest. Our millennium celebrations involved dragging Mum and friend, Mark McColl, up to the top of Dumgoyne Hill in the Campsies. Only a hill was fitting to welcome in such an important year of my life and we savoured the moment as the bells struck midnight and a million fireworks lit up Glasgow. It was brilliant and I was keenly philosophical, pondering what the New Year was going to bring; would it be more celebratory fireworks or a burnt-out squib in a few months time?

7 – Just Another Day and a New Millennium.

So the Champagne corks had been popped and the year 2000 got off to a flyer. I'd decided that the only option left was to hire a motorhome. With slight trepidation, Mum and I went along to Melville's Motorhomes in Glasgow. We shook hands on a very good deal. I left feeling like a huge weight had been taken off my shoulders, knowing the final large piece of the jigsaw was in place and I only had to sort out the smaller bits now – Thunderbirds were GO!

There were, however, quite a few smaller bits that had to be sorted and this again was a time-consuming process. Philip at Lochaline was in the process of selling his boat and wouldn't be able to help. He did, however, gave me the number of some other contacts and I managed to come to a deal with Alan Livingstone who said he'd arrange a back-up boat and crew for me.

I now entered a process of churning out quite a few begging letters to various companies asking if they would be willing to donate some of their products for the run. I was fortunate in the companies I received positive responses from. For instance, Porelle Drys (now Sealskinz) were providing waterproof socks that I knew would be necessary with typical Scottish 'summer' conditions. Saucony were providing my running shoes, which was great as I had used them for years and found them a good fit for my broad feet. Paramo were giving me a Trail shirt and letting me buy other items at cost price.

Training was a bit of a mixed bag at this time. January started quite well, getting back into it all after the Christmas break. February was even better, getting in the miles and some quality sessions. March and April, although very good by normal training standards, just weren't good enough. I felt I wasn't getting in enough running miles to pound the legs and I knew this would be vital for the continuous pounding they were going to take. I couldn't have been that far off course, though, as I took almost three minutes from my personal best at the Clydebank Half Marathon.

I had a slight scare in April when I went down to the Lakes with the family. I had gone on a little training run over Place Fell above Patterdale, when near the top I slipped and fell, hitting my leg off a rock in the process. I looked down and saw a hole on my right shin with copious amounts of blood pouring from it. My predicament was that I'd only carried some water in my bum-bag and had nothing to stop the bleeding. Luckily, just before I'd slipped, I'd seen some walkers descending down below me so I set off downhill after them. I caught up with the trio and asked if they could help. Whereby one man produced a Swiss Army knife, his friend produced a roll of elastic tape and the lady of the party took out a spotlessly clean white cotton handkerchief. With this in place I jogged on down the hill feeling guilty for ruining this lady's hanky. Once back in Glasgow, I got my tetanus jab topped up and had the wound treated; the bad news was that I had to avoid the swimming pool for the next few weeks until it healed over. If something like that happened during the Munro run while I was on my own, hours from help, then I could be in serious trouble, so I immediately put together a little emergency pack that would fit nicely into my running rucksack.

So April ended and from a training point of view, it was now all too late; the next few months would reflect whether I'd done enough. The idea was to wind things up with a few easier training stints in the first half of May and then allow myself two weeks of complete rest to recover fully and prepare my body for the onslaught.

The reduction in training in May freed up my time to allow me to tie up all the loose ends, and there was plenty of tying to do. I'd first approached my fellow Westerlands club-mates in March asking who would be able to lend a hand, and by mid-May, I'd sorted who was going to be able to give me company and support, covering about half of the days. I'd also decided to employ the wonders of modern technology – two mobile phones and the Internet. I wanted a website that gave all the background details about the run, but more importantly, daily updates on current progress, so that any hill company could adjust accordingly if I was up or down on schedule. The man who was charged with being my technical wizard for all this was a good friend, Mark McColl. I had met Mark through my postie job and I found out he was a keen cyclist. Being okay on the bike myself, we teamed up and often went for training runs together. Both being quite competitive, it helped to boost our fitness levels. Mark put in many hours during May to get the website built and running. He had kindly said that he would act as webmaster, but we only managed to get the website completed the day before I was leaving. With slight hiccups, it was launched on the second day of the run.

A few other areas were finalised over the last couple of months. I asked the managers at my delivery office if they would let me save all my holidays from 1999 and carry them over to 2000 so I could then have a block booking of eight weeks away from work. They normally wouldn't allow this, but both Hugh and Roddie understood that it was for a one-off special event and it would bring some publicity for Royal Mail, and so I was allowed my two months of freedom away from the pavements of Glasgow.

I'd not originally thought of doing the event for charity as I usually like to keep a low profile so that if I fail at attempting something, then I'm not letting anyone down. However, with the amount of time and effort I was putting into this project, I felt it would be stupid not to go the whole hog to try to raise some money for a worthy cause. With this in mind, it was a case of going down to the local library for a perusal of the charity listings. I thought of what charities were close to my heart and really meant something. This was relatively easy as young people and children who have terminal illnesses stir the emotions. I appreciate all the things I've been able to do and experience in life and yet for them it's not going to be possible. As I was reading through this category in the listings, one name stood out and made me take notice. I decided I would raise money for Dreams Come True charity – here I was trying to make my own personal dream come true and if, in doing so, I could raise funds for them then all the better. I contacted the relevant person and they were more than happy to have me on board, sending all the necessary promotional items; t-shirts, stickers, sponsorship forms, and the like.

With this sorted, I wanted to get some promotion and publicity for the run. It was around April time that I decided to do something about this. I thought it would be a simple case of contacting the newspapers and relevant magazines, but here I was with what I thought was a fairly worthwhile event and no-one was interested. No-one apart from big Dave Hewitt, that is.

Dave is a bit of a character in hill-walking circles, producing *The Angry Corrie* magazine or 'Hillzine' as he likes to call it, and at about six foot seven he does literally stand out from the crowd. I had known the name for several years so it was nice to finally speak to the guy when he made contact about the run. Dave at the time was writing an outdoor column for the *Scotsman* newspaper. He got all the necessary details and the column appeared in print on Saturday 27th May. At last I was feeling that someone had taken notice and that this thing was for real and going to take place.

I had also been making inquiries with regards to getting the whole record attempt filmed, as I had thought an adventure challenge of this magnitude might be fairly interesting from an armchair point of view, but again this didn't come to anything. This only left me the option of self-filming, and as Mum had wanted a video camera for years, we took the plunge and splashed out on a top of the range model. A complete printed copy of my daily run schedule was left with Mark Rigby and Brian Bonnyman, who were helping to co-ordinate back-up, Mark McColl for website updates, and Dad at home.

I started my break from work the last week of May, to allow myself seven days to tie up the very last of the loose ends. This involved running about like a blue-arsed fly meeting people, phoning people, buying all the food and a thousand and one other little items that needed done. The Scottish news came on the television and whilst deeply engrossed in an OS Landranger, my ears caught 'Caledonian MacBrayne ferry strike.' WHAT! Putting my eyes back in their sockets, I turned to the TV in total disbelief. I knew that everything had been going too smoothly, and now came the glitch.

How the hell was I going to get myself and the motorhome to Mull for my Bank Holiday Monday start? With panic bells ringing, it took me a very long time to fall asleep that night as the mind went into overdrive churning through all the possible solutions. One quick phonecall in the morning and the problem was sorted. If the strike went ahead, it would only affect the bigger ferries on the mainline routes and not the smaller ones, so I'd still be able to get to Mull from Lochaline rather than Oban.

All that was left for me to do now was to collect the motorhome from Melville's, but this didn't go smoothly either. I was originally supposed to be picking it up on the Wednesday, but I asked them if I could make it Thursday instead. Mum and I duly went out there the Thursday lunchtime and were informed that the motorhome wasn't ready; there was some problem with an electrical fuse, plus they didn't have the portable generator we had asked for. The manager paid for our lunch but when we came back an hour and a half later, the vehicle still wasn't ready. Finally, the vehicle was good, and one of the mechanics gave us our pre-hire inspection. The immediate thing that struck us was the relatively poor quality of the van, considering it was only two-years old, but there were no other motorhomes available and with two days before leaving, I was in no position to do anything else but accept it.

Having originally planned to travel up to Mull on the Friday so that we could then have a relaxing couple of days before the mayhem began, this went totally out the window because there was so much left to do. The Friday now involved buying all the food, and also still trying to finalise the website with Mark. The Saturday gave us a boost with Dave Hewitt's *Scotsman* article published but there was still more running about, buying last-minute items and trying to sort the bloody website. The preliminary packing of the motorhome started and I got to bed after two o'clock so I didn't even get a final good night's kip, which was annoying as I knew it was my last opportunity for at least six weeks.

The packing continued Sunday morning and Dad discovered the inside tread on one of the front tyres was below the legal requirement. No problem, just swap it with the spare, but then we discovered that the spare was flat. Dad went round to the local garage, where they mended the flat and inflated all the tyres to the correct pressure. With packing finally finished, my good friend, Mark Pacitti, phoned from Melbourne to wish me good luck. Mark McColl had just about sorted the website problem and came up to wave us off and then that was it; Mum, June, Shaw the dog and I finally left sunny Craigend Street at two o'clock in the afternoon. with thoughts running through my head of how soon it would be until I was back here again.

As with any Campbell family endeavour, there was one last hitch just to spice things up. I'd have to catch the ferry across Loch Linnhe at Corran at around half past four to make the six o'clock crossing from Lochaline to Fishnish on Mull. Well, we'd been on the road all of ten minutes when I suddenly remembered that I'd forgotten to pack my padded cycling shorts. This was a pain in the ass, or would literally have become so, as the first day of the schedule called for one hundred miles of cycling. So I had to get them.

Although close to home, I felt I couldn't afford anymore time wastage, so to solve the problem I decided to call Dad, tell him where the shorts were and then he could catch us up quickly in the car. When I got to Dumbarton (ten miles from home), I pulled into a lay-by and thought Dad would only be a couple of minutes behind. Ten minutes later I left, thinking that he'd catch us on the next long stretch. We drove slowly along, constantly checking the mirrors for the car. I realised that once we were further up the loch-side, Dad would never catch us with the narrower road, traffic and over-taking problems. I wrote off getting my shorts and started thinking of the pain of doing a ton on the bike sitting on a razor blade of a saddle.

By the time we got to Tyndrum I had to pull over and nip into the public loo to spend a quick penny. Back into the motorhome and ready to pull away, what drives in behind us but our red Toyota, Dad looking slightly flushed but with a smile on his face at finally catching us. The three of us could hardly believe it, and I think even my arse had a smile as Dad handed over my good cycling shorts and my old pair as well for spares. It turned out that he had no problem finding them in my wardrobe and had started off after us in the car only to realise that it was very low in petrol. He then discovered that he had no money in his pocket so had to go back to the house to get his bank card, get to a cash dispenser, fill the car and then employ his best rally-driving skills to catch us after fifty miles.

We pulled into the Corran ferry terminal at twenty to five. Luckily the ferry was still on this side, and we drove on. The first ferry was in the bag but it would still be close for catching the other at six o'clock, as the road down through Morvern isn't exactly motorway status. Steady driving was the order of the day on the winding curves, but it was enough to get us into Lochaline by ten to six; we gave a huge sigh of relief when we saw the ferry. I was looking at a vast stretch of white horses on the water, the cold air giving an extra edge, and my thoughts were definitely apprehensive. We rolled off at Fishnish and could now afford the luxury

29

of a relaxing drive through Salen and down Loch na Keal. We found a perfect spot just off the road and settled in.

June and Mum were busy with little jobs in the motorhome. I therefore took the opportunity to sneak out and have some time to myself. There were pleasant views, although the hill tops were covered in cloud, but that didn't matter as I was so happy finally to be here. Although I had envisaged this day, it had always been something far away in the future, a possible dream, but now here it was. There had been so much planning and organising and training and financing to get through, but I had managed all that and now this day was very real. I set up the camera on the tripod and, like a video-diary, recorded some thoughts and feelings of the moment. I could only give it my very best effort and see what happened.

We had some dinner, turned in for ten, and with a mixture of apprehension and excitement, I tried to get some sleep. The talking was over – it was now time for the walking.

Summary of Charlie's Route and Location of Maps

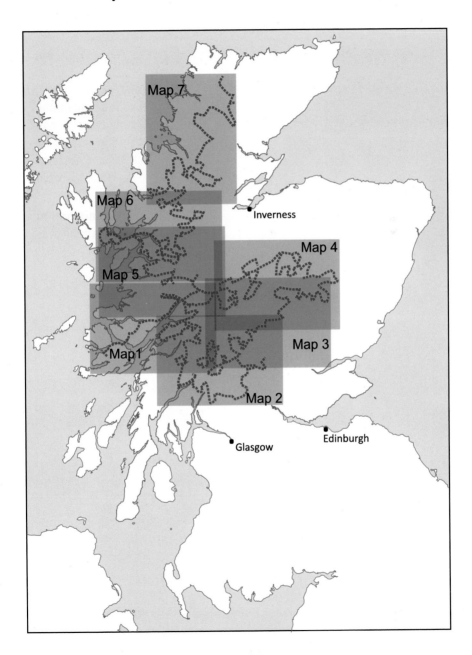

Part II: The Journey

Don't fret if you find your body cannot run. Just remember to feel the ground beneath your feet – every stone and tussock. Become part of the earth.

Week 1

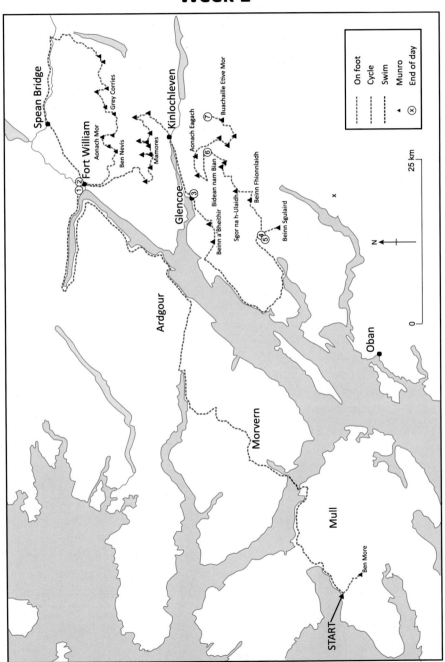

Week 1 – Too Much, Too Soon

Days 1-7

Day 1 – Monday 29 May

Trying to adapt to sleeping in the van meant that I had a fitful, restless sleep and I was up like a shot when the alarm went off at a quarter past three. June was going to join me, so we got ourselves ready and had some light breakfast and lots of coffee. With Mum now in charge of the video-camera it was certainly going to be interesting to see what the results would be. With a few final adjustments, I spoke to the camera and raised my watch to the lens to show exactly four-fifteen on Monday 29th May, 2000. Lao-Tzu may have uttered his pearl of wisdom more than two thousand five-hundred years previously but it still held true today and I stepped forward for my journey of a thousand miles. Although the clock was now ticking, there was no great rush, and June and I walked across the road, starting over the boggy ground.

We climbed steadily, chatting now and then. Once up onto the shoulder, the early morning sun started breaking through the clouds. The colours were absolutely fantastic and I was hoping that this beautiful scene was going to be a good omen for the rest of the run. Being misty at the top of Ben More, there were no views to greet us as we hit the trig point at just before six o'clock – just a rusty piece of drain pipe lying there (it's amazing what people take into the hills). June was happy at completing her first island Munro and as we crouched for the self-timer photo, I gave the finger to the camera. No, not being rude, but just signifying that one was down, only two hundred and eighty-three to go. I got back to the van at about quarter to seven. More fluids and some light food down the hatch, a quick change into my cycling gear and it was now time for the bike.

36

I took it steady along the single-track road, weaving in and out of the sheep sitting about. By the time I turned off the A849 for the jetty, I was getting slightly apprehensive as there was no sign of the motorhome and I knew we were cutting it fine with time. Still, just as I got to the jetty at Fishnish, Mum and June rolled in behind. A pint of coffee to perk me up and it was time for my pervert bit; plenty of vaseline on the frictional parts and then slip into the rubber suit. Well, neoprene actually, but anything would do for protection at this point. David Fergusson was already waiting in his boat at the jetty with his young friend, Kevin Lindsay, who was going to be keeping me company for the crossing, and I suppose, pulling me out of the drink if the proverbial hit the fan. The turn of the tide was just after half past nine and in my reckoning I'd need to split my swim equally either side of that, so that if I was slightly pushed one way, I'd get the opposite effect when the tide changed and hopefully still end up on course. I figured the swim distance to be a mile and a half and I estimated it would take me ninety minutes to cross, so I had to be in the water for about ten to nine. Over a year spent planning for this and now it was too late for worrying – it was time to get my feet wet.

June seemed to be excited by the whole thing but although Mum was hiding behind the camera, her apprehension was showing. I walked down onto the jetty, exchanged a few words with the guys, then the feeling of cold concrete was replaced with cold water around my shins. With a final turn to the camera and a thumbs up to give an impression of confidence, I donned the goggles and splashed in at five to nine. The cold immersion immediately caught my breath and I started off like a crazed frog on adrenalin, but I knew I had to calm it down to a steady breast stroke and settle into the pace. With a slight swell, I was rising up and down between the peaks of some of the bigger waves. I asked the guys to go on my port side to give me some protection from the wind, which was blowing spray in my face. They cruised about five to ten feet away and kept watch for other vessels, asking every so often how I was doing, which at this point was 'okay.' Then about a third of the way across I started getting twinges of cramp in the back of my right leg, which was worrying. The Sound of Mull isn't in my top ten list of best places to get cramp. I had never had this before on a long swim. I suppose I had never climbed a mountain and cycled fourteen miles beforehand, either, so maybe that explained it. Steadily ploughing onwards and trying not to think about the cramp, it gradually eased off after a while – phew!

About halfway across, the Cal-Mac ferry went by around a quarter of a mile to starboard, with Mum and June on board. The skipper gave a few blasts of the horn, and I did my best to raise an arm out of the water to give a feeble wave. At this point, I was starting to weaken, gradually slowing up, and the opposite shore didn't seem to be getting much closer. Swimming into batches of floating seaweed kept things exciting and I remember my right foot getting caught up in something, but I managed to shake it free. Three quarters of the way across, my target – the old pier at Lochaline – was now looking larger, but I was really starting to struggle with the arms and legs. Just for extra measure, I'd noticed on my left a large dark cloud gradually moving down the Sound. When it reached us, it produced a light shower of rain. David could see that I was just inching along now and suggested that, instead of taking the slightly longer route to the old pier, I should take a more direct line for the shore. Anything that was going to help me complete this sooner was welcome, so I agreed and altered course, but the last couple of hundred metres seemed to take an eternity.

There at last, but the coastline wasn't a nice sandy beach, just large rocks and boulders with waves breaking over them. I was left with the dilemma of how I was going to get ashore without injuring myself. The decision was made for me when, as I got close, a large wave pushed me onto a rock that I grabbed and stuck to like a limpet. With my feet not touching the bottom because of the depth, and being too exhausted to haul myself up onto the rock, I just had to cling there, wallowing in the swell and thinking what a pathetic sight I must have looked to the guys in the boat. A couple of minutes catching my breath were enough to recoup some strength and I managed to pull myself up onto the top of the rock before playing hopscotch over the big boulders to dry land. David and Lindsay said 'well done' and managed to get my sandals and a goody bag from Mum to me. Since I'd come ashore about a quarter mile up from the old pier, they kindly offered me a lift along in the boat, but of course I had to decline as that wasn't self-propulsion.

They motored along and I was left to climb onto the raised beach area and make my way along, fighting through some gorse bushes on the way. The stinging of the thorns on any exposed skin managed to bring back some reality as I was stumbling along, spaced out of it. Luckily my goody bag contained a packet of caramel wafers and two small bottles of Irn-Bru which I consumed, and whilst doing so I checked my stopwatch: one hour and twenty-nine minutes stared back at me, so I'd been spot on with my swim estimate. Feeling better when I got to the road-end at the pier, June and Mum were waiting with a big hug. I could see the relief on Mum's face that this part was now over, echoing my own thoughts precisely. I thanked David and Lindsay for their good work and gave them their pay including a few bottles of beer, just wishing that I could have joined them for a couple of cold ones. Beer, however, was the last thing my body needed at this moment and anyway, since it was only late morning, I still had a day's work to do.

My half hour rest in the motorhome was great and after plenty of tea and soup, it was time for another cycle. As anyone who has travelled over the A884 will know, it is not the easiest road for cycling. Starting from sea-level at Lochaline, it is rather undulating and basically climbs to nearly nine hundred feet in about thirteen miles. You then have a fast downhill all the way back to sea-level at Loch Sunart. By the time I got there at one o'clock, I was starting to feel tired and sleepy so I stopped the van and lay down for thirty minutes. Although I couldn't sleep, it was nice just to switch off and close the eyes. I got going again, the sun now strong as the road turned north-east up the side of Loch Linnhe. I pulled over for a minute so that I could water the bushes. Whilst mid-flow, safely hidden behind a few trees, I could hear an engine noise steadily increasing in volume and sure enough, round the corner comes the motorhome. Before I had the chance to jump out and wave, it went straight by me like a shot. 'Shit!'

Although I had only half a bottle of water and a caramel wafer in my pocket, I wasn't overly concerned for I knew that Mum and June would get up the road a bit, realise that they must have missed me, turn around and come back. Continuing at a steady pace, I kept my eyes open for the van but there was no sign of them. I turned west again, on the road heading along the south side of Loch Eil, and now I was struggling into a strong headwind. Still no sign of the van, so the profanities became more free flowing and directed towards certain members of my family. With no cycle cap, it felt as if the back of my head was getting cooked and dehydration was now a problem as there were no fluids available. Pushing the bike was becoming a struggle. Finally, just as I got to the end of Loch Eil and the junction with the main A830 road, the motorhome appeared, as if by magic.

By now I'd actually gone past the point of anger and frustration to one of total disbelief. Mum and June's story was that they had driven all the way to the Glenfinnan Monument car park where I was supposed to be going, sat and waited until it dawned on them that they must have missed me. Eh? Did they think I had been averaging fifty mph on my push-bike, to keep ahead of them on that long circuitous road? They should have realised ages ago that they had gone too far, and turned around. I tried not to be angry as I know what a thankless task a support crew have when they're trying to back up a record attempt. The more worrying thing for me was that if they couldn't get this correct down here on the main roads, how the heck were they going to manage it up north on some of the little back roads that I'd be needing to rendezvous on? I certainly learned the lesson though: if I stopped for a pee on a cycling section, then damn the tourists, I'd make sure that the backup crew could always see me from the road.

Anyway, the damage had been done; I was suffering from the first signs of sunstroke, and was also dehydrated. Looking at the clock, it was twenty to five and sitting in the van, I mulled things over in my tired mind. In the previous months I'd been telling myself the importance of sticking to the daily schedule, but now reality was staring me in the face. In training, I'd already been round the route that was planned, and considering it was a hard five to six hours for the three next Munros when fresh, I was looking at about seven hours minimum. The traverse from Sgurr Thuilm across to Gulvain wasn't exactly in my all time favourites of easy hill routes. Feeling a midnight finish would be pushing my body over the edge for the first day, I reluctantly told Mum and June that we'd head towards Fort William.

We turned into Lochy Holiday Park just before Fort William at six o'clock and it was time to call it a day. Luxury was the shower and the dinner to follow and it felt great to put my feet up for a while. No time yet to totally relax however, as since it was my first day people were calling on the mobile phone to see how I'd got on, and I was already telling them that the schedule would need to be re-jigged. Mark still hadn't managed to get the website online but at least he now had some information to put on it. On turning in for ten o'clock, I reflected that yes, I was already behind schedule and it was probably my own fault for planning too much for my first day. But at least the island Munro of Mull was in the bag, the big swim had been successful, and I'd completed the single biggest cycle of the trip, so all in all not too bad a day. Still it was just the first of many and I had started it fresh and strong; tomorrow, with tired legs, the hard work would start in earnest.

Day 2 – Tuesday 30 May

I did not have a restful night's sleep as my body was a bit jittery from all the exertion. To make matters worse, our old Staffordshire Bull terrier, Shaw, decided to whine a few times during the night and wake us all up. Before leaving Glasgow we had been unsure whether to take him or not, but figuring that he'd probably pop his clogs soon, we thought it would be nice to give him a last holiday. We had packed a small spade in the van so that, if we had to, we could bury him en-route. After being woken by him several times I was thinking of using it sooner than that. The alarm went off at five and, to start what would become my familiar reveille, I drank a load of water and then a pint of coffee to get me going.

Six o'clock, and it was time to finally get going on the bike, but the first thing I noticed was a painful twinge at the side of my left knee when pushing down. I know that I get this every now and then when I suddenly step-up the training mileage on the bike. This must have been the case now with my big day in the saddle the day before. Along the A82 by Spean Bridge the pain was bearable but going by Roybridge, where the road starts climbing, I just couldn't put any substantial pressure on the left pedal as the pain was too sharp. Stopping briefly, aspirin and paracetamol didn't seem to help matters. I made painfully slow progress, until finally I turned off down the little road that took us to Fersit and Loch Treig. Taking time over getting hill gear ready, I let Mum treat me to a monster fry-up.

Starting about nine o'clock with just a steady walk over Stob a'Choire Mheadhoin and Stob Coire Easain, I went from sunshine to cold mist on the tops but the run down and across the Lairig Leacach warmed me up nicely for Stob Ban. Stopping briefly for food at the top, a cold sleety shower hit me with a strong wind and a temperature not much above freezing level, so I was very quickly chilled. Putting on my full body cover, I was too late getting my hands in my mitts and whilst descending I had tears in my eyes from the very painful re-warming.

The hands came to life again as I climbed up Stob Choire Claurigh and some running was managed along the tops of the Grey Corries, but I started flagging on the drag up to Aonach Beag. Another roll was in order, but by this time I was sick of them. Good old cheese and tomato is a favourite of mine when on the hills and since I'd bought a couple of huge tubs of Branston Pickle and spicy salsa sauce, I had expected maybe a few rolls of each and some left plain. After the seventh roll the old taste buds were beginning to revolt.

I had more fluid as well and it did the trick, as I was feeling better on the way across to Aonach Mor, but it was still hard work as there was a good snow-covering to hamper progress. The long climb up the east ridge of Carn Mor Dearg seemed to go on for ages. The view of Ben Nevis from the top was daunting. It had to be done, though, so I traversed along the top of the Arête, as fast as I dared in the snowy conditions, with thoughts of how I had taken a small slip at this point a few years back and almost gone over the edge. If it hadn't been for Ian MacPherson grabbing and steadying me, I would have done.

Going up Ben Nevis, I had to get the compass out to make sure I hit the top, as I was in the thick mist. This I did at exactly eight o'clock and, as I stood alone at the top of Britain, the wind dropped, silence abounded, and I felt very alone in the white grey eeriness. Before leaving, I made a quick call on the mobile saying I'd be down in about an hour. It was careful navigation work off the top and the bearings given on the Harvey map were handy for getting it spot on so that I didn't do a header over Five Finger Gully. Around the four thousand feet mark I came out of the grey murkiness, through the bottom of the cloud layer and into sunshine with lovely views along Loch Eil. This lifted the spirits and jogging down the scree by the Red Burn, onto the big loop in the path, I could see someone waiting. On approaching I saw it was June and with her was a Rabbi gentleman and his two sons that she had been conversing with. The two young boys from London seemed fascinated that I was trying to run mountains and were asking numerous questions, which I did my best to answer.

After saying goodbye, June told me that the Rabbi had given her a tenner for the charity, a great start for our collection as we went along.

Getting to the glen at half past nine, I touched the phone box beside the Youth Hostel as my marker. It had been quite a hard day with twenty miles and over twelve thousand feet of climbing, never mind the cycling, but at least the Munro tally had jumped from one to eleven and my left knee pain had disappeared. It was a happier man who hit the sack at midnight.

Day 3 – Wednesday 31 May

Up at six with a big coffee and an even bigger fry-up breakfast. I jumped on the bike for the few miles along the road from the phone box to where I would be starting the climb. I managed to start climbing at nine o'clock, going steady on the lower slopes of Mullach nan Coirean, the most westerly of the Mamores. Fluids would be crucial today as once up on the ridge there was no water to be had, so my CamelBak reservoir was filled to capacity with three litres. Having no support for this stage, I had managed to plan ahead and get a food/fluid stash put roughly halfway along the ridge so at least there was this to look forward to.

I progressed steadily along the tops going from patches of sunshine to patches of cold, misty rain, and at the summit of An Gearanach, I dropped about thirty feet to the west side to find a big angular rock and my parcel tucked safely underneath. Donald Smith from Westies had kindly come up a few days previously and put this in place. Two litres of water helped to top up my reservoir, two bottles of Coke gave some variety after all the Irn-Bru I was drinking, and a wee malted loaf and bag of sweets were nice little treats. On Binnein Mor, the highest of the Mamores, I enjoyed some views but the climb to Binnein Beag saw me slowing down and even more so on Sgurr Eilde Mor, the last hill of the day. I had descended south south-west to Loch Eilde Mor and started running along the track when I noticed a slight dull ache in the lower part of my left shin. Being generally sore all over, I didn't think twice about it and was more concerned with getting to Kinlochleven, finally arriving at about half past eight. A quick change into cycling shoes with some more fluids and I started out along the B863.

On the steep wee climb out of Kinlochleven, I recognised Mark Rigby's white Ford Escort coming in the other direction, but I was hanging onto the handlebars and could only give him a nod of acknowledgement. Once over the hill I managed to spin the pedals better and after a short while his car went by again, this time with June also inside. They stopped and Mark quickly got out his bike to join me for the last few miles to Glencoe Village.

Mark had enough room to pitch his tent beside the van and then we all tucked into a load of macaroni cheese that Mum had rattled up. Mark bailed out eleven-ish and before bed, Mum massaged the front of my left shin/ankle as it was still aching; I was hoping that it would be better in the morning as another big day was planned.

An above-average ridge day had yielded ten Munros so the tally was now twenty-one in three days but I didn't know that the wheels were about to start coming off. Maybe I should have realised that breaking a tooth today (which wouldn't get fixed until after the trip) was an omen.

Day 4 – Thursday 1 June

Up at six o'clock, feeling tired, my lower left shin still aching, and to crown it all, last night's light rain had turned much heavier and was dropping from a blanket of grey cloud over the hills – this was definitely a day to turn over and go back to sleep. Riggers joined us for breakfast. I donned full waterproofs, and with hood up, took the little cycle round to Ballachulish. Starting at eight o'clock, Mark and I steadily climbed south-west up the steep ridge of Sgorr Dhearg. Bright spell over, it was back into the cloud and over the summit of Sgorr Dhearg and although my ankle hadn't felt too bad when climbing, while running down to the bealach it was hurting. This eased again as we went over the top of Sgorr Dhonuill and then descended west and north-west. Further down we managed to find a route through the tree plantations until finally we emerged onto the A828, south of Kentallen with the motorhome *in situ*. We were both happy to get into the warmth and out of our wet clothes and before we could say 'Yes please,' two hot bowls of an exotically flavoured Baxters soup were in front of us with loads of sandwiches to munch and dip.

Tea finished, it was time for the pair of us to get on the bikes for the cycle round to Invercreran, with this giving my left ankle a welcome rest from the pounding of running. The rain was light during the cycle but by the time we were packing our rucksacks in the van for the next stage, we could hear the drops getting louder and louder on the roof.

A steady plod up Beinn Sgulaird became gradually slower in the worsening conditions, then it was compass bearings for the descent and the long traverse north-east. It is only about three miles between the two mountains but it is over undulating, hard-going terrain and it seemed to take ages, not helped by my increasingly painful ankle. At one point we were stopped in our tracks by the river that flowed into Glen Ure, which by now had become a raging torrent. Going up stream for a distance didn't really help matters. I saw Mark jump straight into the river mid-thigh level, with a few deft moves of the hands to grab boulders, and before I knew it he was on the other bank having just crossed thirty feet of raging river. To say I was well impressed was an understatement and after I'd managed to shilly-shally across, he simply said, 'Sometimes you've just got to go for it.'

Swimming lesson from the master over, we continued through the driving wind and rain to finally get to the south side of Beinn Fhionnlaidh, and pulling back my hood to stare up, my heart sank. What stared back was a seemingly vertical wall of grassy outcrops, permeated with hundreds of little waterfalls, and the whole damn lot just disappeared upwards into the mist. There was no way I was going up there and although Mark said nothing, I think he was of the same opinion. We decided to chuck it but that didn't mean the end of our problems; how were we going to get back round to the motorhome in Glen Coe? We trudged on down towards Glen Creran, and I managed to get June on the phone. I felt as if I'd just won the Lottery when she said she would soon be back round for us, and about forty-five minutes later, as we walked slowly down the road, Mark's white Escort came back into view.

The pair of us were so relieved to get out of our wet gear and back round to the van, where Mum had a big nosh-up waiting for us. It was phone time again to tell the other support people that I'd dropped more hills. It was frustrating but with such big days planned, if you were not one hundred percent fit and didn't have the weather, then it was going to be very difficult to stick to schedule. Mark's help had been great today, but I was just hoping that the pain and inflammation in my left shin and ankle would calm down, so that I could get back on target.

Day 5 – Friday 2 June

Thinking that it would be an easy day if I was only trying to catch up the four hills dropped yesterday, I allowed myself the luxury of a lie-in until seven o'clock. It was now a lovely morning with the sun shining brightly, but any elation I felt was quickly dispersed by a visit to the toilet block. The twenty yard walk there and back had been more of a hobble and a wobble because of the pain in my left shin and ankle. Yesterday's antics in the wet must have made it worse, and over breakfast, I pondered what to do. To try to force it on just because of the schedule would have been foolhardy and the obvious answer, although I didn't want to acknowledge it, was to take a day's rest. Allowing for no rest days in the plan, I'd figured that maybe three or four hard weeks on the go would have forced one naturally, but to have a day off only four days into the whole thing seemed incomprehensible to me. Reluctantly I accepted that if the body needed a rest then so be it.

Fortune was shining a bit, however. Mum had informed Dad about the ankle problem, and he phoned his chiropodist cousin, Pamela. She knew a fellow practitioner in Oban that possibly could help us out, so my left foot and I headed for Oban Infirmary. Podiatrist, Douglas McNab, turned out to be most helpful, cutting new insoles for my trainers from a sheet of highly shock-absorbent material, and also taking me to get an X-ray done. A surprise was in store, however. As Douglas brought the X-ray back, he confirmed that there was no stress fracture, but he could see where there was healing from a previous fracture. Puzzling at this fact, since I'd never broken any bones before, the penny dropped that it must have happened back in June 1998, when I'd taken a header down the stairs after the Scotland-Brazil World Cup game. My left ankle had been very bad then but not one of the three physios I saw had said to go for an X-ray to check for a fracture, so it's a wonder that I managed to get through all the training at that time, never mind the Ironman a few weeks later.

Well that was then, this was now. I thanked Douglas for taking time out of his busy schedule and he passed me onto one of the GPs for further consultation. I explained the situation, getting ready for the usual retort of 'Stop running and rest.' I was pleasantly surprised to gain a sympathetic ear. He placed his hand on the front of my left shin and told me to flex and extend the foot. Immediately, I could feel a rough grating sensation, and this was the tendonitis that was giving the pain and the problem. His advice was to scale things down for a few days, by walking and using boots to give the ankle more support, while hopefully the ibuprofen would let the inflammation ease up. With that relatively good news, I limped out of the hospital.

We enjoyed the warm, sunny day as we wandered about Oban replenishing provisions, and I managed to buy a half decent pair of lightweight Hi-Tecs. Leaving around five o'clock, we headed back up the coast towards Loch Creran and decided to pull into the campsite at Barcaldine. This particular site has a huge circular stone wall encompassing it so it feels unique as you drive in, a bit like entering an ancient fort, I imagine. The site manager was friendly and since we'd be leaving early in the morning, gave us a nice pitch just beside the exit.

The usual phone calls were made and I reflected that my enforced day of rest had actually been quite enjoyable, a welcome break from all the normal, frantic effort. Tomorrow it would resume and, if things went well, it would be all go until the finish. Everything hinged on the medicine man's prescription.

Day 6 – Saturday 3 June

Up at half past six, we headed back to Glen Creran. What a contrast to two days earlier when I'd been battling the elements with Mark. It was still before nine o'clock but already the sun was blazing down, so maximum water was taken on board whilst dusting off my sun hat. From the road end, I cycled the private road by Elleric, and onto Glenure farm with June jogging beside. Although it was only one kilometre, any pounding saved from the ankle was a bonus. June turned and took the bike back, and I looked forward to my walk.

The long ridge east north-east felt easy, and wearing a tight-fitting neoprene support along with the boots seemed to be doing the trick, as my ankle felt much more secure and strong. Soon I was up and over the top of Beinn Fhionnlaidh, but the descent north-east to the col was frustrating. I encountered numerous small rocky crags and terraces, and had to retrace my steps several times. Finally getting to the col, it was like an oven, however, I was fortunate that there was a stream where the cool water was delicious, and then a straight slog up the south face meant that I came out bang on top of the Peak of the Treasure. Managing to skirt around Stob an Fhuarain and descending to the bealach, it was then another traverse north north-east to meet the steep south-west slopes of Bidean nam Bian. Still hot, I cut right for a more direct line to the top, but this took me onto steeper, bouldery ground meaning that I had to keep left of my intended line.

At least here there were two other walkers up ahead, so to take my mind off the sweltering heat, a game of cat and mouse seemed appropriate. They must have been fairly fit as it took a while to pass them, but then the angle of the slope eased and it was faster going to the 1150 metre summit, the highest point in Argyll. I descended south-east to the col and for the short pull up Stob Coire Sgreamhach. This new addition to the Munro list in 1997 is certainly worthy of inclusion and it gave an ideal vantage point with which to observe the hundreds of ant-like people who were crawling all over this group of hills. Glen Coe on a glorious summer Saturday will always be busy and some of the sights I saw whilst descending kept me amused. Briefly chatting to a Glaswegian who was huffing and puffing his way up in all the latest shiny gear, I knew he would be fine and make the top, as a big bottle of Irn-Bru was safely glued to his hand.

Fellow runner Stevie McLoone, a stalwart of Greenock Glenpark Harriers, was coming up to give a hand for a few days. The plan had been that Mum and June would meet him off the bus in the glen, then he and June would head up the hill a bit to try and meet me. Getting to the valley floor, there was no sign of them, so putting it out of mind, I concentrated on trying to follow the path through the huge boulders and, getting to the other side, made the final descent to Glen Coe. The volume of traffic in the glen was incredible, with every available space taken, and although there were a few motorhomes in the big car parks, I couldn't see ours. Deciding that I'd need to start walking down the road, I just caught a glimpse of what looked like a van with a yellow poster on the back. Walking up to have a closer look, it turned out to be ours after all.

We didn't have long to wait for June and Steve, so we turned and headed down the glen. Steve had paid his money and put his tent up in the Red Squirrel campsite, but we were already based down at the Invercoe site, so on promises of much food and beer, we helped him dismantle and come with us. Arriving back about six o'clock, I grabbed a brief rest and shower while Mum made food, then we all tucked in, during which time

Dad and my brother Colin duly arrived. Later, we waved June and Dad off, with Colin settling in for his new co-pilot role, and before lights out, Stevie casually chipped in that he suffered from vertigo. Oh great, guess where we were heading the following day?

Day 7 – Sunday 4 June

Over breakfast Stevie confirmed that he did indeed suffer from vertigo; with a grand total of four Munros under his belt, he really hadn't the chance to dispel it, but then again perhaps that's why he had only done four Munros. Our sunny two-day spell was now at an end, so it was a return to waterproofs as I was dropped off at yesterday's finishing position. My bike was bottom of the pile on the carry racks so rather than undo all the straps, I jumped on Colin's smaller mountain bike and took off down the glen yet again. Two miles further down, we pulled into the lay-by, and because this next section would be short, I just stuffed my hat and gloves into my jacket pockets and took the bum-bag with some water, as it would make for easier scrambling further up. After quite a steep pull from the road to Sgorr nam Fiannaidh and slipping a bit on the wet grass, we got to the summit, and once by the top of Stob Coire Leith, onto the ridge proper. For my third visit, Aonach Eagach held no worries but the drizzle would spice things up on the rock and I had to be considerate of Stevie who was undergoing something of a baptism of fire. Give him his due though, he did well, and it was only on the airier outcrops, when the mist briefly parted to reveal the views to the road far below, that he caught his breath and the palpitations became evident. Meall Dearg in the bag and over the top of Am Bodach, we jogged down to meet the van in the big car park again.

Gillian Irvine from Westies had arrived in the meantime and brought a huge bag of bandages, dressings and herbal remedies with her. Being an infection control nurse, over a long lunch she explained what everything was for and told me that I might find the Arnica beneficial for my injured ankle, as it was supposed to help the body to reduce inflammation and bruising. Feeling thoroughly stuffed from all the food, the cycle was now much harder. Warm-up over, Stevie, Gillian, and myself climbed steadily from the road, south south-east, to Stob Coire Raineach, another new Munro from 1997, then along the backbone of Buachaille Etive Beag to the high point of Stob Dubh.

A nearly five hundred metre rough descent to the Lairig Gartain, and without trying, I was descending quicker than the other two, getting to the pass before them. Going up the other side, I was now struggling to keep up with the other two as we climbed into the mist again and slipped about on the rocky ground. It was at this point that Stevie cracked and stated, 'You'd be just as well walking about in a bloody quarry all day.' The abundance of wet rock and mist was finally getting to him, but his take on it put a smile on my face.

Another new addition from 1997, Stob na Broige was added to our tally, and then it was a case of walking the whole ridge of Buachaille Etive Mor. Despite all the earlier food, by the time we got to the middle top, I was getting light-headed, and a quick look in the rucksack confirmed I had very little left. Gillian had carried some spare grub, so after a short break to refuel, we continued onto our final summit of the day, Stob Dearg. A contrast indeed compared with two and a half years earlier when it had been my last Munro; the weather was the same, but this time there were no celebrations. We descended the steep, stony headwall of the coire together and then finding myself ahead again, I decided to get back to the motorhome, and put an end to this damp dreich day.

The van was sitting in the A82 lay-by at the foot of the Devil's Staircase so it was easy enough to find with no other vehicles there, the total opposite of how the glen had been only twenty-four hours previously. A few quick and welcoming mugs of tea, and we headed back to the Pass of Glencoe to drop Gillian at her car. Saying thanks for the support and some hugs all round, we waited for Gillian to leave for Glasgow. Turning the key in the ignition, there was no response, totally dead, and it was at this point Gillian realised she had left her car lights on nine hours earlier – not a clever idea on a cold and wet night in Glencoe. Colin, being a bit of a mechanic, got stuck right in but realised that, because Gillian's car was an automatic, we couldn't push it to try and give it a bump start.

Scouring the motorhome we found there were no jump leads, meaning that we couldn't connect the vehicle batteries to give it a charge – damn! Stevie now decided that enough was enough, and walked out onto the main A82, wanting to end his miserable quarry day. Thankfully, he was not suicidal, just trying to flag down any passing motorists to obtain a set of said jump leads. Stevie was not having much luck when suddenly a boat whizzed across. Now, although a boat was an appropriate vehicle for the glen in these conditions, it was in fact being towed by a kindly gentleman in a Subaru Forester. It contained jump leads, so the owner and Colin set them up. A few attempts later and Gillian's car burst into life. It was another quick goodbye, with profuse thanks to the Subaru boat man and, at last, we could head back to the campsite.

Being the Sunday night, I could at least congratulate myself for surviving the first week, but it had indeed only been a case of survival. The ankle held up okay today as we were mainly walking, the boots and ankle support helping, but I could feel an old injury deep inside my right gluteal muscle – a literal pain in the arse – niggling away as I finished the last hill of the day. If it wasn't one thing, it was another, and this was annoying me, as I hadn't expected all these injury problems so soon. Looking at the schedule, I was effectively three days behind and instead of sitting on fifty-five Munros, my tally was a meagre thity-four: if things kept progressing at this rate then in a couple of weeks, I could forget about the record. For the time being, the game was still on and my built-in leeway was doing just that.

Week 2

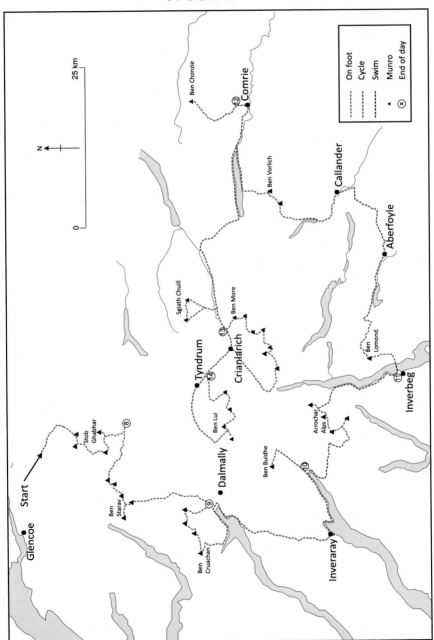

Week 2 – Bloody Weather!

Days 8-14

Day 8 – Monday 5 June

The start of the second week was not like seven days previously. This time the beautiful sunrise was replaced by dull clouds which threatened rain. With the re-jigging of the schedule, an easy day was planned, so there was no rush to get out the door. After our leisurely breakfast, we drove back to the Devil's Staircase, where I was duly ejected for my nice little warm-up cycle to the White Corries ski centre. It was then back to the familiar pairing of running shoes and rucksack for the steep wee climb with Stevie under the ski tow paraphernalia. Despite the cycle, my calves were aching, and the dull pain was again present in my right glute muscle. The slope eased and with it the muscular strain, and before long the pair of us stood on top of Meall a'Bhuiridh. It was cold with the wind and mist, so we wrapped up well and munched some food as we jogged down west south-west. Another short little climb saw us come out onto the summit ridge of Creise. Heading north, there was still quite a bit of snow cover with some cornices, so we erred to our left as it was sometimes difficult to see where earth ended and thin air began. A quick reversal at the summit cairn and we followed our tracks back. Then with the mist, we decided to go straight to the summit of Clach Leathad. This gave us an exact aiming-off point and we got down to the Bealach Fuar-chathaidh spot on, dropping below the cloud level and allowing Stevie's keener eyes to pick out a small green tent with an enviable view of the world.

Across the bealach and climbing south onto the long ridge of Aonach Mor, the legs were starting to feel heavy, so a steady walk was all I could manage. I remembered reading in the guidebook that there were a few rocky knolls to be climbed, but they seemed never-ending and this helped to increase my tiredness and irritability. Finally, the slope levelled off and then the final pull up to the top of Stob Ghabhar gave us a welcome seat, despite being damp and misty, with three other walkers saying a quick hello and heading on their way. Stevie and I enjoyed our five minutes of rest, then we continued along the summit rim and promptly caught them up again before we descended north off the Aonach Eagach. Crossing the col, I spied a rucksack and walking poles sitting all by themselves, but it was only as we started climbing that the owner became evident further down, crouching with his camera and no doubt annoyed that a couple of joggers had come by on this quiet Monday afternoon to disturb his nature photography. A steady plod led to our final Munro of Stob a'Choire Odhair. Turning south south-west, gravity didn't help my sore legs, thus I could only muster a slow jog, with Stevie having to hold back for me. The path by the Allt Toaig was easier going all the way down to the big track, where we turned east and followed the river back to the car park, by Victoria Bridge.

The motorhome safely in place, the side canopy was out and our portable generator was sitting underneath, so we proceeded to peel off our socks and shoes and were immediately set upon by swarms of midges, the warm still air being ideal for the little critters. About twenty seconds and one hundred bites later, we had a seat inside, and although Colin and Mum were keeping us entertained with their stories and questions, I was descending into a funny sort of mood for some strange reason. I decided to crack open a bottle of beer to see if it would lift the spirits. It didn't. It was probably a result of tiredness, despite an easier day, combined with apprehension at the huge day that was planned for tomorrow, which was getting to me. Picking at my stew in a lacklustre manner and not even finishing it, my retorts to the others were rather curt, certainly not fair with the good job they were doing. I needed my bed. Only eight days into the game and I put a final 'P.S.' at the bottom of my diary page: 'Almost feel like being on the point of chucking it.' This summed up my immediate mood, but I was still thankful for little mercies as I snuggled under my duvet; Stevie was stepping outside into midge-fest territory to sleep in his tent.

Day 9 – Tuesday 6 June

The alarm came far too soon at five o'clock, and a quick glance out the window confirmed that it didn't look good for a long day in the hills. Stevie had managed to get some sleep and drop his tent without getting completely devoured, and we both ambled over breakfast, knowing that if the day went as planned then this was our last hospitality for about thirteen or fourteen hours. Prising ourselves away at twenty to seven, we started with the waterproofs and managed an easy jog back along the track in the light rain, then climbed slightly to come out by Clashgour farm. Then we headed west north-west round the bottom of Meall an Araich. After a fairly rough traverse north-west to cross the Allt Dochard, we were left facing the south-east slopes of Meall nan Eun which disappeared in the mist at about the five hundred and fifty metre mark. It was difficult to judge from the map how hard these slopes would be, as I've seen similar OS markings which have been a doddle to climb, and others which have been nigh-on impossible. The guidebook wasn't too hopeful, saying that this little dumpy Munro was well defended on most sides. Still, there was no other way from here so we went straight up, and although worried that the mist would present us with an impassable rock outcrop, we managed to work our way between them and steadily climb. Our trainers were fairly slippy on the steep, wet grass and I could tell Stevie's vertigo was beginning to play up, but very quickly, it seemed, we came out on top and jogged the last few hundred yards to the summit cairn; this wasn't such a tough nut to crack after all.

By now the drizzle was of a thicker composition and combined with a slight wind, it just wasn't a nice day. Map and compass work were called for and I almost made a mistake right away. Aiming for the col before Meall Tarsuinn, I felt that we were descending too far and realised that we had overshot the col and were heading down into the gully towards Coirean Riabhach. A short climb back up and heading west south-west, we climbed over the little top and onto the next steep wee climb, coming out on the south-east ridge of Stob Coir' an Albannaich. We had a brief stop at the top for some fuel and then we faced more compass work in a south easterly direction to make sure we hit the col before Glas Bheinn Mhor. Stumbling upon a ptarmigan and her chicks, (who scattered everywhere tweeting as they went), we found it amusing that the mother with her pretend injured wing climbed the path faster than us in an effort to draw us away from her brood. With heavier legs now, it was good to get to the top ridge, and as we headed to the summit I thought back to when I was last here in 1994, a baking hot day when I had run out of water and become dehydrated. We descended to the col, and were now faced with the climb to Ben Starav. I was tired and could only manage a plod, with Stevie ahead, but this soon reversed when we came to the airier ridge and the rocks. Stevie's vertigo kicked in again and he didn't like this bit, especially in the wet conditions, but we scrambled over it and round the summit rim to the trig pillar. We reversed our direction but only a little way, as Stevie said that he was not going back over his 'bad bit!' We dropped east south-east into the coire then contoured south-east to come out at the col, north north-west of Beinn nan Aighenan. Slow to the summit, and we had number five under our belts, then initially a steady descent south, but progressively steeper down the side of the Eas an Eich Bhain, saw us to Glen Kinglass. During all this time the rain had got heavier and the cloud lower, so it was a couple of tired wet and bedraggled wanderers that stared from dripping hoods at what were to be our next hills, lost from four hundred metres upwards in a sea of wet mist. I just kept staring as if waiting for divine intervention. Stevie wasn't offering an opinion. Mulling over the options, I knew I didn't want to drop any more days, but even though my head was still telling me to stick to the schedule, the heart just wasn't there. We'd been out for over nine hours in the rain and with my present slow pace, I figured it would take another six or seven hours to try and complete the next four Munros. I certainly didn't fancy a late night finish with probable mild hypothermia by that point, so I just turned to Stevie and told him we were not attempting them. Stevie still didn't say much. Being the loyal foot soldier, he'd have gone for the four if I'd been up for it, but I think inside he was quietly relieved.

There was to be no easy end to this day yet, though. The only viable escape route involved a climb from sixty to six hundred metres over the Lairig Dhoireann. We crossed the bridge and got on with the plod. Eventually cresting the pass and dropping south south-west on the path, my knees were aching and my left ankle injury was hurting, but it was time for crossed fingers and giving the mobile phone a try. As far as Mum and Colin were concerned, we were going to be appearing at about eight o'clock at the Cruachan Visitor Centre, so there was no telling where they might be at the moment. The mobile didn't work so continuing on down, we got below cloud level and could see Glen Strae and onto Loch Awe. Time for a second attempt, and the line connected, getting through to them. They were not that far away so we told them we'd be coming out on the B8077 near Stronmilchan, but when Stevie and I finally got to the track end, there was no sign of them. A quick call found that they were waiting half a mile up the road at another track end, so a few minutes later we were inside the motorhome and winding our way back along the A85 to Bridge of Awe. Colin and Mum told us that the highlight of their day had been shopping in Oban only to return to the van and find that it had a flat tyre, which was fixed easily enough at one of the local garages.

Approaching seven o'clock, which meant it had been twelve hours on the move, and getting to the campsite, Stevie quickly erected his tent. There were fewer midges this time and at last a bit of low evening sunshine came out to brighten the day. A warm shower and fresh clothes were rejuvenating and now we could all enjoy a couple of relaxing hours. Dropping the four hills today effectively meant that I'd lost another day from the schedule, so nine days in and already four behind – shit! What was going wrong?

Yes, I'd developed an injury which slowed my speed, and the poor weather was hindering progress, but it wasn't just that. Had I actually been too ambitious in my plans and were these days just too big, just too much for me? Well, whatever, there was nothing more I could do at present.

One bright point, however, was going to lift the mood of the moment. Colin told me that Rory Gibson had called earlier and had left a number for me to get back to him, so it was with slight nervousness that I dialled. Rory's polite accent came on and it was great to finally speak to one half of the duo whose record I was attempting to beat. He wanted to meet up whilst I was south on my journey, so I suggested that, if things went to plan, then I'd be at the campsite at Inverbeg on Thursday evening, two days hence. He agreed to drive through from his home south of Edinburgh, and would share some advice gained from his record-breaking journey of 1992. I looked forward to it and turned in at quarter to eleven.

Day 10 - Wednesday 7 June

Half past six in the morning and the day was brightening up nicely, typically ironic as Stevie was returning home after enduring three dismal days in the hills. But it wasn't all bad; at least his Munro tally had jumped from a lowly four to a mighty nineteen. Starting again from the track end in Glen Strae, I thanked Stevie for his help and said goodbye, Mum and Colin dropped him at Tyndrum for his bus. Although there was bright sunshine on my back, it wasn't overly warm but the tonic was more mental than physical. Strong legs today and a new vigour saw me quickly to the top of Beinn Eunaich, before continuing with a pleasant jog to the col and another steady climb to Beinn a' Chochuill. Ascending south-west from the Lairig Noe slowed my pace, then it was over the north-east top to the summit of Stob Diamh where a rock with a view was acquired. It was great just to sit and appreciate it all for a calming ten minutes: the solitude, the scenery, the warmth of the sun fleeting in and out of the clouds. I was even inspired to get out my little pocket camera for a few self-timed snaps, just to prove that not all my days were a grey gloom.

Skirting to the south side of Drochaid Ghlas saved some climbing, and with my trainers giving good traction on the dry rock, I could jump between the big boulders, working up to the trig point of Ben Cruachan. Turning south, I followed the path for a while. Looking for a more direct line, I veered off left, quite steeply at first, through rock and scree, but giving way to grass further down in Coire Dearg. A quick flashback to my Scottish history reminded me that this was Clan Campbell's favourite mountain, and with echoes of their war-cry 'Cruachan!' in my head, I jogged on down to the reservoir. By now the heat was building and with it, a slight headache, always one of the first signs that I'm getting dehydrated: too much sun exposure on the back of my head. Almost there, though, and the final descent down through the trees brought me out to a very busy visitor centre by the power station. Mum had put Shaw outside to enjoy the warmth, and I sat in the van doorway and peeled off sweaty socks and shoes. Enjoying a few cool drinks, Mum worked her magic again by going to our little freeze box in the fridge and producing an ice cream cone. Dropping Stevie in Tyndrum, she had seen them on sale and her thoughtfulness was now much appreciated as it helped to cool me down. Being quite happy with my time of five hours round the hills, a leisurely late lunch seemed rewarding whilst changing into my cycle gear.

Fed and watered, it was time for a spin on the bike, with sun hat in place and the wind at my back. The hour's rest must have worked, as I zipped along between twenty to twenty-five mph. This soon changed when I turned right onto the A819 with the wind now coming diagonally across me, but the view to Kilchurn Castle took my mind off things and it was weird to see a sleek speedboat crashed in a ditch by the side of the road, obviously having broken free from a driver's trailer. By Cladich, the road climbs for about two miles to over two hundred metres, but once over the high point, a long freewheel allowed the motorhome to draw alongside and I sank a couple of refreshing cans of juice. Straight through Inveraray, where the motorhome stopped to get refuelled, and with the wind in my favour again, the miles went quickly up the side of Loch Fyne. Nice timing ensured that the motorhome just caught up with me as I pulled off the road to the wee parking area at the head of the loch.

Still enthused and keen to get on with it, I carried a bare minimum in my rucksack and took off up Glen Fyne on the mountain bike, soon arriving at Inverchorachan. The clouds were darker and more menacing by now, but it was still warm and humid, so even climbing in just my shorts, there was still a constant drip of sweat running off the end of my nose. High above the corrie, the mist started coming in, so finally succumbing to putting on my top, I popped up onto the windy summit ridge of Beinn Bhuidhe. A quick trot east south-east to the summit trig, then it was just a case of reversing my route all the way back to the house. I flew back along the track as fast as I could on the bike but about a mile from home, the rain came on. A five minute soaking wasn't going to spoil my day, though, and I was chuffed with my time of two hours and fifty minutes for this section. With no pain from the ankle, I was now looking forward to an easier day over the Arrochar Alps.

Day 11 – Thursday 8 June

Heavy rain bounced off the roof of the motorhome, and with the vehicle swaying in the wind, I had a pensive breakfast knowing that I'd soon have to step outside, all of yesterday's elation getting washed away with the downpour. Tuesday had been a downer, Wednesday a high, so it looked like I was heading down into the trough again, the weather playing a bigger psychological factor than I had bargained for. Venturing outside and getting on my bike, at least there was the consolation that it was a smaller day and there would be company. The first mile along the A83 gave me a warm-up, then the incline felt hard, but it was only when the road turned east that I got hit by the full force of the wind funnelling along Glen Kinglas, as if a giant hand was pushing me back. For a Thursday morning there seemed to be a large volume of traffic, with the spray from the cars bearable, but big articulated lorries cutting in closely and soaking me in clouds of moisture. Mum's face looked concerned as the motorhome went by, and then the increasing steepness of the climb to the Rest and be Thankful pass ensured that my face didn't look a pretty picture either. Crossing over the high point meant that the tension could come off the leg muscles and about a mile down the road, I pulled into the lay-by behind the van.

Five minutes later, I recognised the Peugeot estate car that drew in beside us, and Kevin Holliday jumped out. He was my companion over the big guns of the Arrochar Alps and after a fifty-three minute soaking for a lousy seven and three quarter miles on the bike; it was good to have a friend along. Over mugs of tea with lots of biscuits, I changed into fresh gear and then it was that time again. We only had to jog about a quarter mile down the road before turning left and climbing north-east, progressing up the right hand side of the water, and managing a fast steady walking pace in the waterlogged ground, over the Bealach a'Mhaim and up to the top of Beinn Narnain.

A quick reversal to the bealach, north north-west over Beinn Ime, and then on, reaching Glas-Bhealach, it was accurate compass work for the descent north-east to make sure we hit the Lag Uaine. The torrential rain had turned the grass slopes into giant water slides, and the thought was in my mind of possibly aggravating the ankle injury again. This didn't stop Kevin, however, as he took full advantage to produce some long energy saving bum slides, not caring about his already saturated clothes. Starting to slow on the climb to Ben Vane, I managed a little jogging over the summit and also on the descent north-east, however, further down, the increasing angle of the slopes meant that we had to walk and work our way through some rocky outcrops. We finally emerged out of the mist just above the wall of the Loch Sloy Dam.

61

It was at this point that Kevin announced he was not going to climb Ben Vorlich, and that he was going down the track instead. He said that he'd go and meet with the motorhome, collect the two bikes, and bring them back to the track end later. A steady pace was maintained on the unrelenting angle, with a quick hello to a descending walker, and once on the top ridge, a gentle jog north north-east past the trig point saw me to the summit cairn. After a steady run all the way back down, the mist thinned out and I could see Kevin approaching the track end with the two bikes, timing it to perfection. A few minutes later and we were whizzing down the single road; it was only about two and a half miles to the main road but this little bit helped save already tired legs from an extra pounding.

The motorhome was sitting at the viewpoint car park by Inveruglas power station. It was still only quarter past four when we arrived so there was no rush, and now that the rain had finally died, we could sit outside and enjoy some leisurely mugs of tea. A point of amusement was when Kevin peeled his socks off. Although the smell wasn't amusing, I noticed a bulge that looked like the top of a boiled egg on both his left and right forefoot. Colin and I were intrigued and we asked how he had sustained these injuries. Kevin's face broke into a smirk. The lumps under the skin were no injuries, but the natural consequence of avid dinghy sailing in his younger days. The act of leaning over the side to counter-balance wind strength on the sail, whilst feet were anchored for support, had developed the small forefoot muscles to such an extent that they were now permanently enlarged.

Despite the usual traffic on the A82, I was enjoying my easy cycle down the loch with views over to Ben Lomond, giving a quick wave to the van as it went by. They were taking Kevin back round to Glen Croe for his car, and it was now that I thought more fully about Mum's parting words to me, 'Would you like us to get you a chippie on the way back through Arrochar?' Refusing at the time, with protestations of sticking to a good diet, now that I had almost finished, my taste buds were starting to kick in. I debated this in my head for several miles. Stuff it! I pulled over to the side of the road and got on the mobile to Mum, hoping that I'd catch them before they passed back through Arrochar. Luck was on my side and I ordered a fish supper. Salivating the last few miles, Inverbeg soon appeared with the Holiday Park entrance on the left, where I pulled in and stopped, as my day's work was done. Five minutes later and Kevin's

Peugeot drew alongside where he offered me a seat as we awaited the motorhome; just as well, for Colin and Mum didn't appear for another half hour.

Saying goodbye to Kevin, we drove into the caravan park, adjacent to reception, where Mum went to book us in and pay for the night. Emerging a few minutes later, she got into the van looking visibly flustered, and upon inquiring, wouldn't say anything except to go and find the pitch for the van. Driving round the small track, our pitch was only about fifty yards from the loch shore, ideal for tomorrow's early morning start. Safely parked and upon further urging, Mum then proceeded to tell us that while at reception, the older man behind the desk had spotted our 'Munro Run 2000' signs on the side of the motorhome. He had then launched into a diatribe directed at my mother, saying that this was no way to be doing the Munros, that he had no time for runners as they ruined the hills by causing erosion, and that we wouldn't be able to appreciate the Munros anyway.

Instantly my hackles were up and I could hardly believe the audacity of this guy; to take our money and then shove his views down Mum's throat. I would have left instantly, and presented him with a Glasgow kiss, but this point of land gave the shortest swim crossing of Loch Lomond and I had already arranged to meet people here. Yes, everyone is entitled to their opinion, but the fact that I'd already appreciated the Munros, thank you very much, when walking my first round, and was now in the process of raising several thousand pounds for charity, was of no consequence to this plonker. Did he think I was running blindfolded? The compounding factor for me was that my mother had been the focus of this outburst, which was just not fair as I knew what a sterling effort she was putting into a difficult job. Still, no time to dwell on fools. I calmed myself down, for we had to ready ourselves for an important guest, a true gentleman.

Enjoying the fish and chips whilst still warm, it was a nice little treat from my usual fare. A pleasant shower removed the sweat of the day and I smartened myself up a bit, then hurried back to the motorhome for eight o'clock. Sure enough, a few minutes later and bang on cue, Colin said, 'That looks like him now,' and a cursory glance from the window confirmed that it was Rory Gibson. Wanting to know as much as possible, Rory gave an account of the 1992 record and what Andrew and he had experienced. His first-hand rendition was intriguing and, unbeknown to

63

me at this point, it would be Rory, who in his own little way, would help me out a few weeks later.

We walked to the shore to have a look at the swim, and I remembered from the film how the two of them, with seemingly effortless front crawl, had quickly crossed this stretch of water. Asking if in any way he could help out, we looked at my upcoming schedule. With a really huge day planned in the Cairngorms a week on Tuesday, I decided it would be a great help if Rory would take up a food/fluid parcel and leave it on the top of Cairngorm itself. On that note, he wished me luck and departed, our brief hour an uplifting boost to my motivation.

Day 12 – Friday 9 June

This time the alarm went off at five o'clock, then it was the mandatory huge coffee and some very light breakfast. I was excited, and not in a nervous way, as I knew this swim was going to be so much easier than Mull. Chris Fuller, another friend from Westies, was already waiting at the entrance barrier to the site at six o'clock. I let him in and whilst he sorted himself and his kayak for the crossing, I made my own final preparations.

Standing on the little sandy shore, the conditions were perfect for swimming. Just before starting, another kayaker appeared to my left and it was only when it came closer that I recognised the paddler as Damien Theaker, from Helensburgh A.A.C. Damien, as well as being a good runner, was also a keen sea kayaker, and it was a nice surprise to have his accompaniment for the swim.

No time like the present, so with lots of 'oohs' and 'aahs' wading out to waist level, I finally took the plunge at about twenty past six. Immediately, the coldness of the water took my breath away, followed by hyperventilation. What Loch Lomond lacked in terms of tides and swells, it certainly made up for in temperature, much colder than the sea swim. Gradually catching my breath and settling into a steady rhythm, my new goggles were misting up, so I just pulled them down round my neck. As Chris and Damien's kayaks glided on the flanks, each swim stroke contrasted, one of cold black water rushing over my head then one of bright warm stillness, giving a surreal quality to this early morning experience.

Twenty-five minutes later and I was wading through the shallows to a small audience of Dad, Mark Rigby, Donald Smith, Brian Bonnyman and Mark McColl. With a quick thanks to Damien and Chris, they turned to paddle back across the loch and hurry themselves for a day at the office. Walking to the vehicles beside the Rowardennan Hotel, we enjoyed some coffee and malted loaf whilst changing, and Mark McColl, obtaining more digital pics for the website, was now heading home with my father. Donald was taking my wetsuit and swimming gear to the motorhome at Drymen before returning home and Riggers, who I'd not expected to see this morning, was driving Brian's car round to the next stage.

One hour after diving into the loch, Brian and I started on Ben Lomond. It felt great to climb without a rucksack, Brian being the packhorse for this stage. The trig point was soon reached and we savoured a quiet couple of minutes to take it all in, Glasgow in rush-hour in the distance but peace and solitude at almost three thousand two-hundred feet. Descending north a little, we then turned east north-east for a steady jog towards Comer farm. A small point of amusement came during a quick fuel stop, ever-helpful Brian said he would get me some water from the stream whilst I munched my biscuits. Giving him my little collapsible plastic cup, he duly returned a minute later with exclamations of 'Wow, this cup really is minimalist and lightweight' and passed me about five teaspoons of water. Laughing at this, Brian hadn't realised that the malleable material could be folded out to give a normal size drinking cup, so I showed him how it worked. Several cupfuls later and science lesson over, we passed the farm, continued on the track and over to the B829, by Loch Dhu.

Brian's silver Ford Fiesta and the motorhome were in place, with Mark Rigby inside keeping Mum and Colin entertained with stories. Although it was still only twenty past ten, the day was starting to warm up and I was feeling slightly dehydrated, so lots of fluids were downed, whilst attempting some stretching for tense muscles. Having worked up a good appetite, brunch was now the order of the day and I just couldn't resist Mum's offering of a mince pie smothered with ravioli. Being a lover of sandwiches, however, I took it a stage further, bunged the lot on a couple of bread rolls, and munched happily away. Saying goodbye to Mark and Brian, I set off on the bike.

Charlie started early this morning with his swim across Loch Lomond in perfect conditions with near to no wind and a flat calm loch. Unfortunately, for the bleary-eyed spectators (Rigby, Donald, Mark, Charlie's Dad and myself), the conditions were also perfect for the clouds of midges enjoying an early breakfast. Charlie was accompanied by Chris Fuller and Damien Theaker of Helensburgh in their canoes, and he asked me to pass on a big thank-you to them for their help – especially as they were both up before 5 a.m., and had to return straight to work! Charlie seemed to enjoy the half-hour swim (less choppy than the Sound of Mull and no jellyfish to contend with, but noticeably colder than the sea) and after a couple of cups of coffee, was off up the Ben with myself in tow. We had good views over the clouds looking back down the loch and were up to the summit in an hour and a half, down the far side by Comer, and along the forestry track to meet Charlie's Mum, brother and Rigby waiting on the Aberfoyle road. Charlie was feeling his ankle a bit after the swim, but was descending and running well on it, which he hadn't been managing a few days ago. After a change of clothes and some scran (a pie roll with ravioli!) he headed off on the bike towards Stuc and Bens Vorlich & Chonzie. Tomorrow he's aiming for the Crianlarich hills (Beinn Chabhair to Ben More).

Along through Aberfoyle, the A81 and then the climb by Loch Rusky with the long descent to Callander, I turned and headed up the A84 to Loch Lubnaig. Arriving at our pre-arranged meeting point just before one o'clock, the motorhome hadn't caught up yet and although they were stopping for some provisions in Callander, I thought Mum and Colin would only be a few minutes behind. After twenty minutes, I decided to get back on the bike and slowly cycle up and down the narrow lay-by to try and keep myself warm. Unfortunately, whilst attempting a tight turn at one end of the lay-by, gravity intervened and I couldn't release my pedal clips in time, the resulting crash no doubt providing amusement to passing motorists. Sporting a nicely cut knee, I was now really pissed off, so when the van arrived not long after, several politically incorrect phrases were directed towards the occupants.

Calming me down, Colin and Mum explained that the first pharmacy they visited would not sell them Ibuleve gel and ibuprofen tablets at the same time, so they had to source a second chemist shop. Since I was averaging a daily intake of a couple of grams of ibuprofen just to keep the ankle injury at bay, it was always necessary to top up supplies where we could. It had also taken them a while to find a suitable source of drinking water to fill up the van's tank, another necessary task, as I would simply have ground to a halt without my large daily volume of water. This demonstrated how absorbed I'd become with the here-and-now and time, time, time, not realising that the half-hour sacrifice was for elements that would keep me going much further in the long run. Keeping an eye on the bigger picture was difficult, however, with the knowledge that I was still only halfway through the day.

We enjoyed a leisurely lunch and for all my earlier time-consciousness, the relaxed feeling continued as I walked up the path to Glen Ample. Once at the highest point of the pass, it was then a matter of climbing and traversing the open hillside north-east, just skirting to the west of the 735 metre spot height. Arriving at the foot of the final slopes, a steady plod saw me to the top of Stuc a'Chroin and now the downhill was enough to coax the legs into an easy jog to the bealach, and then another walk to the 985 metre trig point of Ben Vorlich. A few minutes of rest were enjoyed but, gazing along the flat summit plateau, the cairn at the far end looked higher. This is a trick on the eyes that we are all familiar with when looking along at objects of a similar height, and normally I wouldn't have thought twice about it. My omnipotent Ordnance Survey map said the cairn was one metre lower than the trig so that should have been that – except it wasn't exactly.

For the last few months before the run, there had been a bit of a debate going on in one of the outdoor magazines about the height of a Munro that I would be traversing the following day, Beinn a'Chroin. Some walkers had disputed the OS heights, and which of the cairns was the highest along its summit ridge: west, middle or east. Now, if they were disputing a few metres of OS height with that hill, I figured that it would be just my bloody luck if they re-measured Ben Vorlich and also discovered a discrepancy. Stuff it! What's an extra hundred odd metres in a journey of a thousand miles? Leaving the rucksack, I was soon along at the other summit cairn. You've guessed it. Staring back along, the trig pillar did indeed look higher and in this case, I'm sure the OS got it right. Huge boggy and eroded areas meant that it was a case of zigzagging all the way down to avoid the worst bits, and by the time lower Glen Vorlich was reached, my left shin and ankle were aching, a result of all the jumping about.

The motorhome was parked on the main road by Ardvorlich House, and it was good to get a seat with a nice mug of tea, times three, and the obligatory 'mountain' of Tunnocks biscuits. By now, the very slight brightness and warmth of early afternoon had given way to an overcast grey layer that was producing a fine drizzle. Break time at an end and starting on the bike again, a quick glance at my watch showed twenty past six; twelve hours since jumping into Loch Lomond. Feeling I was going to get equally wet this time as the light drizzle turned into a light rain, I trundled along the A85, doing my best to avoid the large puddles.

Comrie soon came into view and a sharp left-hander took me onto the small road that leads up into Glen Lednock. Iain Barr's grandparents had owned a static caravan in Comrie and over the years, I'd enjoyed a few holidays here, so I was relatively familiar with the area. Moving slowly up the glen, I reached our stopping point by Invergeldie and made another change from cycling to running gear. Whilst doing so, Iain Barr pulled up in his car with his mother and a friend for company. With Colin's week as navigator and assistant at an end, he was returning to Glasgow, and Big Iain would be taking over for the next nine days. I said goodbye and started for the hill at ten to eight, aware that the light was starting to dim.

The initial jogging turned into a fast walk. Getting onto the broad plateau and taking a compass bearing north in the mist and cloud, I soon picked up the fence-line and followed it round north-east all the way to the summit of Ben Chonzie. At about ten past nine on a Friday night in mist and low light, this was definitely a case of touch the cairn and get the hell out of here. Reversing my upward route and arriving back at the motorhome at ten to ten, I could sense Iain's neophyte enthusiasm in his new role as he prepared my bike for me – how long this would last when having to put up with a tired and moody hill runner remained to be seen.

Gravity could now be put to full advantage, and I turned the pedals lightly, descending the three miles back down the glen, a nice little cool down for the day. We found a suitable parking place off the road near the Deil's Caldron waterfall and pulled in. It was now almost dark and my watch read twenty past ten, sixteen hours since the swim start. We enjoyed the dinner. I turned in at eleven thirty. For all that it had been a long day; with half a mile of swimming, nine thousand five-hundred feet of climbing, twenty-four miles on foot and forty miles of cycling, it had also been a good and enjoyable day.

Day 13 – Saturday 10 June

I must have been one evil dude in a past life, and now it was payback in this life. Despite being up over eighteen hours in yesterday's long outing, I had to struggle awake at six. Another big day was in the offing but this was one that I had quietly been looking forward to. Years ago, when Mum and Dad used to take us on a car run to Glen Falloch, as the A82 climbs away from Loch Lomond, the views to the right never failed to impress, and they still impress today. From the Falls of Falloch, the hills that rise up have always been fond to my eye, and knowing that seven Munros nestle in there, it had always been an ambition to climb them all on a grand day out. That day had now arrived.

I managed to get going on the bike by twenty past seven, first along the A85 to St. Fillans and then into a noticeable headwind along the north shore of Loch Earn. A quick right at Lochearnhead was followed by the three mile climb of Glen Ogle. The legs seemed to be firing pretty well, and once over the high spot, I enjoyed a rapid spin down to the Lix Toll. Now the real test began: as the A85 left the shelter of the trees, I was hit full on by a very strong headwind. Bending horizontally over the pedals didn't seem to help much and it was a slow crawl all along Glen Dochart to Crianlarich. Spying today's helpers in the little car park, I was more than glad to have the excuse to get off the bike and talk to them. Malcolm Finbow of Shettleston Harriers had brought along a friend, Stephen Owen, and there was also John Donnelly, formerly of Shettleston Harriers, who had recently defected to the hallowed gold and black of Westerlands CCC.

Not stopping long, I headed down the A82 and Glen Falloch, with the exhausting cycle continuing. Finally, I pulled in beside the Drovers' Inn. A hard thirty-six mile cycle like that would normally have been deemed a good day's training and I would have headed in for a few golden thirst quenchers, but hey, it was only approaching ten o' clock and there was still a proper shift at the coal face to be done. The guys joined us in the camper van and Mum rattled up loads of bacon rolls to feast on. Shaw

69

stirred to life from under the table, and although half deaf, his old nose was working fine, and I gave him the strips of fat from my bacon.

With the three guys being kind enough to carry all my spare gear, I could enjoy the luxury of only having to tie a bum-bag around my waist, and we headed off at half past ten, jogging the first bit of road and track by Beinglas farm. The steepness of the path soon saw us walking, up past the waterfalls, and it was a steady plod all the way to the summit of Beinn Chabhair, with jokes aplenty. Gazing south, we could make out the small lump of Duncolm in the Kilpatricks and it suddenly made me feel very close to home. Continuing on, we dropped and climbed north-east to An Caisteal, then south and south south-east to the col before Beinn a'Chroin. With the jury still being out on the exact height and summit of this Munro, I made sure we went over every top, which wasn't a problem as they were all on our route to the next hill.

It was a longish descent to the col before Stob Glas; we contoured east below its crags and continued on a diagonal climb to the main ridge of Beinn Tulaichean. A quick trot south-east gained the summit, and a gentle jog back down the ridge led to the climb onto Cruach Ardrain. By this point we had noticed a distinct change in the weather, as the cloud was lowering closer to the tops with spits of rain, and the wind speed picking up again. Excluding sweaty hill runners, John Donnelly must have got a whiff of something else in the air, for he now announced that he had a party to go to in Glen Coe that evening and wouldn't be joining us for the last two hills.

Once over the summit of Ardrain, Stephen advised us to keep high and also go over Stob Garbh to avoid the crags. With dark menacing clouds overhead, John left us for a speedy descent to his car at Crianlarich. Malcolm called him a 'Jammy Dodger', for as we reached the low point of the col between the two glens, the heavens opened. We were now faced with the daunting two thousand feet climb up the side of Stob Binnein. I tried hard to hang onto Stephen's heels, with Malcolm flagging a bit a further behind me. His emergency Mars Bar came to the rescue and he soon joined us on the summit, where it was wild. The jog northwards to the bealach had the wind aiding us, so we were there in under ten minutes. Twenty minutes later and we were standing on the summit of Britain's sixteenth highest mountain, and boy did we know it. It took me all my strength to hang onto Ben More's trig pillar in the gale-force wind, but I managed to get the camera out for a quick photo.

We wanted out pronto, and headed down the north-west ridge where we continued to take a battering – even a thousand feet lower there was no appreciable drop in wind speed. Continually slipping, sliding and falling to the ground, the other two appeared to be enjoying the water-slide and were soon a fair distance ahead. I was certainly not enjoying this, however, as the injured shin and ankle were aching painfully from the constant strain. Getting back to the motorhome in one piece, the contrast could not have been more complete. Knocking on the door like three drowned rats, Big Iain opened it, adorned in bright Bermuda shorts, and a simultaneous blanket of warm air exuded from the van. Quickly inside, Mum promptly produced three black bags for us each to drop all our gear into, and whilst I had spare shorts and t-shirt to put on, Malcolm was left standing in only his classic men's Y-fronts. That wasn't a problem, but when we drove back along to Crianlarich, Malcolm realised his dry gear was in Stephen's car, which was. Iain and I had no choice but to video a certain scrawny professor as he scampered across the busy A82 on a wet Saturday evening. Heaven only knows what the coach-load of tourists that had just pulled into the hotel opposite thought.

Seeing off Malcolm and Steve, we went to the caravan park a few miles along Glen Dochart, and after all the cold rain, the warmth of a hot shower was welcoming. Saturday night required a bottle of beer, so Iain and I cracked open a couple from my onboard stash, whilst Mum told me her story from earlier in the day. A minibus full of older ramblers had turned up beside the motorhome and the driver had asked Mum many questions about what we were doing. She gladly answered about a record-breaking attempt and raising money for charity, to which the driver said that they would have a whip-round when they returned from their walk. Arriving back a few hours later, he came up and gave Mum their collection before heading off. Mum looked into her hand: one two-pence piece and two one-pence pieces. Still, four pence is four pence, and it had been duly dropped into the Dreams Come True kitty. Feeling very tired, a weary head hit the pillow.

Day 14 – Sunday 11 June

Up at seven and still feeling lethargic from the previous day's effort, I certainly didn't hurry over breakfast. Finally getting on the bike at nine, at least it was only an easy two miles along the glen to the road by Auchessan farm. I set off north north-east over the open hillside with the heather making for slow progress, and the overcast conditions making a plod seem appropriate anyway. Sgiath Chuil came and went easily enough, followed by the descent to the broad col and then a traversing climb west and onto the summit of Meall Glas. The long descent south south-east over roughish ground made for a mixture of walking and jogging. Iain was down at the bridge filming as I approached, so a jog was put on for the camera.

Over lunch, Brian Bonnyman arrived. I told Brian I'd see him along in Strath Fillan and, starting on the bike at twenty past one, I could immediately feel the strength of the wind against me as I pushed for Crianlarich. It was a struggle all the way along Strath Fillan and by the time I'd got to Dalrigh to meet Brian, I was tired and had already changed our plans in my head. I reasoned with him that if the winds were this strong at road level then at three thousand feet they would really be going some. With our planned route taking the Ben Lui group east to west, into the wind, it would make progress very slow and difficult indeed.

Agreeing that we'd reverse the route and do them west to east, I got on the bike and headed for Tyndrum. Taking the A85, as the road bends south-west in Glen Lochy, I was turning more into the direct line of a very strong southwesterly wind and it required ever more effort to push the bike forward. After a seeming eternity, the car park sign came into view and I turned in and down to the motorhome. Stumbling off the bike, I collapsed on my bed inside the van. Lying there for five minutes feeling shattered and catching my breath, the stats spoke for themselves; ninety minutes to cycle sixteen miles, when normally that sort of effort from me would have delivered twice the distance.

Half an hour of rest helped, and Brian offered to carry all my bulky gear for the hill, meaning that I could travel light with just a bumbag and essential nibbles en route. Setting off at twenty past three, it was still windy but there was a touch of brightness, and it was a warm humid air stream, so much so that I peeled off my top five minutes after starting and just ran in shorts. The pair of us set a good sharpish pace up the path through the forest and at one point, bumped into a walker on his way down. This young guy had on the full range of foul weather kit with two walking poles, and he took one look at me and exclaimed that it was blowing a gale up there and that he hoped I wasn't going up top like that. Fair enough, standing there in only a pair of shorts, bumbag, trainers, and with tape over my nipples to prevent chafing, this guy must have thought that I was some sort of lunatic. I did assure him that Brian was carrying all the adequate gear for both of us and that we were quite experienced at all this stuff, but the look on his face said that we still hadn't convinced him.

Breaking out from the trees and over the fence, we continued up the middle of Fionn Choirein, where I finally gave into the diminishing temperature and put my top back on. Climbing onto the col, Brian dumped his rucksack and we climbed south-west to the summit of Beinn a'Chleibh, then trotted back down to collect the pack again.

It was dull and overcast for the plod up to Ben Lui, but at least the wind was giving us a helping hand. The climb to Ben Oss saw the first spits of rain and by the time we got to Beinn Dubhchraig it was falling steadily. Coming off the north-east ridge, we managed a steady run all the way until we met the track by the river and the jog round to the motorhome in the car park at Dalrigh. Getting to the van door, Iain displayed clairvoyant tendencies by announcing that we had met a youngish guy on our first climb, hadn't we? We nodded in agreement, and Iain proceeded to tell us that whilst still round in the Glen Lochy car park, the guy had spotted our emblazoned van and came up to tell Iain and Mum that he was very concerned because there was a runner climbing the hill wearing only shorts, and with Micropore tape over his 'titties'. We all burst out laughing and I asked Iain how the heck the guy knew it was Micropore tape that I had over my nipples? It transpired that the guy was a nurse from the Royal Alexandra Hospital in Paisley, hence explaining his concern for a semi-naked, potentially fatalistic, hill-goer.

Brian left immediately for Glasgow and I settled in, getting changed and listening to the wind and rain outside. Now, although there was a big sign in the car park saying 'No Overnight Parking Allowed', we were hoping that on a late dreary Sunday evening we would get away with it. The loud knock on the door came at about half past nine and the three of us stared at each other. I kept out of the way and told Mum to play the sympathy card about the charity run. She and Iain opened the door and it was indeed a local who informed them that there was indeed no overnight parking. Mum was very calm and cool and just explained the situation and fortunately, the guy accepted and we could stay. Mini panic attack over, we relaxed again, and I took stock of the last seven days. The left ankle had held up, so that was a bonus, and at thirty-five Munros for the week, it was one better than the previous week. However, I'd dropped another day, hence four behind now, totalling thirty-four Munros fewer than I'd planned for the first fortnight. It wasn't the best of starts, but at least I was still moving, and although the weather was crap, I lived in hope for a few more sunny days.

Week 3

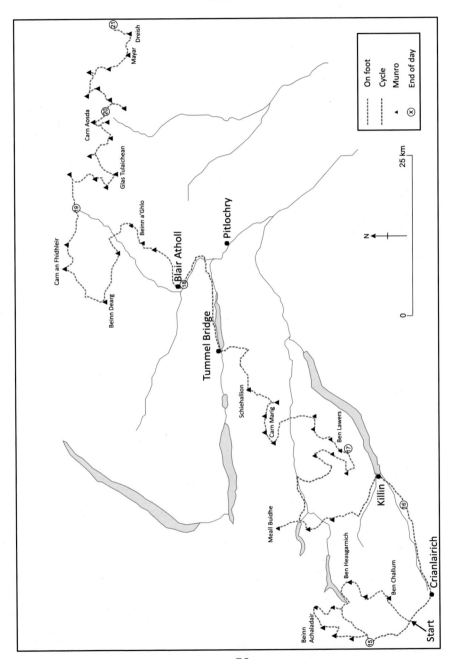

Week 3 – Sweeping East

Days 15-21

Day 15 – Monday 12 June

The start of week three soon drowned all hope of sunny days. A very big day had been planned to swallow all the Munros from Strath Fillan to Bridge of Orchy, eight in all, hence the alarm bell rang at twenty past five. I groggily stirred and pulled back the curtain to wipe the misted window. This resulted in no difference to the view, and it was then that my tired brain deduced that the mist was on the other side of the glass. My heart sank as I could hardly believe the clag and cloud were only a few hundred feet above road level. I just couldn't drag my tired body and mind out into the dull grey dampness, and at twenty past six I told the other two I was going back to bed. I knew this meant another day was being dropped from the schedule, but at that point I just didn't care, a bit more sleep was more appealing than anything. I only allowed myself the luxury of ninety minutes extra kip, so the alarm went off for a second time that morning at ten to eight.

Unfortunately, the mist was still there, both internally and externally, and not even breakfast and coffee number two could dispel the mental lethargy. The inevitable could be delayed no longer, so I said goodbye to Iain and Mum at half past nine, trudging along the side of the main road before turning off on the track by Auchtertyre farm. A bit further up from the farm, at the end of Gleann a'Chlachain, there was a new, incomplete metal bridge over the river, supported by scaffolding tubes. It was taped off, but with so much rain, the river was basically in spate, so I decided to use it anyway and tiptoed across on one of the steel girders. Getting to the other side safely, a new track (not shown on my map) had been bulldozed up the right hand side of the river. It must have been done relatively recently as there was still loads of soft earth around that hadn't been compacted, and although this slowed progress, I decided to follow the track as far as I could. This helped to take me up the glen a bit, then I left the river and started a slow climbing traverse towards Ben Challum's north-west ridge, hoping to bypass the south top altogether.

Plodding uphill, the wind and rain were gradually increasing, and just for good measure, there were several electric fences across the hillside, turning me into a contortionist to try and climb over them. Physically and mentally, I was just not in the mood for all this, and then the mind games began. I questioned why I was putting myself through all this discomfort and how easy it would be to stop and put an end to it all. For the first time since starting the run, I opened the waist belt pocket on my rucksack and pulled out the little cards I'd made for myself. Knowing that low moments like this were going to occur, I had cut some motivational quotes from a magazine and had them laminated so that they could be carried all the time. There were only four but I read and re-read them to drill them into my mind to keep going, even if it meant being zombie-like on autopilot; to keep on keeping on was all that mattered.

Getting onto the ridge of Ben Challum, I turned and climbed east south-east to the summit cairn. Then I started to doubt myself; both ridges from the west looked very similar on the map. Shit, in all the low cloud and rain, and with my below-par performance, had I inadvertently come up a ridge too soon and was I actually standing on the summit of the south top? Finally grasping that the south top didn't have an east ridge, if this was the true summit I'd very quickly find out about it. Descending eastwards for a bit, I was indeed soon on a ridge which levelled off after half a mile, so I had been correct all along.

It was now a case of dropping steeply north through the crags. Dropping below cloud level and continuing north over the many burns and streams, a steady climb north north-west back into the cloud and traversing below Stob nan Clach saw me come out onto the ridge and follow it round for the final climb north-east to the summit of Creag Mhor, Munro number two for the day. Knowing that the guidebook said to avoid the crags to the north of the summit, I retraced my steps a little way, then descended north-west, north and east north-east. By now, the rain was very heavy, bordering on torrential, and just stopping for a minute, I raised my head and peered from the hood to see the dark crags of Creag Mhor rise up on my right and disappear into the swirling mist. Looking around, I felt a million miles from anywhere and really lonely, like a diminutive character transported to Tolkien's Middle-earth; this was indeed a day where someone's company and support would have been priceless.

There was nothing for it but to lower the head again and squelch on through the boggy ground which gave way to quite a steep climb. Reaching the long summit ridge, by now the wind speed was very strong, I thought at least fifty mph, and gusts were frequently blowing me off balance. I crouched at the cairn of Beinn Heasgarnich to take a bearing and then jogged north north-west, leaning at a thirty-degree angle into the wind, but still getting knocked to the ground a few times. Down the long ridge of Stob Garbh Leachtir and then more steeply north-west, I kept slipping and sliding on the wet rocks and grass, the sore ankle taking a pounding.

Whilst climbing some Corbetts here back in April, I had noticed a new track that was not shown on my map, cutting along the south-eastern side of Loch Lyon. I now made a beeline for this in the hope of easier going. Upon reaching it, there was the task of crossing the Allt Fionn a Glinne which, although just a large stream, was flowing at a tremendous rate into the loch. A bemused herd of drenched cows watched as I dilly-dallied up and down the bank until I finally had a 'Rigby' moment and took a hop, skip and jump across, only re-soaking my feet in the process.

Leaving the cattle to their misery and returning to my own, I had to cut away from the south end of the loch for several hundred metres before being able to cross the extremely full Abhainn Ghlas and head round to Srath Tarabhan. Whilst doing so, I gazed up the length of Loch Lyon and was amazed at the size of the waves and the white horses blowing off the top of them; this was reminiscent of the seaside in winter, not an inland loch in summer. I pulled back my jacket hood and held up the camera to snap myself with the loch in the background. Months later, the developed photo would reveal an extremely tired and battle weary person, with a dull bleak background, one of my most vivid memories of the run. Gaining the track end, it was a case of head down and switch off for the five mile trudge along Auch Gleann, and by the farm I managed to get reception on the mobile to tell Mum to come up from Tyndrum and collect me. They arrived just as I got to the A82, at half past seven. Ten hours was indeed slow for only three Munros, but it was a very bad-hair day in every sense of the expression, and I've got the photo to prove it.

Showered and fed at the campsite, as expected I was now another day behind schedule, and with the wind and rain increasing, it was not a good omen. Trying to sleep in the swaying motorhome, at least there was comfort in the knowledge that tomorrow I would have hill company.

Day 16 – Tuesday 13 June

Don Reid from Westies was driving up from East Kilbride to give me a hand, so this meant I could afford to lie in until seven o'clock. Don duly turned up, and driving back to yesterday's finish, we started at ten past nine. Last night's fears were confirmed, with the weather once more horrendous with heavy waterproof jackets and trousers from the off. Crossing the railway line, we had a steep pull up the southern flanks of Beinn Dorain, but at least this was partially sheltered, the full force of the wind only being appreciated on the summit. Continually buffeted in the wind and rain over Beinn an Dothaidh, it all cranked up another notch on Beinn Achaladair. Don and I could just about manage a leaning jog, but we were often getting blown to the ground and falling over. Despite having the hood drawn as tight as possible to my head, the wind was still managing to pound the fabric like a road builder's jack hammer, with the result that I was developing a headache.

Fighting this all the way out to Beinn a' Chreachain, some respite was afforded as we turned and headed south-west and south-east to Beinn Mhanach. A quick summit photo, and then I was off as fast as I could manage. Slipping and sliding south south-west down the steep wet slopes, the rapid staccato of the hood gradually eased, so that shouting from more than a couple of feet was now possible. Meeting the track in Strath Tarabhan, we got our heads down for the long run out, but such is the paradox of mountain weather that, now running in the opposite direction from the tops, we still had the wind in our face all the way along the glen. Almost back at the farm, my trip along Auch Gleann had been much quicker than the one twenty-four hours previously, but once we were back at the A82 again, Don confessed he was knackered. Yes, it had been tough physically, but Don's help had been immeasurable for the companionship. After yesterday, I really couldn't have faced it on my own.

79

I met up with Charlie at 08.30 at the Tyndrum campsite. It wasn't difficult to spot the van, it was the only one with a Tunnocks caramel wafer on the side. The winds had eased down to mild hurricane force as we climbed Ben Dorain directly up the steep side. Bearing in mind the weather he has suffered recently, I suggested to Charlie that he had good justification for claiming the fastest winter ascent of the Munros! I was impressed how philosophical Charlie was about the conditions, he just didn't let it get him down. Although the clag was down, navigation along the ridge was fairly easy. All we had to do was follow the erosion trail. A couple of times Charlie slipped on the wet rocks aggravating his ankle injury again. I just hope for his sake it doesn't get any worse. Beinn an Dothaidh, Beinn Achaladair and Beinn a' Chreachain were climbed in succession, the wind on a couple of occasions blowing Charlie and I off our feet. It was a good feeling to turn and head for home via the final peak of the day, Beinn Mhanach. I was getting tired by this time but Charlie still looked strong, and I began to wonder who was supporting who! Typically, the weather started to improve when we met up with the van at Auch farm. Charlie amazed me by jumping straight onto his bike for the cycle down to Glen Dochart. As for me, after the beating we had just had, I was glad just to stagger back to the car for the drive home!

We waved goodbye to Don, and I took the road bike for the trek through to Glen Dochart. The weather finally breaking in the last hour, it had calmed down to just windy with light squally showers, and it was also being kind for a change as the wind blew at my back, heading east along the A82. Stopping again at the Glen Dochart caravan park, I called it a day, but a busy evening still lay ahead. After such a poor publicity response, except for Dave Hewitt's article before the run, we finally had someone from an agency who was interested, and had made contact regarding a newspaper article. Driving down to the Drover's Inn, Tom Martin of Freelance Journalism looked like a young sleuth with his long overcoat and notepad, and as we chatted he took down the answers to his questions. Tom's photographer, Chris, wanted to get a few shots as well but first I had another appointment to deal with.

I had arranged for Ian Struthers, one of our resident GPs in Westerlands, to come up from Glasgow and take a blood sample from me for testing. I figured that after sixteen days of the campaign, if I was starting to become deficient in anything then it would show up in the blood and Ian would be able to advise me accordingly. Ian had duly arrived, so in the motorhome he drew blood, and headed back to Glasgow saying he'd phone through the results when he got them. The rest of us headed back up Glen Falloch for some late evening photographs. The only suitable place we could find was the long lay-by about a mile before Crianlarich, where at least there was the pleasant backdrop of An Caisteal. This all took longer than I thought, involving a change of gear, with and without the bike, standing still and moving – photographers can be demanding people. Done and dusted, we wished the guys good luck with persuading the papers to pick up the story and headed back to the caravan park about half past nine.

I had last seen proper sunshine on Friday, so the late evening brightness of this Tuesday was most welcome after surviving four days of abysmal weather. Hopefully tomorrow would be better.

Day 17 – Wednesday 14 June

Six a.m. and the sun's rays were poking through the clouds – hurrah! I started on the bike along Glen Dochart at quarter to eight, leaving Mum and Iain to finish tidying up in the van. What a difference a day makes. With renewed enthusiasm for life translating to the pedals, they spun effortlessly at twenty mph and boy, was I happy. I was singing along to the music of my personal stereo, thinking of my postie pals pounding the pavements of Glasgow, and here I was on a beautiful morning living my dream.

I sped through Killin, and turning left into the small road up Glen Lochay, I pulled in just by Tullich farm, and it was time for work. I stuffed down more food, as today was fairly big, with around twenty-one miles on foot and over eleven thousand two-hundred feet of climbing. The statistics didn't perturb me, however, and it was a contented man who hit the steep southern slopes of Meall Ghaordaidh at nine o'clock.

Climbing steadily, I was soon high above the glen, over the summit and running down the long ridge north north-west, not giving much thought to the rocky outcrops of Creag Laoghain that were shown on the map. I was taking a straight line for the bridge by Stronuich, and as I descended more steeply, I soon found myself stuck amongst small cliffs and rock terraces. This was a bit of a nightmare, with tenuous grassy holds and edges over steep drops. Several times I had to nervously retrace and re-climb to try and work my way out of the maze. Wasting much time before getting to easier ground, I turned round and realised why I had got into trouble. OS Landranger 1:50,000 maps have been my bread and butter since my teenage years and it's my map of choice, but if I have one complaint, it's the extremely wide range of meaning that one symbol can take. I've known the outcrop symbol to cover everything from the odd wee bit of rock on slightly steep ground, to near vertical cliffs which are impassable and dangerous.

Excitement over, I crossed the bridge and could feel the heat beginning to build despite the thin layer of cloud. The sun broke through on the long traversing plod north-west, so the white hat came out. Next came the Stuchd an Lochain ridge with a final wee climb up to the summit. As I took a breather, I could see someone coming along, and quickly greeting them I jogged back around the ridge and descended to the east end of Loch an Daimh. The motorhome in place at the road end, at the back of one o'clock, I enjoyed a light half-hour lunch before the ninety minute trot up and down the relatively boring, but easy, Meall Buidhe.

Searching my memory, I thought I remembered that the small road down to Bridge of Balgie was not in the best of conditions, so I opted for the mountain bike with its fatter tyres for this leg. The two hundred metre drop over four miles gave an easy descent, but this was followed by a right turn and a three hundred and fifty metre climb over the same distance again. At least one pint of sweat lighter, the high point of the road was reached, and pulling in below the cairn, the motorhome managed to find enough room to squeeze off the road as well.

Another half hour break to allow for rehydration after the hard cycle, and then it was time to head for Meall a'Choire Leith. Jogging over the rough ground, but still feeling slightly squeamish with the start of a light headache, I knew that dehydration was still having an effect, so I just walked to the summit, putting on my large white hat to protect me from the sun. After descending to the col, I then had a long walk up the ridge to Meall Corranaich, by which point I was feeling much better, enjoying a fast descent all the way to the dam wall at Lochan na Lairige. It was now about quarter past seven, so I didn't waste anytime at the motorhome, jettisoning as much gear from my rucksack as possible and shoving in some more biscuits and water.

I climbed strongly to about halfway, but ten thousand feet of climbing had started to affect me, and I slowed to a plod again. Popping out of the shadow, the hazy evening sunshine graced the summit ridge, and I headed a short distance south to the cairn of Meall nan Tarmachan. A couple of minutes to take in the view, then it was jogging south-east by the knoll and continuing east south-east down grassy slopes. Finally gaining the little track and bridge back onto the road, it was a short walk down to the Lawers visitor centre car park where the motorhome was *in situ*. It was only nine o'clock, so the usual update phone calls were made before a leisurely dinner and turning in.

Day 18 – Thursday 15 June

Waving goodbye to Mum and Iain at quarter to eight, for some reason I set myself the little target of trying to get to the summit of Beinn Ghlas in one hour, and made it just in time. I always feel that when you get the first Munro under your belt, you have broken the back of the day's climbing. Then again, that was in the good old days when only two or three hills were the daily target – today my premise might not hold.

The weather was not as good as yesterday morning, with thicker cloud, but at least it was above the hill tops, and it was still dry. From the top of Beinn Ghlas, I could make out someone just getting to the top of Ben Lawers, so the competitive instincts kicked in and catching this person was now my aim. A good run down to the bealach and climbing to Ben Lawers, then continuing north down the ridge, there was no-one in sight until a figure popped up on top of An Stuc. Damn, this walker must be fast, as I was not gaining much ground. Over An Stuc myself, a steady and sure descent down the steep and eroded north-east face, before the next little pull to the summit of Meall Garbh. Again the person was already about half a mile down the ridge towards the next hill, and making my efforts seem decidedly average.

Settling on a full blown run, I finally passed him just before the grassy col, but don't remember my wave being acknowledged. Continuing strongly, I soon reached the cairn of Meall Greigh and returned along the plateau before descending north north-west. The sun had broken through now as the broad undulating ridge twisted north-east, and I took the left hand fork which turned north and descended quite steeply through the bracken and heather to the farm at Dericambus. Up to the road by Invervar at a quarter past twelve, lunchtime beckoned.

Mum had paid a visit to a bakery, and for lunch she presented me with a large bridie which she had kept warm in the van's oven. Having just gone hard over five Munros, and with the temperature in the glen starting to build, I wasn't overly enthused by this offering, but I didn't want to disappoint her, and it did make a change from the sweet hill fare I had been consuming. Half of another bridie was washed down with a big mug of tea and, rucksack restocked, it was time to hit the trail again at one o'clock.

The trees provided shade for a short distance, soon giving way to the open path, and the heat of the sun was palpable on the climb up the eastern slopes of Carn Gorm. By the summit, I was not feeling too great, and after the jog down the ridge, felt queasy, so had to settle for a steady walk, constantly sipping water from my CamelBak. Over Meall Garbh, then Carn Mairg, it was only by the summit of Meall na Aighean (formally Creag Mhor) that I started feeling better, returning to the previous col with a jog, then traversing north-east to the broad col between Meall Liath and Meall nan Eun. Schiehallion filled the view a couple of miles to the north. My immediate problem was that this broad col was covered in dark watery peat and often when following a rake of ground, it would abruptly end in the mire. Nine out of ten Munros was a good mark for this schoolboy, but to get a full ten out of ten, a final ball-buster straight up the southern rocky flanks of Schiehallion was needed.

Although it was after six in the evening, the sun was still beating down strongly on my back, so I had to put on my hat. Every so often a breather was required, with a quick glance back down the slopes revealing how quickly I was gaining height, beads of sweat dripping from the end of my nose. The slope very quickly rounded off and I was on the ridge, where a right hand turn and an easy amble took me to the summit. A can of juice I'd kept in reserve was an elixir as I took in the great views all round; I was surprised to see how far away Ben Lawers now looked. I was certainly in a buoyant mood, pleased at getting a big day of ten Munros in the bag with no problems. Tomorrow would see the magical one hundred mark reached, all being well.

I met the motorhome in the Braes of Foss car park, changed into bike gear whilst downing more fluids and biscuits, and set off again at a quarter past eight. I enjoyed a fast descent to Tummel Bridge, and I managed to keep up a good speed and cadence along the undulating B8019. We trundled into the Blair Atholl caravan park at half past nine. Waddling off for a shower, Mum and Iain set up the van and by the time I came back, dinner was almost ready. Turning in at a quarter past eleven, I was pleased that I'd managed to complete another big day and hold to the revised schedule; the more this happened, the stronger my psyche would become for the weeks ahead.

Day 19 – Friday 16 June

Waking at the back of seven to a sunny morning, I had a bee in my bonnet. At breakfast I announced, 'Right, I want a pair of fell shoes!' All my recent hills were fairly runnable over quite good terrain and my trail shoes were fine for that. Now, however, I was heading into rougher country, not in terms of rock, but hills of heather, cut through by rivers, small glens and quite a lot of peat for good measure. I figured this would put a much greater strain on the ankle, so a new pair of traditional fell running shoes with a lower profile and sharp studs, seemed like a good idea.

Fellow Westie, Gordon Robinson, lived down the road in Perth, so I phoned him to ask the name and address of a shop where I could get some Walsh PBs. Campus Sports in the High Street was the answer, so off we set at nine down the A9, thinking that we'd do the round trip in about ninety minutes. Lying in my bunk, the van slowed unexpectedly after a few miles, and a quick glance out the window revealed that we had run into road works by Pitlochry – bollocks! It was the back of ten before we finally got to Perth. A five-minute walk took me to the shop, and there were my hallowed PBs sitting on the shoe rack. 'Great' thinks I, 'A pair of those in size eleven please.' The assistant disappeared into the back and promptly returned to say that they only had them up to a nine and a half. My mind immediately jumped to a favourite Blackadder quote – 'I think the phrase rhymes with clucking bell.'

I couldn't believe it. They did suggest I try the outdoor shop down the road; no luck there either, but they gave me the telephone number of the appropriately named Munros outdoor shop back in Pitlochry. We hit the road north, and this time with the savvy to phone ahead. They didn't have any PBs, but their other outlet in Aberfeldy did. A swing off the A9 and we were soon there, finally getting size elevens and throwing in a couple of pairs of medium-weight walking socks to give a little more cushioning.

With all the messing about, it was after midday when we pulled back into Blair Atholl, and I was aware of the late hour considering the twenty-seven miles and ten thousand feet of ascent that lay ahead. Taking the mountain bike for its lower gearing, and starting again from the caravan park, I was soon puffing and panting up the steep little road that lead to Loch Moraig. Getting a good lunch on board, I was off at twenty past one, doing my best not to dwell on the fact that with about a twelve hour jaunt ahead, it was going to be a very late finish.

Ah, it was a good feeling to have sharp new studs that bit strongly, and the summit of Carn Liath was soon behind me. A quick adjustment of the laces and a steady jog saw me over Braigh Coire Chruinn-bhalgain and onto the summit of Carn nan Gabhar, the highest point of Beinn a'Ghlo. The sun was strong as I ran northwards down the ridge and over the little point of Meall a' Mhuirich, then after steady slopes, a final steep descent north-west into Glen Tilt. Crossing the bridge over the river, it was very bright and absolutely sweltering in the glen, so for the third day in a row, out came the sun hat. The original plan had been to head back down the main track for a couple of miles to pick up the hill path near Forest Lodge, but I just wanted to climb out of this heat as soon as possible. The change of plan involved going north up the opposite side, and although I'd be sweating buckets with the very steep incline, at least I could follow the Allt a' Chrochaidh and sup cool water to my heart's content.

Following the stream round south-west, then taking a direct line west south-west, I climbed gradually for a couple of miles to the summit of Carn a' Chlamain. By now I felt that my first break had been earned, so I had a quick seat for five minutes to appreciate the surroundings and have a snack. Beinn Dearg looked far enough from here, and I didn't dare look north for my final two hills. Still, it was turning into a lovely evening, so I trotted off into the sun and admired the steep sided gash of Gleann Mhairc. Pulling up and over the intervening ridge between Beinn Mheadhonach and its northern outlier of Carn a' Chiaraidh, I descended north-west into a broad basin of little water tributaries, and with the legs waning slightly, climbed the final thousand feet up to the top.

As I had been approaching, patches of thin wispy cloud were gently grazing the summit of Beinn Dearg, and by the time I got there, a thin blanket touched the broad plateau. This resulted in a strange lighting effect that I've never seen before, or since, on the hills. One could look clearly into the greyness for about one hundred metres all around, and below see a very bright halo where the sun was trying to shine through about ground level. It gave the feeling that I'd just been enveloped by a giant flying saucer and I have to admit that it was eerie. A quick snap on the camera didn't do it justice. At twenty-five past eight, it was time to get a move on, so I headed off north north-east towards the source of Tarf Water. Immediately out of the cloud and I glanced back to witness how finely heaven and earth kissed each other, a unique experience indeed. Anyway, it was not heaven where I was heading, but more like hell.

A friend had joked on the website that Charlie was now heading into MAMBA country, and if I had to define that, then this area would certainly come close – nothing to do with poisonous snakes, just Miles and Miles of Bugger All! Crossing what little there was of the headwaters of the Tarf, I nearly jumped out my skin when almost standing on a grouse with its throaty alarm call. Looking down revealed a nest of six perfectly formed speckled eggs. I took a photo, having never seen them before, and moved quickly away to let the mother get back to them. Climbing to the west of Meall Tionail na Beinne Brice, I then descended east before another steady climb beside the Glas Feith Bheag brought me to the top of Carn an Fhidhleir just before half past ten.

With the light fading and the cloud cover thickening above the tops, I wanted to get to the final summit before darkness set in. A run down to the broad col, and then nearly a thousand feet up the other side, which I hit as hard as my legs would let me. Thankfully, I got to the summit plateau of An Sgarsoch at ten past eleven, just as the last glimmers of light were going; despite the wispy cloud, this was enough to let me find the cairn. I hadn't bothered with lugging a head torch around all day, but instead carried a couple of glow sticks. Cracking one open to allow me to read the map, I took a bearing. Still just being able to make out the ground, I dropped down to the next col. Darkness now reigned, and rather than climb onto the next ridge of tops and risk coming off the wrong side, southwards, I used my altimeter to contour between the seven hundred and the seven hundred and fifty metre lines on the north side for the next two kilometres east. Figuring this would take me about twenty minutes, it was more like thirty by the time I had staggered through the thick heather, by chance finding the col to the north of Coire na Creige.

Descending east into the gully a bit, I looked in vain for any sign of light, then after a few minutes of contouring north-east, a tiny point of light appeared far below. It was a slow descent in the darkness as I didn't want to risk injury on the rough ground, but the light kept enticing me and gradually grew bigger. Nearer Loch Tilt itself, it dawned on me that Iain wasn't at our prearranged meeting point of the cairn, but down nearer the north-east edge of the water. Contouring round the bottom of the wet ground it was great to finally reach the tent and say hello to Iain, who had been dozing. With the watch reading ten to one, I dearly hoped that this would be my latest finish of the trip. It was then, after a few minutes of sorting stuff and wanting a drink, that we realised that between us we had very little water. Damn, this wasn't good after nearly twelve hours on the hill and the necessity of rehydrating fully. I had just presumed that there would be enough at the campsite, but there was no running water nearby and we had no purification tablets for using the still water of the little loch, which I wouldn't risk drinking direct. Leaving enough for a coffee in the morning, and drinking the last little bit in my CamelBak, over some quick nosh Iain said that Mum had given him a couple of little bottles of Mixed Doubles. So, although five days later than planned, we toasted hitting the one-hundred mark, and enjoyed our after-dinner tipple.

Day 20 – Saturday 17 June

Six hours of fitful sleep later and getting up at half seven, my mug of coffee had a perceived effect of zero. The mind and body stupor continued but with baggy eyes, a smile managed to break on the face when Iain asked me to hold up a little card he had made for a photo. Ah yes, 'One hundred down, only one hundred and eighty-four to go.' That little milestone should have stirred some vigour, but not this morning. Sorted by nine o'clock, I left Iain to pack away the tent and ambled over a small rise by the cairn, then dropped across the watershed between the River Tilt and the Dee. It was then a long, rising traverse to the south of Geal Charn and over the south-west top of Carn Bhac, with another easy walk to the summit. Knowing that fellow Westie, Gordon Robinson, was coming out to give some hill support, I scanned all directions whilst eating, but there was no sign of anyone.

With my legs suitably warmed up by now, I managed to break into a jog south-west down the broad grassy ridge, but it was soon back to a plod up steepening rocky slopes onto the ridge of Beinn Iutharn Mhor. Turning right and jogging to the summit, I glanced back and sure enough at the north-east end of the ridge there was a figure running in my direction. Five minutes later, it was great to have Gordon's company for the next section, and we jogged off south to the col, then descended more sharply south-west. Dropping to about seven hundred metres meant we were presented with quite a steep climb of around three hundred metres, but my mind was taken off matters by all Gordon's news, and we were soon at the summit of Carn an Righ. We continued east south-east then south-east and this time it was a three hundred and fifty metre pull up to the summit of Glas Tulaichean, before turning north north-east and running down the ridge. It was at this point that I first noticed a slight twinge in my right calf muscle, which increased quickly, so much so that by the time we were passing Loch nan Eun, it was really painful with each stride. I was almost limping. Stretching didn't seem to help very much, so we were now down to a slow walk.

To add to the mood, the cloud level had thickened and dropped to cover the tops. As we climbed the final steep slopes of An Socach, a grey murk started to ooze a fine drizzle, necessitating the use of rain jackets at the summit. Since Gordon had come in from Glen Ey this morning, he now had to return that way to his car, so he headed north whilst I took a compass bearing and headed south-east. Descending beside a stream for a long way, the surrounding ground was wet and boggy, so I did manage to jog most of the descent without too much complaint from the grumbling calf muscle. The steady walk up the long grassy slopes of Carn a' Gheoidh didn't really irritate it much either. Managing to find the cairn on the misty flat top, the realisation came to mind that this was a Saturday and that, if I got a move on, I might be able to get a beer with Iain in Braemar. The smooth, gentle slopes made for steady running, with the compass bringing me past little lochans and then round the top of the coire south east to the Cairnwell. After a reversal north and a little climb to Carn Aosda, it was time for the final descent of the day. Normally this would only be a few minutes to the ski centre but, with left shin aching, right calf hurting again and just being plain knackered, I struggled to jog and ended up walking most of it. I met the motorhome at a quarter past six.

As Iain drove down the A93, the cloud that had been sitting over the ski centre gave way to broken sunshine and, by the time we parked up in the Invercauld campsite, it was a lovely evening in Braemar. A warm shower was fantastic and I made an effort to spruce myself up with some fresh clean clothes, feeling invigorated. Dinner was followed by phone calls, and then Iain and I walked into town and went to the public bar at the Invercauld Arms Hotel. Sipping pints, we remembered that the Euro 2000 football tournament was on. Tonight was one of the big games, England versus Germany. Whilst enjoying the game, I spied bottles of Smirnoff Ice behind the bar and felt an unexpected craving for lemon; Iain and I were soon going round for round on these. The game ended with England beating their old adversary one-nil, and we rounded the night off with a few G&Ts each. The return journey to the motorhome was certainly slower than the outward one and once back, I had more food. Good old Mum got to work with the Ibuleve gel on my left shin and right calf, and whereas the vigorous massage would normally bring forth some howls of protestation, my alcohol anaesthetic was working its magic. After twenty days, I had been ready for this wee blowout and it felt good.

Day 21 – Sunday 18 June

Although today would be another 'eight' day, the stats were only about four thousand five-hundred feet over eighteen miles of runnable terrain, so I only stirred at about half seven, and then enjoyed a leisurely morning. Returning along the A93 to the ski centre, Iain drew into the car park and I jogged back over the road to where the van had been parked the previous evening. Rucksack sorted, I waved goodbye to Iain and Mum at ten thirty and, still feeling a bit bloated from breakfast, took it easy up the track by the ski tows towards Meall Odhar. I continued traversing south at just above the nine hundred metre mark and, despite the hard going on stony slopes, came out onto the small col. Continuing south-west on the ridge, it wasn't long before the summit of Creag Leacach was reached. The sun briefly breaking through the cloud, it was warm here, but I could see there was slightly more cover north-east where the next hills lay.

Returning along the ridge, I was starting to get into my stride and there was apparently no aftermath from last night's indulgence. I powered north-east up smooth grassy slopes and onto the summit of Glas Maol. After a quick snack, I descended north, travelling fast over runnable slopes. My good mood increased, and even more so as there were no aches or pains, even in my right calf, which at some points yesterday had been excruciating. I've heard that quinine is supposed to be good for stopping muscle cramps, so perhaps all that tonic with the gin had helped. A fast walk brought me to the summit of Cairn of Claise then north north-west and west north-west to Carn an Tuirc. Thankfully, despite all the running, I wasn't overheating as the cloud cover was total and above the tops: perfect conditions. Traversing and descending east south-east, I switched OS sheets whilst enjoying the excellent view into the deep cut of Glen Callater. Another little pull followed, up to the summit of Tolmount.

Another descent and reascent, to the top of Tom Buidhe, saw me gazing for miles over the south-east expanse of the Mounth plateau to far-away Mayar, the next Munro. My mind cast back five and a half years to a cold, windy, sleet-filled January day in 1995 when, with Iain and Ian, we became disorientated in the mist on this barren upland. In fact, it was Ian's new altimeter watch that had helped extricate us from the situation, prompting me to buy my own a few months later. Today, the cloud was still just above the tops, but the odd wisp came lower every now and then, so I was keen to get across this MAMBA country while a line of sight was still available. Steady little jogs were interspersed with walks as I encountered undulating peat hags, and it took about an hour to gain the summit of Mayar. Continuing a gentle descent east, I soon arrived at the col and the steeper little climb up to the broad top of Driesh.

With the cloud level starting to rise again, I ran towards the Scorrie and down its steep snout. An easy walk to loosen off the legs brought me to the car park just after five, and I was pleased with my time of six hours thirty-five minutes for the easiest group of eight Munros of the trip. Dad was already there with Colin and Mark McColl, and over soft drinks we started the generator to plug in the laptop Colin had brought from Glasgow. Having not been online for three weeks, there were dozens of e-mails waiting. It was soothing to spend a few leisurely hours in the evening sunshine before Dad had to leave with Mark, and take Big Iain home to Airdrie, his stint as navigator and all-round helper now at an end.

The third week had certainly been much more productive than the previous two. The terrible weather at the start had meant another day dropped, and I was now five days behind schedule, but I had managed to hold the last five days, and fourty-seven Munros for the week was bowling nearer the mark. Sitting on one hundred and sixteen and passing the psychological number of one hundred had helped, so to keep on a roll and start the fourth week well, we turned in at nine for a good night's sleep.

Week 4

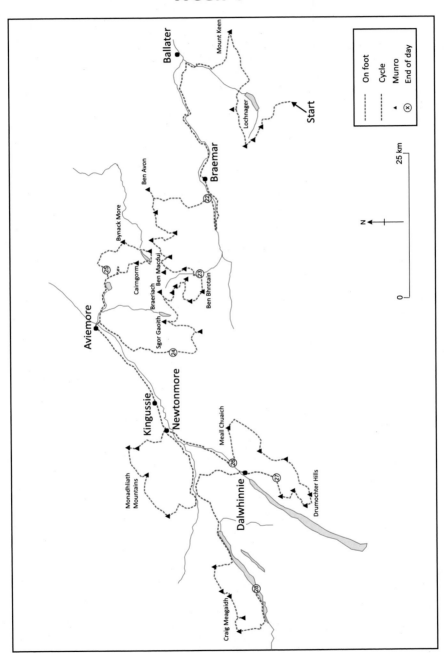

Week 4 – Feeling Low on High

Days 22-28

Day 22 – Monday 19 June

Fat chance of that! For some reason I wasn't tired, and it was a warm and humid night, so sleep was sporadic. The result was a lethargic Charlie getting up at six o'clock for another Monday at the office. Gordon Robinson turned up again to give a hand, and we hit the road at ten past eight. A gentle jog up the track by Moulzie, to the head of the glen at Bachnagairn, was followed by a climb north and west north-west to the summit of Broad Cairn. The other summits of Cairn Bannoch, Carn an t-Sagairt Mor and Carn a Coire Boidheach came and went easily, mere undulations on this high upland, and we were soon on Cac Carn Beag, the highest point of Lochnagar. Like my first visit here, there were no views from the trig, which was bathed in mist and light drizzle, so after a short rest, Gordon and I got going.

Following the main path over Cac Carn Mor, we missed the path junction, but quickly realised we had strayed, so it was only a few minutes' climb back over to the path we wanted, along the coire rim. Whilst jogging along this in the mist, we encountered an American guy who stopped us and asked if we could tell him exactly where he was and how far away the summit was, all the while unfolding some paper. Gordon and I, expecting to see a detailed map, were a bit taken aback to see that this guy was trying to climb the mountain with a book of tourist walks in Deeside, containing a general little map of the whole area; no wonder he was having difficulty locating his position. The fact that we had gone off course whilst using a good map and compass played in the back of our minds, but we gave him directions and set off again, just as his wife plodded up. Both of them were in jeans and trainers, which was not reassuring, but then again we were wearing shorts and trainers, so each to their own.

Continuing down the path, my left shin and ankle were aching again. Turning onto a stony, uneven track, I was struggling to jog, again slowing Gordon up. It was about ten past two when we got to the car park at the Spittal of Glenmuick. Upon arrival, Colin greeted us with the news that he had done a bit of mechanics and investigated the grinding noise we had been hearing in the van for the last few days: we had no front brake pads left, and the brake discs were scratched. Colin was going to phone Melville's later and see where we stood on this matter so, putting it to the back of my mind, I tucked into lunch. It was amusing to see that, even after his morning's outing of five Munros, Gordon only had a few handfuls of his own dried fruit mixture; no wonder he cut such a lithe figure. He was off again, over the Capel Mounth track back to his car, as I restocked my rucksack for the afternoon session.

The time had now arrived for a part of the overall journey I had not been looking forward to; quietly wishing over lunch that it would somehow disappear didn't work. Hugh Symonds had said how traversing this landscape had been difficult and tiring – gulp! If an athlete of his calibre found it hard, then how would a punter like me fare? There is no easy way to get to Mount Keen from Glen Muick so it was going to be the old scenario of head down and bust a gut.

Stepping out of the van at just before half past three, I slowly climbed southeast up the path, just along from the car park. After a while the path faded and gradually I emerged onto a bleak upland. Even with good visibility, I was finding it difficult to tell which low rounded top was which. The full benefit of the lunchtime calories were kicking in, however, and feeling strong, I switched on my personal stereo for an additional boost and attacked the rough ground with what I thought was a good speed. Jogging sometimes burst into running over the undulating heather and tussocks but, as soon as this had been achieved, I'd just as quickly drop over an edge and grind to a halt in the black mire of a peat hag. This went on for a while, and I realised that the constant oscillation in speed and climb was sapping my energy and adding dozens of extra feet of ascent that I hadn't accounted for.

Originally wanting to traverse about a kilometre south-east of Fasheilach, I realised that I must have drifted further east when the slopes started to drop more steeply down to a river on my right, heading in a northerly direction. The map told me that this must be the start of the Water of Mark, so what to do? The ground was still rough and undulating, but at a more acute angle, so progress was even slower. Down by the river there appeared to be green grassy strips on either bank, which looked much more appealing and runnable. Reluctant to lose more height, I really had no choice, and so dropped fifty or so metres to the river. At least I had the consolation of sparkling water on tap, and the going beside the river was indeed much easier.

Following the water for a mile and a half, I eventually headed up steep slopes by Little Hill. As the angle eased, through beads of sweat, Mount Keen came into view, at last looking within striking distance. I put a bit more effort into the final six hundred feet and touched the trig at twenty past six. It had been a hard three hours to cover approximately eight miles for this lowly Munro, but the relief at finally getting there was more symbolic than physical. Mount Keen being the most easterly Munro, this was not only a literal turning point in the journey, but also a psychological one. I had started three weeks ago in the far west, sweeping through central Scotland, and now this part of the journey was over. Twenty hills shy of the halfway mark, I was now heading west again, back to the rugged areas I love, and I almost felt this was the start of the long run for home.

Managing to get a photo of myself pointing to a beautiful sun in the west, I devoured some biscuits, put the headphones on again and charged downhill. The burst of new-found vigour was amazing as I passed Head of Black Burn, jumping over tussocks, cutting through runs in the heather, plunging through bogs and dropping over the upper tributaries of the Water of Tanar. The odd little peat hag and the gradual slopes to the south-east of Creag Dearg slowed me to a fast walk but, with dance tunes in my ears and the sun in my face, the work rate remained the same. Breathing hard and sweating, I was soon over Creag Dearg and bounding down through the heather north-west to the track. What looked like a lonely figure further down turned out to be Mum, and meeting her just as I rejoined the track for the final half kilometre, she passed me a welcoming little bottle of Irn-Bru.

At the motorhome, Colin told me that, after several phone calls with Melville's, he had arranged to take the van to the nearest approved garage, which happened to be in Aberdeen. This would necessitate the van being away for most of the day but, fortuitously for me, would coincide with the big Cairngorm jaunt I had planned for tomorrow. The angst was laid more at Colin's door, for he and Mum would have to make the long drive to Aberdeen, find the garage, hope the job got completed in time, and then make the long drive back. Colin then had a six mile walk-in with all the gear for our overnight camp in Glen Dee that evening. Fine by me.

Trundling down the glen, the evening sun was pleasant but I wasn't overly enthused at the thought of the thirty mile cycle. Wee Damon was en route from the Central Belt and I was looking forward to seeing him. Balmoral came and went and the van did the usual leapfrogging trick with me along the A93. I carried onto the Linn of Dee, then back along the other side of the river, where the van finally caught up. With diminishing light, it looked like there was a figure on the road ahead. Sure enough, just behind Mar Lodge, the imp that is Damon came bounding along, telling me that he had been fed up with waiting and had decided to stretch the legs. I kept going, and was soon at the road end at Linn of Quoich, closely followed by the others. Stepping off the bike at ten past ten, an average of just fifteen mph for the stage showed that I was tired. Damon put his tent up while Mum got cooking, and we all enjoyed a late dinner and catching up on news.

Day 23 – Tuesday 20 June

This was planned as the biggest day of mileage on foot for the whole trip, approximately thirty-six miles and over twelve thousand feet of climb along with it, so a five o'clock alarm was necessary. After yesterday's outing, though, it was a struggle to get up and the groggy feeling never really left me. Damon and I set off at just after six thirty, initially following the track up Glen Quoich, and then branching right onto a small path climbing north between Carn Elrig Mor and Carn na Criche. Even on this very gentle incline, my jogging was laboured, and bouts of fast walking were injected to give some respite. It was a grey and drizzling morning. Damon was sprightly and effervescent as ever, and I could tell that my relatively slow progress was frustrating for him, to the point where he diplomatically exclaimed, 'I thought there would be more running than this.' This has to be put in context: Damon is a two and a half hour marathon man with a pixie-like frame. I felt truly cumbersome trailing in his wake, the carthorse trying to keep up with the thoroughbred, but in my fourth week, I just couldn't cajole any more speed from the old nag.

Once past Clach a'Cleirich, we were into the mist, the increasing angle slowing the wee man a bit but, alas, me also. Turning right at The Sneck for a final climb up to the plateau, we jogged across and scrambled up the summit tor of Ben Avon. On the return, Damon thought it prudent, seeing as he now had phone reception, to call the wife to wish her a happy wedding anniversary. He struggled to hear in the increasing wind, but maybe it was just as well Anna's words were snatched away. Up the other side of The Sneck, we needed careful map and compass work in the mist, but even so, after reaching the plateau of the north top of Beinn a' Bhuird, I noticed we were starting to descend slightly. Damn, we must have missed the cairn, so we separated to about thirty yards, the limit of our visibility, and started sweeping round the summit plateau. Sure enough, after six or seven minutes of this, the cairn appeared out of the mist and was tagged with mitted hand.

Annoyed at losing even a few minutes, I was aware that our navigation had to be spot on for the long journey out to the next Munro, over featureless terrain; if we screwed this up, it could be hours lost rather than just minutes. This task was really mine alone, as Damon's forte was certainly not map and compass work. One clear and sunny evening the previous year, whilst leading the Kilpatricks hill race, Damon took the wrong route on part of the course, dragged the next five runners with him, and before they realised their error, the rest were away and fellow clubmate, Brian Bonnyman, won the race. Damon has never been allowed to forget this and, although I never mentioned it today, the compass was remaining firmly in my safe hands (at least I thought they were safe).

Over the next few miles we steadily worked our way down and round in a south-westerly direction, went by what we reckoned was the 858 metre spot height, and then started a rising traverse towards the summit. Arriving at the top, I looked at the map more closely and considered that the two summit tops looked similar in size and shape, with only four metres height difference. Were we definitely on the 931 metre top and not the 927 metre one? Surely we couldn't have drifted about six hundred metres over the last mile? Stranger things have happened, though, and with my altimeter not being able to distinguish height variances of less than five metres, I was just wishing that Beinn Bhreac would give us a break in the mist to check our surroundings. It wasn't to be. Logic prevailing, if we were to head west north-west, we would either descend or hit the other top, depending on where we were starting from. Heading off, the slope descended slowly for a while, but then gently climbed and we were soon at the cairn on the other top; our first one had been the true summit all along.

I had been aiming north north-west to hit the bottom of the eight hundred metre contour line on the west of the Moine Bhealaidh, then follow it north. But after a while we started descending fairly steeply. Telling Damon this wasn't right, I figured that we must have overshot the turn north and had inadvertently dropped into the gully where the Glas Allt Mor flowed. This wasn't really a problem, however, for if we now headed north, it would just be a short steep climb up the other side and then we would be on course again.

Not a problem, that is, until there was a fleeting break in the mist and we caught a glimpse of long slopes descending steeply away in front of us. This didn't tie up with being near the stream, so where the heck were we? Getting flustered, I was even desperate enough to give Damon the map. He made a few suggestions but could not work out our position, so we dithered for ten minutes until another fleeting gap in the mist revealed more. This time we could see across what looked like a large valley and then up steep slopes on the far side. Finally the penny dropped; we had drifted too far to our left after leaving Beinn Bhreac, gone straight over the featureless area of Craig Derry, and then started descending down towards Glen Derry itself – now that would have been a major *faux pas*! Climbing north-east, we got back to the edge of the Moine Bhealaidh, trudged through the boggy ground north and north north-west, then finally to the top of Beinn a'Chaorainn.

By now I was physically and mentally drained and even here, on this uninviting summit, I just wanted to lie down and sleep. This was not an option, so the next best thing was an extended lunch break. Whilst stuffing my face with food, over the next twenty minutes Damon and I discussed the many options. It was already two o'clock and, with my flagging performance, the planned big day was just not on. Damon finally came up with the right solution, which my tired mind quickly agreed to. Drop the three hills to the northwest, we could do the final three to the southwest today and still make the tent rendezvous with Colin tonight. I would just need to pick up the other three hills in two days' time, so one more day would be lost from the schedule.

Plan sorted, we managed an easy jog and descended south-west to the Lairig an Laoigh. Dropping below cloud level as we reached the pass, there was a brief period of brightness, and it actually felt warm for the first time that day. This didn't even last to the Hutchison Memorial Hut, and climbing steeply south-west we were back in the grey drizzle. Through a gap in the rocky outcrops, Damon was soon way ahead, but as the angle eased and the mist thickened, he waited for me. By the time I caught up, he was complaining of feeling cold, understandable considering he had only brought a light running jacket with him. Having no hat, I gave him a spare balaclava that he folded up to cover his head and I jokingly chastised him for not bringing more gear – did he not realise that this was Scotland in summer?

Through the mist and along the wet boulder-strewn ridge of Derry Cairngorm, we rounded the cairn and headed straight back. This was another long slow plod for myself, and further on, Damon walked with hands in pockets and head down, looking dejected. I felt sorry for him, as he had probably been expecting a lovely day where we skipped over Cairngorm giants in warm sunlight; the reality was more a cold and protracted crawl over these inflated contours. Across the final plateau and we were on top of Britain's second highest mountain. A metal plate giving names and distances to faraway hills was testament to the fine views on a clear day, but the only thing we had a chance of seeing was the Big Grey Man of Ben Macdui.

Taking another compass bearing, it wasn't too difficult to find the top of the Tailors' Burn, but the long stony descent south-west played havoc with my aching knees, and it was with relief when we came out of the mist to reach the grassy col at the bottom. It was at this point that Damon finally cracked and started running across the col, to which I responded by breaking into a shuffling jog. The first incline of the long Carn a' Mhaim ridge brought me straight back to walking pace, however, and I shouted to Damon to keep going himself. He came bounding back and we completed the rest of the ridge together, the summit flitting in and out of the cloud. To add a sting in the tail to an already exhausting day, we were then subjected to over a thousand feet of steep heather, full of half-hidden boulders, and giving a slow and painful descent. This seemed to take forever, but the angle and terrain did ease, and we finally got to the path in Glen Dee.

Arriving at the track end meeting point about eight o'clock, there was no sign of Colin. We looked about and waited a while, and then decided to walk very slowly southwards. After about three quarters of a mile, a faint figure appeared in the distance. We waited, and gradually the shape of a giant red rucksack with a pair of legs became apparent – Colin hadn't let us down, and was powering up the track to meet us. He arrived and we hurried putting the tents up, filling water bottles and getting the food cooked. Over a dinner of noodles, he filled us in with the motorhome story. They had left not long after us this morning and found the garage in Aberdeen. Having assured Colin yesterday that they had two types of brake discs in supply for our van, the mechanic had then discovered that neither of them would, in fact, fit. All they could do was leave the original brake discs on the van, and fit the new brake pads. They would wear out more quickly, but at least the van would get us to the end of the trip.

Day 24 – Wednesday 21 June

Having only briefly awoken a couple of times during the night, I was much fresher when the alarm sounded at twenty to seven. Waking the other two and peering into their tent, they both looked in a more bedraggled condition than I was. Always slow to stir in the morning, Colin lay in his sleeping bag whilst Damon and I sorted gear and had breakfast. By eight fifteen I was ready to leave. Thanking Damon for his help in getting me through yesterday, I told Colin I'd see him round in Glen Feshie, and turned back along the track. The eastern slopes of Beinn Bhrotain beckoned. The weather had not changed and I soon climbed back into cloud and light drizzle at about the eight hundred metre mark, then on up to the summit. Monadh Mor was easy enough but, once by Loch nan Stuirteag, it was more difficult on the climbing traverse over the area of Buidheanach of Cairntoul. The bearing was spot on, though, and getting to the top of the Devil's Point, I took a five-minute break before the next three big ones.

Despite this, the legs still lacked energy on the stony climb up to Cairn Toul, but I managed a jog down to the next little col, and a fast walk up to Sgor an Lochain Uaine, a new addition to the Munros in the 1997 revision. Down to the next wee col then over another top, brought me to the tributaries of the Falls of Dee, where I drank cold, clear water from the melting snow patches. Watching the compass all the way, another walk took me to the top of cliffs overlooking Coire Bhrochain, and then it was only a short distance round the corrie rim to the summit cairn of Braeriach. Britain's third, fourth, and fifth highest mountains were in the bag but a long trek lay ahead for the last two hills of the day.

Starting to feel cold, it was good to get jogging again and I paid very close attention to my compass over the Wells of Dee. Like yesterday, the cloud level had now risen in the afternoon, and after seven hours of greyness, I dropped through it at just above the one thousand metre mark again. I now had a line of sight and this would be a great aid in getting through the jumble of undulations that made up the ground between little Loch nan Cnapan and the top of the steep rocky outcrops above Coire Odhar. The top of Sgor Gaoith was clear and I could enjoy the rugged scenery dropping away into Loch Einich. Munro number eight for today was four miles away, and looked very distant indeed.

Skirting the western edge of the Moine Mhor, I managed to jog for a while, but this proved too exhausting so I slowed to a steady walk, munching sweets despite them giving no perceived energy boost. Reaching the track made for slightly easier going and I finally cut off to the cairn of Mullach Clach a' Bhlair. This isn't the most inspiring of hills so I left and retraced my steps, taking the track for the descent. Tired quads and knees ached and the hard jarring of the track started to inflame my left shin and ankle again. Many people say that they find descending harder than climbing; I always disagree, but today I was firmly in their camp. The paracetamol and ibuprofen had no effect and it was with great relief that I finally reached the bridge over the Feshie by Carnachuin.

Early evening sunshine now bathed the glen and made the walk up the road more pleasant. A bicycle at hand would have been even better to ease the discomfort. I crossed the bridge to the other bank and this last little stretch by the river was tranquil. Colin appeared and joined me for the last few hundred metres to the motorhome. As it was only quarter to eight, my intention had not been to stop for long; just a quick break and then cycle at least a few miles. Alas, it felt so good being in a comfy seat, with a cool drink in hand, that after eleven and a half hours on the go, I just couldn't face doing any more exercise. Mum passed me an envelope that Damon had left this morning. It contained a nice little note with a cheque towards our expenses. This was kind of him, but I wouldn't be cashing it, as his help on the hill yesterday had been more than enough.

Driving and briefly stopping at Kincraig to make some phone calls, we continued a couple of miles up the road and decided to pull in at Dalraddy campsite. At dinner, Colin and Mum seemed to be bickering over trivial matters, maybe they had spent too much time in each other's company in the last few days. Colin then told me that he was leaving tomorrow.

Day 25 – Thursday 22 June

Up at twenty to seven we drove back to the car park in Glen Feshie where I'd finished the previous night. As it was overcast and breezy, I asked Mum to pass the Paramo windproof jacket which Colin had carried out from Glen Dee. She couldn't find it, however, and had no recollection of what had become of it. Colin said he hadn't seen it either. Then Mum came up with the only solution – it must have gone out with some of the rubbish bags she had dumped in the bins back at the campsite. Bloody brilliant! My good jacket had been binned and I would need to cycle via the campsite again to find it.

I set off cycling back up Glen Feshie with the motorhome in tow. Through Kincraig, with the van speeding onto the campsite, I rolled up a few minutes later to find Colin and Mum coming back out clutching a plastic bag. The story was that, as they pulled in, they had heard the sound of a council refuse truck so had both sprinted round to the bin area, grabbed the lids off the bins and plunged in. After a bit of searching, they had pulled out some recognisable poly bags and, sure enough, my jacket was in one of them.

Our mini drama over, it was time for a sharp exit so I headed back up the B9152 towards Aviemore. After a few minutes, I became aware of a low whirring noise in the background. Admittedly, travelling at about fifteen mph isn't fast, but I was still surprised when a young guy in trendy baggy clothing cruised effortlessly past me on an oversized double-suspension mountain bike with big fat tyres. I turned towards Coylumbridge, the sun beginning to break through the clouds, and the temperature rising as the road wound through the forest. By Loch Morlich, almost a thousand feet of ascent lay ahead on the road up to Coire Cas but, selecting my lowest gear, the climb didn't feel too bad, and we were soon at the car park.

I opted for my lightweight boots to try and give the left shin and ankle a bit more support after the pounding they had taken yesterday. Finding it a struggle to leave the van, I had to depart because Mum was taking Colin back to Aviemore so he could catch the next bus to Glasgow. Colin's help had been invaluable over the last few days, getting the brakes fixed in the nick of time and doing his Sherpa act with the tent stopover in Glen Dee. Saying goodbye to him, I headed out into the sunshine and started upwards at a quarter to one.

My longing to stay in my motorhome refuge, compounded by Colin's departure, grew into a sense of loneliness as I climbed the ridge of Sron an Aonaich. My mind started mulling through all the facts. Here I was, on the twenty-fifth day of the trip, and by tonight I'd be on only one hundred and forty Munros. Passing the halfway number of one hundred and forty-two tomorrow, if I kept up at this rate I would finish around the fifty-one or fifty-two day mark; all I was doing was bursting my arse to repeat the old record. This realisation hit me full on and my sense of loneliness turned to one of despondency. Across on my right, a dark cloud was moving in, and as I climbed higher, I couldn't stop chewing over the situation. Much still to do, with several huge days planned in the weeks ahead. Would I cope? Could I cope? Did I even want to cope? Why continue? Why keep struggling with all this suffering; the tired body and sore muscles, the constant lethargy, the painful injuries that came and went – why? I could put a stop to it all right now: just turn around, go back down and admit defeat. The Munros had won and I had lost, I just wasn't good enough.

But hold on a minute. I had known it was going to be tough. 'When the going gets tough, the tough get going!' rang hollow in my head, meaningless at that moment. 'Come on, pick yourself up,' I voiced audibly, getting the little motivational cards out from my pocket.

The race is not always to the swift, but to those who keep on running.

Yeah, but I'm struggling with walking, never mind running. And this ain't a race, it's a slow war of attrition that I'm losing.

There are defining moments in a life ... when faced with the choice of giving up or going on ...

So true, but it didn't take away the pain and loneliness of the moment. I just wanted the whole burden lifted from my weary shoulders.

Labourers and machinery were at work further over, on the new funicular railway, but it was a world away from the one I was in. My mind wandered to the Good Book and I dwelled on one of my favourite scriptures, Philippians 4:13.

I can do all things through him who gives me strength.

Musing internally in a blue haze, maybe that was the trick; I should have been saying my prayers and asking for divine help.

Icy cold drops of rain instantly grabbed my attention and, gazing skyward, the black cloud that had been out to my right had now arrived and was enveloping the top of the mountain. Hurrying to put on my heavier jacket and pull up the hood, I just couldn't believe what was happening. Like in a cartoon, this one dark cloud, out of all the white and grey ones, had come across and dumped its load on me. Why, oh why? This just wasn't fair. In my head, the whole damn Munro run had now acquired Sisyphean proportions, and it was with a lump in my throat and fighting back tears that I moved over the final slope of Cairngorm.

Motivational books recommend looking for the good in any bad situation. When you are at rock bottom and suffering your own personal nadir, they say, something will present itself to help lift you out of the situation, if you look for it. I didn't have far to look. I covered the last few metres and arrived at the summit cairn. Immediately, I noticed something built into the stones of the cairn. I peered closer at the white paper that was taped to some red plastic and it read 'Please leave for Charlie Campbell Munro Run 2000.' A few seconds passed before the eureka moment: I had totally forgotten. This must be the parcel that Rory Gibson told me he'd leave on Cairngorm, for Damon and I when we were attempting our huge stage. I was amazed it was still sitting here intact, as the summit of Cairngorm is a busy place, but thankfully no-one had touched it. Removing all the stones that encased the parcel in the cairn, I pulled it free.

Spying the little weather station building sitting further along the top, I scurried away like a squirrel that had just found a big acorn, and sheltered behind it in privacy to open my present. Putting my hand in and proceeding to pull out treats, Rory had got it spot on. The best part was that there was two of everything because it was meant for Damon and me. This would certainly have given a welcome lift for the pair of us, two days ago, but it was now a morale-boosting banquet, especially with only a couple more hills to do. There were two bottles of water, two bottles of Coca-Cola, four bananas, two large bars of Cadbury's chocolate and a huge homemade bag of dried fruit, banana chips, little chocolate pieces, nuts and chocolate Smarties – ah, so this was the secret of Rory and Andrew's 1992 record. I ate two bananas, washed down with most of the water, and after taking a large handful of the mixture, I packed the rest away.

Thinking about the parcel, I was struck by the gesture that had been made. The current record holder had taken the time, money and effort to travel, and then climb up here to leave a big bag of goodies to help me try and beat his own record. In a scolding manner, I screamed out loudly at myself, 'You can't quit, you just can't!' Several other expletives and phrases were directed at myself, and I kept moving on.

I didn't feel good but I didn't feel so low either, just a kind of neutral mentality. It was time to slip into automatic pilot and not think, just do. The descent over the lip of Coire Raibeirt sharply focused my attention, and I had to concentrate on the rough path as it dropped steeply down to Loch Avon. I carried on around the end of the loch and across the river, which led to a steep pull south-east and east to come out on the flat col south of Stacan Dubha. Another rising traverse east north-east took me towards the tors and a little scramble up the highest, the summit of Beinn Mheadhoin.

Cresting A' Choinneach slightly to the east and continuing over the grassy plateau, another steady rising traverse found me on the summit of today's third and last Munro, Bynack More. I ran down the north ridge but I must have been too eager to get home. Without paying full attention, I had ventured much too far to my left and found myself above steep heather slopes dropping north-west to Strath Nethy. It was at least half a kilometre north-east to get back to the path I'd been aiming for so, noting that the map showed another path down by the river, I opted to head down the steep slope. Bad choice. I was soon struggling through deep heather, my boots and laces getting tangled, and several times, I tripped and stumbled. Down at the bottom and suitably irritated, I broke into a jog as the boggy path wound its way beside the river and up to Bynack Stable.

Light rain was now falling as I jogged down the track, fading to a steady walk by little Lochan Uaine. I was wondering if Mum would have found the road end, now that she didn't have a navigator with her. I needn't have feared, though, for coming round a bend near Glenmore Lodge, I saw this lonely little figure standing in the rain with my road bike, and it was heart-warming to see her. Although I didn't need the bike, the gesture was appreciated; she had wheeled it up the road and had then stood waiting, for the best part of two hours, amidst the rain and midges.

Wanting a quiet spot, I drove the van up the road to the Sugarbowl car park, which we had all to ourselves. Manny and family were in Kingussie, looking to relocate to the area. He had a job interview the next day, so he drove out to meet us. It was cheering to have him and his own brand of zaniness about for a while. Ian Struthers phoned from Glasgow and told me that the blood samples he had taken were fine, so at least I wasn't breaking down totally on the physical front. It was the psychological front that was under attack at the moment, and what my body and mind were screaming out for was rest. One good twenty-four hour period of food and sleep would have seen me right, but it was a luxury that I couldn't afford whilst the clock was ticking.

Day 26 – Friday 23 June

Up at half past six, coffee, grub, sort gear, drive back down to the Glenmore Lodge road end, step out into a grey rainy morning, sort the bike, and I was off at eight o'clock. The first few miles passed easily on a gradual descent, and gave a nice little warm-up, which was just as well. Having been sheltered in the forest, I turned south-west onto the B9152 and was promptly hit face on by a strong wind blowing north-east. Oh great, here we go again! It took ages to cycle down the road and, by the time I was going through Kingussie, I'd decided to change the plan and switch the hill direction so I'd have a tailwind. The only problem was that Gordon Robinson was giving support today and was meeting me at the wee road end above Newtonmore, so in the village I jumped off the bike, collected Gordon in the motorhome, then continued cycling south-west. It was still a struggle into the wind all the way to Laggan and then onwards to our stopping point near the Spey Dam. The thirty-one mile cycle plus change of route had eaten up time, so it was with relief that Gordon and I started running at twenty past eleven.

Heading north up the track in Glen Markie for a couple of miles, we crossed the burn and climbed into the mist up steepening slopes, through rocky outcrops, and onto the top of Beinn Sgiath. Compass bearings then took us to the top of our first Munro, Geal Charn, and after grabbing a quick snack we set off for the long slog to the next one. Keeping slightly lower on the leeward east side of the fence line, which crested the highest ground, we paid very close attention to the map and also any physical features that could be distinguished in the mist. Cutting the corner to the south of Carn Odhar na Criche saved both height and distance; climbing gradually to the east and south-east, we then came to the summit of Carn Dearg. The lowly little cairn didn't look much, but it meant enough to me, as it was my one hundred and forty-second Munro – halfway at last! Gordon took a photo and then I snapped one of us at arm's length, just as the cloud lifted momentarily to let us glimpse our surroundings.

Returning north north-west to Carn Ban and picking up the district boundary line fence posts, we followed these but cut corners and took direct lines where we could to save time and effort. On the summit of Carn Sgulain, we passed the first cairn and moved onto a second, but I wasn't sure if there might be others, so we walked on through the mist for a further hundred yards. There was nothing else. Returning and dropping south south-west, crossing a stream, we climbed north took to our last Munro, A' Chailleach. Not far down the other side, we dropped below cloud level.

Running and jumping through the heather, we saw a distant figure climbing towards us. After a while we were with Manny, who had decided to come and see how we were getting on. Manny, whose job interview had gone well and was in a good mood, kept us entertained as we jogged the last bit of track to the motorhome.

Gordon was leaving and I wouldn't be seeing him again until the final week of the trip, if I made it that far. He had come out and helped get me through three grey and rainy days that week, and it was appreciated. Saying goodbye and getting on the bike again, I had a good little run down into Newtonmore and out along the B9150, but I wasn't too enthusiastic about having to join the A9. There was no other route, however. Pulling into the lay-by just beyond Cuaich, it was the back of seven and the schedule for the day was already scuppered. The plan had been to continue on and do the three Munros to the east of Drumochter with Manny's help, but even though he was still keen to go, I had to renege.

Putting the bike on the rack, Mum and I headed down the A9 and took the Dalwhinnie turn-off a few miles later, managing to find a suitable little spot for the van. Knowing two monster days were planned for Knoydart and Torridon, I realised that, after my Cairngorm 'failure', there was just no way I'd be able to do them. They would need to be split, meaning another two days lost. And I still had to pencil in the three Glenfinnan hills I'd dropped on day one, so that would effectively be another day gone. If I could hold all the other big days, and that was a big if, then I might still sneak in around the fifty day mark. But I wouldn't have liked to bet on it: seven days dropped by halfway meant I could only afford to lose three more days in the second half of the run – the odds didn't look good. The whole thing was still just about possible, but today had been fairly tough for only four Munros and, as my diary entry noted – 'Hope my enthusiasm starts to pick up.'

Day 27 – Saturday 24 June

Getting up at seven o'clock, we could afford a leisurely start, as Mark Rigby and Jennifer Rae were driving up from Glasgow. The truckers' cafe was open in Dalwhinnie and we decided to treat ourselves, and give Mum a rest from cooking breakfast. Soon afterwards Mark's car pulled up, with Jen and Damien Theaker also on board. Driving in convoy to Drumochter summit car park to drop their car, I then took us all back to the Cuaich lay-by in the motorhome. It was breezy and overcast when we started at ten, jogging along the aqueduct track. A huge nut and bolt from one of the water pipes was lying on the ground, so I held it to Mark's head whilst a photo was taken – was this the one he had been missing all these years, or was it mine?

A steady climb up into the dreich mist led to the summit of Meall Chuaich, a few nibbles, and then a good descent south south-east to the col. Chatting, Mark said he had brought up a newspaper cutting for me that I might find inspiring. It was an article on Jamie Andrew, who had lost both his feet and hands to frostbite in a climbing tragedy in which his friend had died. But now, with the use of prosthetics, Jamie had managed to climb to the summit of Ben Nevis the previous weekend. This was indeed a remarkable and inspiring triumph, and a story I had been following. Jamie and I had been in the same year at Kelvinside Academy and, although we didn't mix in the same circles, had shared some classes in our lower years, and registration class in sixth year. I thought it cruel that, in our own separate and individual ways, we went to the mountains to pursue our love of the outdoors and now, by a twist of fate, Jamie was a quadruple amputee and here I was running over the hills. It kept things in perspective with my recent mindset.

Mark forged ahead through the boggy undulations and then the ridge climbed slowly up to Carn na Caim. Damp, windy and misty was how I'd found this Munro the first time, five years previously, and it was still the same. It had been my hundredth Munro and the boys had brought me a celebratory bottle of beer – chilli beer! The gits made me drink every last drop, starting a routine whereby, whenever one of us reached a significant Munro, we'd have some sort of weird and wonderful alcoholic concoction that had to be downed by the recipient. Thankfully today, the others were far kinder and offered more appetising sustenance and drink.

Continuing south-west over undulations, I was beginning to tire by the 902 metre spot height. With a final little slog, we came up to the trig pillar on top of A' Bhuidheanach Bheag. Just as we got there, the cloud lifted from the top, the sun shone through, and our summit photo belied what it had actually been like for the previous few hours. Descending south-west, we made our way through final steep heather and rock slopes and down to the motorhome.

Mum had warmed up a large pot of soup, so upon getting into the van and sitting at the table, we all immediately had a bowl in front of us with as much bread as we wanted. Toasted cheese rolls were also on the menu, perfect for dunking in the soup, and more than compensated for the five and a half hours of calories that had just been burned. Mark, having a copy of my schedule at home, brought out some plans that he had written up. Over our late lunch, he quickly explained how I could rejig days and hills during the following week and get to Skye early. If I managed it by the following weekend, we could take advantage of our friend George Reid, whose climbing skills would be invaluable on the Cuillin ridge. Jen presented me with of a couple of pairs of new running socks and a big box of home baking treats, which were more than welcome. In the back of my mind, however, was the fact I was still only halfway through today and would have to go back out into the dreich hills, this time on my own. As I started to pack my rucksack, they must have been able to read my mind;

Jen suddenly announced that they'd join me for an hour up the first hill and then come back. Unbelievable – this was just what I wanted to hear.

Leaving again at half past four, we headed down the road a bit, then cut over the railway line to pick up the track leading into Coire Dhomhain. The hour came and went, but the other three had decided to continue to the top of Sgairneach Mhor. Once we reached it, I sincerely thanked them. In the mist and drizzle, I paid very close attention to the map and compass to ensure that I found the col, before climbing north-west and north to the top of the gloomy mountain, Beinn Udlamain. It lived up to its name today. Feeling strong, it didn't take me long to get out to A' Mharconaich, before dropping below cloud level at the col above Coire Fhar. I was promptly straight back into it for the last climb up to Geal-charn. Enjoying a relatively fast descent, the soft peaty ground further down made for less pounding on the joints, and I got to the motorhome beside Balsporran Cottages at half past eight.

Mum asked if I was going to do any cycling, but I politely refused, knowing there was plenty of time for that tomorrow with it being an easy day. We drove back along the A9 and pulled into the Invernahavon Caravan Park in Glentruim. Feeling great after a thorough wash and fresh clothes, I phoned Mark McColl to tell him the latest schedule amendments for the website. It was nice to relax with a bottle of beer and I studied the maps whilst looking at Rigby's amended schedule for the upcoming week. It was definitely a goer. My more upbeat mood was reflected in my last little diary entry, very much in contrast to the one twenty-four hours previously – 'Chuffed with the three of them helping me. Feel like I'm picking up now mentally.'

Day 28 – Sunday 25 June

Leaving the campsite at half past eight it was overcast and dry, but I didn't realise how cold it was until stepping out at Balsporran Cottages again. There was a cutting northerly wind so I needed fleece leggings, thermal vest, cycling top, windproof jacket, hat and Buffalo mitts – all this just four days past the summer solstice. It was a bit of a battle up the A9 for a couple of miles, then through Dalwhinnie and over the A889, but once onto the A86 and heading westwards, the going became easier. In the rather full car park at Aberarder, the sun was breaking through the clouds and, with the wind easing off by the time I headed for the hill at twenty-five past eleven, it had the makings of a pleasant summer's day.

Climbing strongly in the warm heat, I soon had to take my top off. After a photo with Creag Meagaidh and The Window providing an excellent backdrop, I was soon up to the top of Carn Liath, which I had all to myself. It was fast going over undulations for the next couple of miles, and there were a few folk on top of Stob Poite Coire Ardair as I arrived. Passing even more on their way up, I dropped down to The Window, the volume of people increasing again on the other side, all climbing Creag Meagaidh. Many salutations later and I was at the summit and over the other side, where I knew it would be quiet and far from the madding crowd. Southwest for a bit, then a broad grassy spur headed west and made for soft, fast, enjoyable running to the Bealach a' Bharnish.

Aware that the sun had been beating down on my head for a few hours now, the white hat was out. Munching a few biscuits, I enjoyed a steady walk up the north-east ridge, admiring how the steep rocky walls dropped away into Coire na h-Uamha. Over the north top and onto Beinn a' Chaorainn, there were great views westwards to Loch Arkaig, and a plethora of mountains stretching northwest.

It was a steady descent north-west to the col, but my legs were starting to weaken, and I could only manage a slowish walk up the ridge to Beinn Teallach, one of the lowest Munros at 915 metres. Jogging down long heather slopes and starting to get that overheated nauseous feeling, I walked for the last bit by the river and into the forest, managing a final jog to come out on the main road by Roughburn just before six o'clock. Climbing over the big stile, Dad had already arrived with Mark McColl. After a quick change and some juice, Mark took my mountain bike and helped pace me up the road for a few miles to the car park by Luiblea. We were finished for half past six.

Sorting a few bits and bobs whilst Mum made dinner, it was nice for the five of us to enjoy a relaxing meal and catch up. With mobile phone reception lousy, I took Dad's car and drove back down the road for a few miles to the public phone near Tulloch station. Speaking to Mark Rigby to say that we'd go with his plans for later in the week, I then phoned Dave Calder from Westies, who was coming up with his wife and fellow club member, Muffy, to help tomorrow. Returning to the van, Dad and Mark headed for home and I then had time to reflect at the end of week four.

One hundred and fifty-six in the bag but only forty Munros for the week was poor again. Dropping another two days meant that I was now exactly one week behind the planned schedule. I had felt down at times, especially on Thursday, a result of the often poor weather and hills that are not the most inspiring to me. I had found it it all very tiring just to get to halfway. At least Rory's food parcel and the help of others during the week had given me a psychological lift. Now that I was heading west, I was feeling much better. How long that feeling was to last would be tested immediately, for tomorrow's hills involved a grand sweep between Loch Laggan and Loch Ericht, then down to Loch Ossian; eleven Munros in total, all through remote land.

Week 5

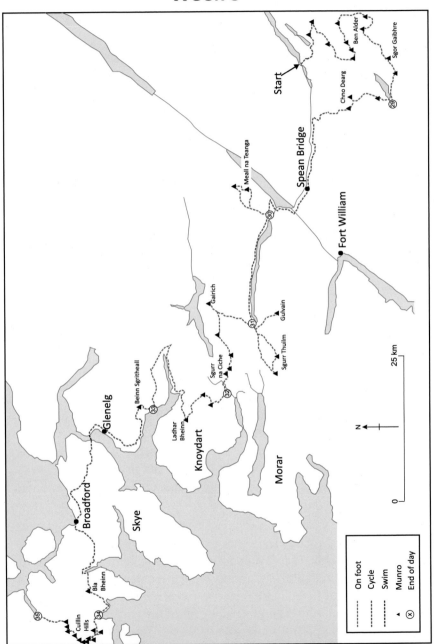

Week 5 – Speed, Bonnie Boat, Like a Bird on the Wing

Days 29-35

Day 29 – Monday 26 June

The start of week five saw us getting up at a quarter to six. I spent a while deciding what gear and food was going to be given to Dave and Muffy to take into Loch Ossian Youth Hostel. As it was a very big day, with no chance to rendezvous at any point, I had to ensure that everything required for the next twelve to fourteen hours was on board. Even my own rucksack ended up fairly heavy. Time was of the essence and I wanted to be away by seven, but that had come and gone and I was tetchy and getting annoyed with June, who seemed to be wasting time; who needs to brush their hair before going on a run at this time of the morning? Was it because I'd mentioned that they'd filmed the BBC series *Monarch of the Glen* near here? Finally, on our way at twenty to eight. June jogged along while I cycled the mountain bike by Luiblea, and up the track to the end of Lochan na h-Earba and its little sandy shore. I was edgy because I knew that a particularly big day lay ahead, and in remote land there could be no slip-ups; I had to successfully climb my hills and get to Loch Ossian in one piece.

Thankfully the weather was on my side and a uniform blanket of cloud sat above the tops, giving clear visibility but screening off the sun. It was cool and comfortable – ideal running conditions. After a steady walk to the first Munro, Creag Pitridh, a short jog got me down to the col and I was soon on top of Geal Charn, before a faster run to the next col. After a steep initial climb, it was a gradual ascent of the long summit ridge of Beinn a' Chlachair, all the while with views north-west to the white dot of the motorhome, still sitting beside the A86. I then moved off the top south-west, then west south-west, on a long ridge down to the stream.

With the warm-up over, it was time to start working in earnest. I had refilled the CamelBak higher up, as there would be no water supplies for the next few hours. I eventually got to the top ridge and round to the summit of Beinn Eibhinn, where I took a five minute breather and had some grub. It felt slightly chilly up here but the good ridge made for quick running onto the top of Aonach Beag. After another little descent, I headed round to the summit cairn of the second Geal Charn of the day. A fast run then took me across the broad plateau to the top of a steep spur, which I descended. Starting to flag a bit, I munched biscuits and walked all the way up to the top of Carn Dearg.

It was now mid-afternoon. The cloud cover had lasted well but, coming off the side of Carn Dearg down steep slopes of stones and heather, the sun burned through and things immediately began to warm up. Concentrating hard on the descent, it was only on getting down to the river that I realised how warm it was. I topped up the reservoir again, downed several cups of water and put on the sun hat for some protection, as I climbed the path on the far side. I had to leave when it swung away to the right, and climbed directly south south-east towards the long ridge of Beinn Bheoil. Gaining this and turning south south-west, it was an enjoyable walk to the summit. Two older gentlemen were coming along the ridge in my direction. Exchanging pleasantries about what a fine day it had become, I told them that they were the first people I'd seen all day. They retorted likewise, although, sitting on Ben Alder, they were sure they had seen a runner on the top of Geal Charn. Replying that it had most likely been myself that they had seen, their faces suggested disbelief. I made my excuses and headed on over the top. Soon down at the Bealach Breabag, another plod saw me to the plateau of Ben Alder and the steadily curving climb round the Garbh Choire cliffs to the summit trig.

I allowed myself a rest; it was turning into a beautiful evening, with great views in all directions. I rattled off a few photos before having a fast run westwards, then turning and dropping very steeply south south-west by the stream for almost five hundred metres. Crossing the upper tributary of the Alder burn, I refilled the water supply, as even after seven o'clock it was still warm. I then continued on a gradual climbing traverse into the lower reaches of Coire na Cloiche. Experience has taught me that the type of terrain now displayed on my map usually meant tough going through heather, bog and peat hags, and so it was to prove. Cutting south over the broad ridge that came down from Meall a' Bhealaich, I veered and managed to jog over slightly declining ground towards Lochan a' Bhealaich, where at one point I suddenly hit the deck. Picking myself up and turning, I saw my foot had gone straight down a hole in the peaty ground, up to about mid-shin depth, and somehow come straight back out without getting jammed. Scraping the dirt off, I felt lucky indeed for what should have been a broken leg; the big person above must have been looking after me, for this was exactly the type of 'no man's land' where I could not afford an accident.

I enjoyed the coolness of some shade on the next steep climb, before popping back out into sunlight on the Bealach nan Sgor. My legs were feeling the burn on the climb up to Munro number ten, Sgor Gaibhre. I took a few minutes to get in some calories, then jogged down to the col before another walk, up to the summit cairn of today's second Carn Dearg, my last hill. It was nine o'clock but the sun was still shining brightly, one of those summer evenings when one feels enlivened. There was no sign of Dave as I ran off and started leaping through the heather, but he suddenly appeared over to my right and caught sight of me at the same time. Down at the hostel for quarter to ten meant it had been fourteen hours on the go - which I had expected for today. I was happy that it had all gone to plan.

Surprised at meeting Muffy with her left arm in a sling, it transpired that she had tripped the week before, whilst running along the relatively benign Kelvin walkway in Glasgow, and had fractured her arm. Still, even with only one functioning arm, Muffy had managed to boil some rice, so after giving myself a brief wash in the loch, I opened a tin of chilli they had brought in and it went down a treat with the rice. The hostel was quite busy with other users so we sat and chatted for a while – Thomas the warden was suitably unimpressed when Dave told him my day's journey, which by this point had caught up with me, so we turned in at eleven fifteen.

Day 30 – Tuesday 27 June

We packed away all the gear into three rucksacks and Dave and I, being true gentlemen, promptly buggered off just before half past nine and left one-armed Muffy to carry it all back to Corrour train station. Muffy said she didn't mind making two trips to the station, as the train wasn't due for a couple of hours, so we had loaded the large rucksack onto her back and she carried one of the smaller sacks with her good arm, returning later for the other one. This was good of her, as Dave and I could then head straight for our first hill without any detours.

Managing a brief jog round the track, the pair of us took to the long, steadily rising slopes of Beinn na Lap. Whilst plodding upwards, I kept my eyes focused on the ground in a vain attempt to find my red Swiss Army knife, lost here back in 1996. After partaking of most of a bottle of whisky for our last Munro of the year with Ian and Iain, I'd thought it a good idea to try some tobogganing in my plastic survival bag. Shooting down the snow was fun, but not when I turned around to see a trail of gear scattered back up the slope – I'd forgotten to re-zip the top rucksack pocket. Despite searching, we never did find the knife, so if you ever happen to find one on this hill, with the initials C.C. etched on it, you know how it got there.

No such shenanigans today as Dave and I headed over the summit and down the north north-east ridge, before dropping north north-west over the Allt Feith Thuill. On the steep climb up the far side, my tired legs were feeling it from the big day yesterday. It took a while but we got to the subsidiary top of Meall Garbh, with an easy little jog down to the next col, where I dumped the rucksack before the final pull up to Chno Dearg. The knolly ridge of Stob Coire Sgriodain again slowed me, but we got to the summit and didn't stop for long before descending north. Further down the ridge, we somehow came off the usual path and ended up descending on the western side of the little 470 metre top. This made for a rough descent and brought us into the trees, but we managed to get through and onto the railway line, which we then followed for a few hundred metres before crossing at the Loch Treig dam wall. Gaining the track on the other side, we jogged up to the car park at Fersit, and the motorhome, at a quarter to two.

After a brief rest, it was tempting to gorge on food and drink, but I resisted as there was still a cycle to come. Heading off at twenty past two, the undulating little road to the A86 warmed up the cycling legs nicely and the gradual descent all the way to Spean Bridge made for fast going. It was a sharp contrast to when I had cycled painfully up this road on day

119

two of the trip. Turning right onto the A82, I noticed a crunched white Fiat Tipo sitting in the local mechanic's forecourt and remembered what had happened to club mate, Archie Cameron, who had crashed just up the road from here a few weeks ago. Despite the coachloads of tourists at the Commando Memorial, we had no such problems, and negotiated the road safely down to Gairlochy. A few miles along the B8005 we stopped at the Chia-aig forestry car park, beside the Witches Pool and waterfall. My day's work over at half past three, it was a lovely spot, so with the sun starting to break through, we shot some more photographs before leaving.

Returning along the same route and continuing on the B8004, it turned out to be quite a busy road with single track stretches. Mum often had to pull over for other cars and vans to squeeze by. On a particularly sharp corner, one of the upper cupboard doors flew open and out fell a plastic tub containing an open bag of sugar. Poor Shaw, who had been peacefully minding his own business on the floor, was suddenly whacked and covered in about a kilo of sugar.

Getting to the car park where Dave had left his car, we met Muffy, who had successfully managed to get all the rucksacks onto the train at Corrour and back to Fort William. Then, to kill some time, she went shopping. Only one functioning arm didn't stop a perusal of the local outdoor shops, or handing over the plastic fantastic, and now Dave struggled into his new roll-neck fleece pullover and emerged like a New Romantic from the 1980s. Thanking 'Dapper Dave' and Muffy for their help as they headed off, the three of us had a cup of tea and a sandwich. Feeling suitably inspired by Muffy, June and Mum decided to go and take a look in the outdoor shops themselves, with myself tagging along for the ride. I spied a zany-coloured Buff and remembered how Damon, having forgotten his own hat last week in the Cairngorms, had still had the temerity to slag off the Buff I was wearing at the time. I decided to buy it for him, posting it off with a cheeky little note inside.

After four weeks of exercise with only one day of injured rest, I'd been toying with the idea of taking advantage of our visit to the metropolis and getting myself a good sports massage. Heading into Marco's on the way back to the van, I thought there was a fair chance they would have a massage therapist on site, but no such luck. We did get the number for a therapist offering a mobile service, but it turned out they were down in Oban that evening. I would just need to stick with Mum's amateur but worthy hands for the time being. Colin pulled up on his motorbike after taking a blast from Glasgow, and we all drove round to the Lochy Holiday Park, where I cleaned myself up with a shave and a shower.

Dave Calder's e-mail to Westies the next day

Monday: I met Charlie bounding off the last of his day's Munros at 21:00, looking none the worse for wear after his longest day yet. He was understandably tired but in fine form as he arrived at the hostel. Conditions had been good with late afternoon sunshine giving tremendous views in all directions. In true Westies fashion, Charlie went for a post-run dook in the loch, however, he wisely declined full immersion. For Muffy and I, the experience of arriving at Loch Ossian was rather different to the normal Westies event. Ok, so I did have to carry in two rucksacks from Corrour Station, but at least I didn't also have to struggle in with multiple poly bags containing Archie's carry-out and homebaking! And it was still daylight when we arrived, with no puddles to dodge on the track. Thomas the Warden viewed us suspiciously when we arrived, quickly clocking that we were from Westies, although we sensed his relief when we adjourned to bed obediently at the 23:00 curfew. This must rank as some sort of club record! It was rather ironic that despite 167 Munros and 4 weeks continuous running, Charlie has so far avoided major bodily damage, however, Muffy was there complete with fractured radius after tripping up on the Kelvin walkway last week. Despite this, Charlie did remark that she was still able to prepare a mean boil-in-the-bag rice.

Tuesday: The day started a bit claggy but cleared up later to give another day with fine running conditions. Charlie has decided to have a lie in, so he didn't get up until 07:00! The day was relatively easy, with only 3 Munros (Beinn na Lap, Chno Dearg and Stob Coire Sgriodain) so I decided that this was just about within my capabilities and left with Charlie just after 09:00. Clearly tired from the day before, Charlie nevertheless made steady progress over all three summits. We both cursed the rough descent into Fersit, but at least I had the benefit of knowing that my stint was almost complete. However, faced with the 20 mile cycle to the overnight stop at Loch Arkaig, Charlie suddenly seemed to get a second wind and looked good all the way. To make up for Charlie's relatively unexceptional itinerary, the main day's excitement came on the ensuing journey in the motorhome from the overnight stop back to Fort William. Charlie's Mum skilfully negotiated the vehicle along the single, twisting track, the parallels

121

with Colin Macrae seeming obvious as we avoided with hairsbreadth precision the oncoming juggernauts and coaches. To cap it all, Charlie's sister June was attacked by a sugar bowl, which launched itself from a high level cupboard as we negotiated yet another bend in the road. We left Charlie in Fort William as he was about to enter into negotiations over a massage (I'm saying no more ... !)

Day 31 – Wednesday 28 June

We drove back round to yesterday's finish at the Chia-aig car park, and I got going for half past nine, again with overcast, dry weather, and the cloud at about Munro level. Once up onto the track, I had a good run along the glen, over the bridge and along the Allt Cam Bhealaich, before taking to the south-west slopes of Sron a'Choire Ghairbh. The climb was broken when I spied a little common lizard darting about in the grass; managing to catch it, I took a few photos as it sat in my hand and peered up with big black eyes. I continued up to the summit in the cloud, then made a quick descent down to the Cam Bhealach, before climbing south and south south-west, along the top of the 'Hill of the Tongue' to its summit. Another quick down and up to Meall Coire Lochain then took me westwards, running along at about the height of the eight hundred and fifty metre contour line and cutting below the tops of Meall Odhar. Quickly I dropped out of the mist, and all the way down to the path again. It was now warm and humid, so I flagged a bit on the final run, meeting June and her camera whilst dropping down to the car park just after half past one.

I changed into my cycling gear and then we set off. I wasn't really looking forward to the cycle because I'd driven this road several times before, and knew how undulating it was as it ran along the north shore of Loch Arkaig. Setting off, I trundled along; the relatively poor surface didn't help my progress. At the road end, we found a suitable spot for the motorhome and I packed my rucksack while Mum provided a late lunch. After a month, it was time to pick up the three Munros that I'd dropped on day one of the trip, but it was now four o'clock, so I wasn't giving myself much time. It had only been twenty to five when I had decided not to go for them in the first place – because of lack of time!

With the heat of the sun making a steady walk feel like exertion enough, I followed the track by the houses at Strathan and into Glen Pean, the trees providing a bit of shelter for a while, before coming out to the path by the bothy. This was a lovely spot and, following the path by the river, at one point I noticed ripples darting across a big pool that had dried up a bit and become separated from the main body of water. Always curious, I took a closer look and saw the wake of a fish darting across again; having been an avid fisherman as a boy, I recognised it as a young pike. I thought it strange that this fish was here in the upper reaches of a small river, trapped in a glorified puddle, but despite trying, there was no way I could catch it to return it to the main stream.

Climbing steadily south-west, I worked my way through rocky outcrops further up and, by the time I came out on the ridge to the west of Meall an Tarmachain, it had at last clouded over. Dumping the rucksack and taking the camera, I nicked up to the top of Sgurr nan Coireachan, where there were great views westwards over the end of Loch Morar and out to Eigg and Rum. Collecting the rucksack again, I tried to jog as much as possible along the ridge between the two Munros, but four little climbs over the other tops took their toll, and I trudged up the last bit to Sgurr Thuilm. The jagged outline of the distant Cuillin was silhouetted on the golden horizon and it was exciting to think that I'd be there in a few days, but I had a more immediate problem at hand. It was after eight o'clock, and Gulvain still looked fairly distant, but the main obstacle was the intervening ridges, which would add lots of extra climbing. It didn't take me long to come to the sensible decision, and I headed off down the north-east ridge, before dropping into Gleann Cuirnean and all the way out to Strathan again.

On the last bit of track towards the van, I turned a corner and June was there. I walked by her and mentioned that I had ran out of time and hadn't managed Gulvain. 'Just stop a minute,' she replied. This sounded serious, so promptly obeying and not saying another word, June told me that George Reid had arrived in the late afternoon with a friend, Martin, from the Czech Republic. They had decided to reverse my route and hopefully intercept me on Gulvain. It was five minutes to ten, with the light starting to fade, and they were probably still sitting up there waiting for me. I stood for a moment thinking, and then we strolled along the last bit of track back to the van. In a nutshell, there was nothing we could do. I knew Big George was an experienced hill man so he would wait up there a certain length of time and then they would come back and that would be it; I just hoped he had packed a headtorch. Feeling guilty as I ate dinner and hoping the pair of them would arrive, it didn't happen and I turned in after eleven, crashing out with tiredness.

There was a timid knock on the door at five to two. Stirring groggily, I went to the door and George was just as glad to see me as I was to see him. It turned out that he was only going back to Dundee for a day and that he'd be returning on the Friday, so we'd get to do some climbing together after all.

Day 32 – Thursday 29 June

We were up at seven o'clock and because I only had to carry a bumbag for this morning's outing, it didn't take long to sort stuff, and I was ready to leave by eight. Presuming George would be having a lie in after his late night, I was surprised to see him up and about, and he told me the details of last night. He and Martin had waited a while on Gulvain, but the penny had dropped when I didn't show up, and they had come back down and around the loch over rough ground. This had been difficult in the darkness, and Martin was further hindered because he had been wearing a pair of open-toed sandals. The plan this morning was for George to collect Mark Rigby from the A82 and then bring him along to the motorhome, so I'd see the pair of them when I returned.

The sun was already shining brightly, it was warm as I left for Gulvain. Hopefully now it was a case of third time lucky. It felt good to be able to run without the rucksack and following the track for about half a kilometre, I climbed the fence and headed over rough ground where the River Pean flows into the loch. Finally, the boggy tussocks gave way to good old *terra firma* and the intervening ridge, from Leac na Carnaich to Monadh Ceann Lochairceig, rose steeply in front. From the map, the lowest chink that I could see in its armour was at about four hundred and fifteen metres, so I aimed for that and got on with the work, before dropping over the other side and back down to about one hundred and sixty metres in Gleann Camgharaidh.

Bathed in sunlight, this was quite a pretty glen. I crossed the stream and had a few cupfuls of water before starting on the next eight hundred metre climb. Sweating in the sun, thankfully Gulvain was casting a partial shadow on this side of the hill, and as I climbed into the shade, it made the steep slopes a bit more bearable. A last little walk along to the summit and, thirty-one days late, Gulvain was finally topped. It gave superb views, with this afternoon's hills looking rather distant. The ground didn't make for a fast descent, but I went back over the stream, with some more gulps of water, and then launched on another climb to the ridge, where about halfway up I stopped for a quick breather. Looking back over the glen, soaring high above was a bird of prey; having seen plenty of buzzards, this beauty was almost double the size, so it must have been a golden eagle. Fantastic!

Leaving the eagle to its glen and dropping over the other side of the ridge, I had another battle with the rough ground by the west end of the loch before regaining the track and the van. Ten past twelve meant it was lunchtime, and Mark and George had arrived and were outside the van with Mum and June. They had the video camera running once again. For the umpteenth time she asked, 'How do you feel?' to which I sarcastically retorted, 'How do you think I feel? Bloody hell, you ask that every time … I feel GREAT!' Poor June, she would need to come up with a new question now. Mark, George and Martin were going to walk into Carnoch for an overnight tent stop, which was great as it meant that the original huge day that I had planned for the Knoydart Munros could now be split into two more manageable days.

After lunch, I gave Mark all my gear for tonight and tomorrow and then changed into a white top and sunhat for the next stage. Just as well because, stepping outside, it felt like an oven. As it was twenty to two, it was time to get a move on. I climbed the slopes immediately behind the motorhome, intercepted the path beside the Dearg Allt, and followed it over the broad 450 metres col for a jog down by Kinbreack bothy, where I managed to get a spot to cross the River Kingie. Picking up the path on the far side, I followed it up to where it crossed the Allt a Choire Ghlais, and then found a suitable place to leave the rucksack.

Free of its weight, and despite the five thousand feet already in the legs, I climbed strongly up steep slopes and, as the angle eased, jogged over the broad top of Gairich Beag. Another little pull saw me to Gairich proper and, like my visit here four years previously, sunny views.

A fast run back over small Gairich, carefully down the steep slopes, I then collected the bag and started on the east ridge of Sgurr an Fhuarain.

Climbing high on this hill, it only fell short of the Munro mark by thirteen metres and made a fine Corbett. I'd have to return another day, however, as the effort required for the extra one hundred and fifty metres could not be spared. Traversing westwards at about the seven hundred and fifty metre level and gaining the other ridge, there was a short drop before the climb to Sgurr Mor.

This Munro gave fabulous views over the deep blue waters of Loch Quoich and all the surrounding hills, so I spent a few minutes taking it all in and setting up the camera to get a few shots of my sponsored gear with the beautiful backdrop. It was invigorating to continue running out along the ridge; even the tops of Sgurr Beag and An Eag that had to be climbed en route did not perturb, and I arrived at the summit of Sgurr nan Coireachan. Mark had kindly volunteered, on his way up Glen Dessarry with Martin, to drop the big rucksack and leave me a bottle of water somewhere around this Munro. Scouting about the top, though, there was nothing obvious to see. I needn't have worried, for dropping down to the next bealach, lying right in the middle of the narrow path was a two-litre bottle of pure clear water – lovely! I drank quite a bit and filled the CamelBak before climbing along the summit ridge of Garbh Chioch Mhor. Here I became aware of a distant noise. Continuing to the top, I sat and waited as the volume increased. I recognised the characteristic beating of helicopter blades and then, about two miles to the south, I picked out the bright little dot flying into one of the glens between the intervening ridges. It helped give scale to the whole scene and reminded me of just how puny we are among the mountains.

I dropped north-west into the shade of the col before a final weary climb took me to the top of Sgurr na Ciche at five minutes before ten. Feeling slightly chilly, I put on my jacket and rattled off two panoramic photos of a low sun dropping over Ladhar Bheinn and the distant Cuillin. There wasn't time to hang about and watch the sunset, for although it was all downhill now, my map showed very steep contours with rocky outcrops on my route to Carnoch. I was keen to descend these before losing all natural light. Jogging down the snout of Sgurr na Ciche as fast as safely possible, and then skirting to the north side of the 760 metre spot height, the angle eased off and I couldn't resist one final snapshot for the day. The dark peaks hung below a palette full of colours, from the thin golden line on their summits, through orange and reds to the light and dark blues stretching far above. The ensuing photograph was enriched by my own ruddy pink hues.

The map was correct as, dropping west, the slopes were very steep and rough. Fortunately, I didn't get stuck anywhere. Slow and methodical, the only respite came on the last few metres down to the river bank, and I was glad to make it in one piece. Following the river with what little ambient light was left, at the far end of the sweeping bend, two recognisable tents came into view and I got to them for eleven o'clock. Time for some late-night dinner. Mark and Martin set about cooking, allowing me to crash out in my own little home for a while and drink some juice. The slight breeze afforded us the luxury of leaving both tent porches open to be able to chat without fear of a midge attack. A short time later, a large pot of various ingredients was passed across. I tucked in while the guys told me how their day had gone; winding down, it made a relaxing end to what had been a cracking day for me.

Day 33 – Friday 30 June

After a solid night's sleep, the alarm sounded at seven, with sunlight already illuminating the tent. Not being in the motorhome meant it was much easier to get ready quickly, so by eight o'clock, I was ready to leave. I would see the guys again tonight. Heading by the old ruin at Carnoch, the path started climbing fairly steeply up to the Mam Meadail. Immediately, I was aware that my legs were heavy, but I hoped they'd warm up and get going as the day went on. Unbeknown to me at the time, yesterday's total climb was the biggest for a single day of the trip, at over fourteen thousand feet, which might explain why I was feeling a tad jaded today. Nearing the pass, I had to take my first short rest; glancing back down the path, I noticed that another walker was on the ascent, climbing fast. As is often the case, this spurred me on, but the steep slopes north were hard work. Eventually I turned north-west to the 942 metre top of Meall Buidhe. Dumping my rucksack here, I headed along the ridge for a few hundred metres to the proper summit, then came back to pick up the bag. Just before doing so the other walker came over the top. I said hello on passing, and noticed that the man looked like an advert straight out of an outdoor magazine; broad-brimmed hat, light-weight trekking clothes, two walking poles and a nice new pair of Brasher boots. There was no way I was letting Mr Rambler catch me up, so I set off at a fast trot down the north-east ridge, thinking that that would be the last I would see of him.

Getting down to the first bealach, I didn't want to have to climb over any intervening tops on the way to the next hill, as is suggested in the guidebook, so I dropped into the coire, heading north north-east to some little lochans. The rough ground made it hard work and this certainly wasn't an easy option, so perhaps I would have been better sticking to the path over the tops after all. Turning east, it was a slow climb towards the next bealach, and then veering north and labouring on up the slopes, I got to the ridge and ambled westwards to the summit of Luinne Bheinn. Feeling drained and empty, the legs were still not getting going, and taking a seat for five minutes, I realised that I would be late for my next rendezvous. The arrangement from the day before had been that Mum and June were coming in with the van and meeting me at Kinloch Hourn, where I could refuel and have a break before heading through to Arnisdale. The fact that there were only three Munros to be climbed must have affected my judgement, as I had optimistically told them to expect me by about two o'clock, forgetting the actual distance and the climb involved.

The early morning sun had given way to a blanket of light grey cloud and, as I turned to go, Rambler Man popped up at the far end of the summit ridge. Geed up again, I dropped down the path north-west and tried to break into a jog, but the legs just weren't having it. Across the pass of Mam Barrisdale, the slopes on the other side immediately took away what little momentum I had, and I clawed every inch of the way up into Coire a Phuill. Walking in treacle wouldn't have made me any slower and, as I'd been expecting, a glance across confirmed that Catalogue Man was passing me about one hundred yards to my right, his fusion of metronomic pace and windmill walking poles easing him up the slope. Trying to raise my game from slug's pace to snail's proved of no avail and he got up to the ridge by Stob a Chearcaill, turned left and was away. About five minutes later I was there myself. I turned and climbed up to the little 849 metre top; seeing the view westwards, I decided a break was the order of the day. Although it wasn't warm, I felt like lying down and sleeping, but had to make do instead with some biscuits, while my eye was drawn down the line of the Aonach Sgoilte and two smaller hills, hiding Inverie on the far side. Oh, for an easy saunter over these and a drop down to the only watering hole in this rough land for a few Friday afternoon pints.

Snatching myself from the daydream, the frustrating fact was that I had to drop almost one hundred and fifty metres to the next bealach, only to climb the same straight back up the other side, before being able to continue up the undulating ridge. 'No rest for the wicked,' so getting my head down, I plodded away and eventually came out at the corner of the summit ridge. With no competitive edge left, I sat at the top of Ladhar Bheinn for a quick battery recharge and some food, aware that time was pressing on, but that I didn't have the energy to press on after it. If only there had been a giant zip wire across the water to Arnisdale, I could just have clipped on and flown straight over the intervening four miles. On foot, my journey would involve about twenty miles. It was now also later than my planned meeting time at the far end of the loch, and I wondered what Mum and June would do in the hours that would elapse before my arrival. Would they sit, wait, and worry about why I hadn't turned up? Or think that somehow they had missed me and just head off to Arnisdale? The latter was one scenario I did not want to entertain as by then, I'd have no food or water left.

Starting down the north-east ridge, the view along the length of the loch was beautiful, but also reminded me of just how far I still had to go. My hill friend had about a quarter of a mile on me, but I dropped into Coire Dhorrcail sooner, thinking I could cut more directly and pick up the stalker's path on the far side before him. Having gained slightly, he was still there before me and then, once on the better path, he started to pull away again, all the way round to Barrisdale Bay where we finally parted company. This man was the only person I'd seen all day on the hills, and we had basically shadowed one another – same route, same length of breaks, same speed, for the last seven hours. Despite hundreds of trips in the hills, this had never happened to me before. Anyway, Brasher Boot Boy had kicked my hill-runner ass and, as he headed for even more climbing back towards Mam Barrisdale, I crossed the river and steeled myself for the walk ahead.

With no imaginary competition to distract my thoughts, this was the bit of today's journey that I had not been looking forward to. For all that it is beautiful, the undulating path along the south side of Loch Hourn is no stroll in the park. Trying to tune out the body feedback and tune into the scenery, I couldn't stop thoughts of lovely food and drink coming to mind. This reminded me of the *Great Munros Challenge* film, where Andrew Johnston mentions that he had struggled through the Knoydart Munros suffering from a bad stomach bug. What was not revealed on camera was that Andrew was fond of his grub and that, stopping briefly by a bothy, they found a lunchbox inside. Andrew had opened it and, upon finding some 'fresh-looking' sandwiches, had promptly devoured them. Except of course they were not fresh.

The tarmac of the road end finally appeared, but there was no sign of the motorhome. I wandered on, peering a few hundred yards up the road, just at the track junction. I noticed something dark that resembled a figure sitting down. Eventually recognising Mum, I was overjoyed. How wonderful that she had waited this long, for it was now quarter past six. and she had been here at least four hours. Never one to disappoint, Mum produced a flask of warm tea, which hit the spot perfectly, and a large Bridie. The savoury flavour made a tasty change to the sweet snacks I had been consuming all day. Sitting on a rock to rest my legs, Mum told me that June had been down earlier, waited a while but then had given up and gone back to the van to sleep. Fortunately for me, her protestations that they must have missed me, and should head onto Arnisdale, had been dismissed. I was now reaping the benefit of that – good old Mum!

Having taken a full forty-five minutes of recovery, it was time to get on. Leaving my rucksack, I wore my heavier jacket just in case the ever-darkening clouds produced rain. Through the farm buildings then onto a path that climbed up through trees and over another small hill, I was already regretting not bringing my light jacket instead. Although it was overcast, I was sweating in the humid air. Taking my jacket off, all I could do was roll it up like a rugby ball under my arm. Once over the second gradual climb, it was all downhill for several miles, but I continued walking with only the occasional jog. I was too busy looking about at the scenery anyway, this being a Rigby alteration to the schedule to get me to Skye more quickly. Through Gleann Dubh Lochain, I soon reached the main track in Glen Arnisdale itself, which was freshly bulldozed in several areas. I arrived at Corran at half past nine.

Crossing the bridge to the public road end, the car park looked empty until I noticed a motorbike at one side. As I got closer, I realised it was Colin's, and there he was sitting behind it. It was a welcome surprise, as

I had not been expecting to see him, and even better that he was carrying a bottle of juice to quench my thirst. Chatting for a while, he told me the good news; he had just got his exam results from university, and had done enough to earn his degree. Mark's car rolled in and Colin, seeing Martin's camera bag, soon had a new friend as they discussed the model of SLR camera they both owned. Standing about after the heat of exercise, even with my jacket on, I was starting to feel chilly, so, like an ever-resourceful boy scout, Mark rummaged through his camping gear to produce a stove, and immediately got a pan of water on the boil. I was soon sipping a soothing mug of tea.

My journey from Kinloch Hourn to here had been about eight miles on foot, whereas Mum and June had at least seventy to do in the van, over half of it on single track roads. Pushing half past ten, though, it was getting a bit late. Finally they arrived, closely followed by two other cars. One contained Richard Speirs (aka Tricky Dicky) and his friend John Mitchell, with the other heralding the promised return of Big George and Malcolm Finbow, who I'd last seen when washed out at Crianlarich. The bonus was that this time round he was wearing more than his underpants. It turned out that Tricky and John had already been here for hours, camping about half a mile up the road, but only realised we were down at this end when the Tunnocks biscuit tin had cruised past. Introductions all round, folk talked for a while, then I enjoyed another late dinner and got to bed for about half midnight. Tomorrow a swim, Sunday the Cuillin ridge in all its brutal glory, and with the cavalry now massing to help me do battle, things were getting exciting. Come Monday morning, would it be Charlie two, Skye nil, or vice versa?

Day 34 – Saturday 1 July

Up at seven with a sunny start to July, I had a fairly light breakfast. Whilst getting ready I noticed that, out in the car park, Mark, George and Malcolm were poring over maps spread on the ground. I was interested to know what the council of war was planning, but didn't have time to investigate, preoccupied with getting round to Glenelg in time for the plunge. My written schedule had the times for the high and low water marks, but that was for Friday 23rd June, when I had originally planned to be here. Consulting my Tide Table book, I calculated that the most

131

suitable turn of the tide was the low water mark, due to occur around one o'clock. Working back from that, I hoped there would be enough time to get this morning's jaunt completed first.

I jumped on my bike and cycled the short distance along the road to Arnisdale, then headed up the hill with Tricky at quarter past eight. Having joined my sister at some of her outdoor club meetings over the last few years, I had got to know both Richard Speirs and John Mitchell, members of their mountain activities club. Being a naturally affable guy, Tricky was more than proficient in numerous outdoor sports, and although I was rather meticulous in planning outdoor ventures, he took it to another level. This was probably in part to do with his leadership role for the Duke of Edinburgh Award, but also from an inbuilt thoroughness and deep enthusiasm for all things outdoors. He applied this approach now, carrying food and water for me and asking every so often if I needed anything, as we climbed the steep path to the bealach. Here, I took him up on his offer and we enjoyed a few minutes' break, looking back down the steep slopes to Arnisdale, before we turned left for the last thousand feet.

Over the east top, along the summit ridge, and up to the trig point, which drifted in and out of low cloud, we then took another quick break. Beinn Sgritheall was number one hundred and eighty-four so I was now on the long countdown from one hundred. Tricky was bagging not only the Munros but also their tops, so while I headed down the west ridge, he ran off towards the 928 metre point. Getting towards the lochan, he caught up again and we turned south south-west, ploughing down through scrub to pop out on the road. Our time of two hours and five minutes showed that my legs had recovered from yesterday. John Mitchell was going to be keeping me company on the bike and we set off for the ferry point by Glenelg at quarter to eleven. Despite a couple of longer climbs on this section of road, there was the compensation of having a fast downhill all the way back towards sea level, at which point a black cat ran across the road in front of us with a dead mouse hanging from its teeth. Hopefully not an omen for the upcoming swim?

I arrived at the jetty at half eleven and had plenty of time to prepare for the swim, but what immediately struck me was the velocity of the current down through the strait; the idea of jumping in there was positively frightening. The ferry had to power across at a forty-five degree angle just to get to its target, the Kylerhea landing opposite. Having spoken

132

again with ferry owner, Roddy MacLeod, in the previous week, I at least had confidence in the knowledge that he had organised a small safety boat for me.

I went down and spoke to Roddy who told me, with the experience of a master of his trade, not to worry; the current would calm down nicely. On that reassuring note, I returned to the motorhome. Reckoning that it would take me about thirty minutes to swim the channel with my slow stroke, all things being well, that meant splitting it fifteen minutes either side of the twelve fifty-five mark. I would be starting at twelve forty and I squeezed into the wetsuit and donned my bright yellow swimming cap, before we all headed down to the waiting area at the jetty, where my small back-up boat had now arrived.

Roddy had arranged for Jimmy Watt and his young friend, Gordon McDonald, to pilot the boat, and they had brought along a couple of collie dogs, Pylon and Holly. After a quick confirmation chat with Jimmy, I put on my sandals, climbed down the top wall, and walked over shale and stones into the water. Passing up the sandals, I waded in a bit deeper, set my stopwatch and then went for it, the shock of the cold water once again taking my breath away. With my goggles having steamed up on the previous swims, I didn't bother wearing them this time, but I still needed to see the opposite jetty, so I kept my head above water and focused on the far side. Thankfully, there was neither wind nor waves to contend with, but even so I watched the opposite jetty gradually drift across my field of vision from left to right; even with only a few minutes to the low tide, there was still a slight current pushing south. The guys shadowed in the boat about twenty feet away, with the two collies looking bemused by the yellow swim cap bobbing about in front of them. Still plying his trade, Roddy gave us a wide berth as he came across in the ferry.

Nearing the far side, I was about fifty yards down from where I should have been; adjusting course, I tried to put more effort into the last stretch, and the concrete ramp loomed closer. At the last little bit beside the jetty, I could feel my arms touching seaweed, so put my feet down. Sure enough, I could now stand up on the Kylerhea side of the strait, only twenty minutes after setting off. It was a great feeling to complete this swim for, although it was the shortest of the three, it was the one that I had been worrying about the most. My immediate problem was that the stones on this side of the water were covered in thick seaweed, making it nearly impossible to walk. Tricky was there offering me a towel, so I used him for support while I struggled over up to the wall. Jim Hall from Westies, who I hadn't been expecting, had also appeared. Watching the whole swim unfold from this side, Jim had noticed a seal following me across the strait, probably bemused by the bright-hatted invader in his home patch. Jim, just back from his climbing holiday in France, was also able to lend his vertical skills for tomorrow – great!

The ferry had brought the motorhome across, so I went down and thanked all the guys for their help, then tried discreetly to give Roddy some payment for all his work. He was having none of it, though, so the only thing I could think of was to get the guys some beers. Checking the van, I was dismayed to find there wasn't much left of my onboard stash, but Jim came to the rescue by running up to his car and returning with some bottles of fine ale. Saying goodbye to all the boat guys, we went about a hundred yards up the road to a lay-by where the van could pull in. I took on some more light sustenance whilst changing back into cycling gear. Slipping some money into my back pocket and stepping outside, I found the sun had returned and again my poor ears were being attacked by its rays.

John was accompanying me on the bike again, but there would be little conversation on the first section, as the road climbed from sea level to over nine hundred feet in little more than two miles. Feeling heavy, I had to work hard as the road climbed Kylerhea Glen; just to add to the burden, the bloody chain wouldn't sit in the lowest gear properly. Of course, it slipped out on the steepest section near the top of the road, and it took every ounce of strength and all my weight to stand on the pedals and keep them turning over. John had lower gear ratios on his mountain bike and had no such problem, and we both finally made it over the Bealach Udal. The run down Glen Arroch on the far side was pleasant, with the breeze cooling us, and at the bottom we turned onto the busier A87 and along to Broadford. I had expected the motorhome to have caught up with us by now, but there was still no sign of it as we turned onto the B8083.

I had slipped some money into my pocket earlier, joking to June that I was going to stop at the pub in Broadford, but now that the opportunity had arisen, I couldn't resist. The Munro run was not supposed to be all work and no play! Resting the bikes on the hotel wall, with our cleated cycling shoes, we waddled into the bar like a couple of tap-dancing penguins, got our pints and waddled back out again to take our table in the sun. The cold, crisp lager went down a treat and it was great just to take some time out; I only wished the van would come round the corner, so I could see the look on Mum and June's faces. The effect was just as good when Tricky appeared in John's car. After another quick pint, we headed off down the road; the cycle along Strath Suardal was beautiful and as the road dropped down through Torrin we could look across Loch Slapin to the rugged mass of Bla Bheinn – one of my favourite views.

Cycling round the top of the loch, we looked back to see the motorhome coming up behind, just in time to catch us finishing at the car park. Being a summer Saturday, it was very busy here, but Mum managed to squeeze the van onto a small patch of ground. Big George, who had been waiting, came up and greeted us. By the time I had eaten and had my fourth change of gear for the day, it was after half past four. Climbing in just shorts and trainers, George told me about what he and the others had been up to since I had last seen them at Arnisdale. They had worked out all the logistics and driven down to Elgol, where they had managed to charter a boat to take them and all the gear up Loch Scavaig, and then dumped the lot near the Coruisk Memorial Hut. This was where they were now hopefully setting up camp, and I was looking forward to meeting them there, as I had never been into the Loch Coruisk side of the Cuillin before.

Climbing up into Coire Uaigneich, we veered round to take the gully and struggled on up steep scree and rock. Eventually, we got to the top of the gully, from where it was another little climb to the summit, with its panoramic view of the whole Cuillin ridge. Thinking that tomorrow we'd be attempting to traverse the whole thing was a slightly scary prospect, and I was happy enough to enjoy its beauty from a distance for the moment. Back to the col and up the other side, we moved over the south top then started the long descent of the south south-west ridge. On the last bit of ridge we heard shouts and jeers coming from the area to the north-west of Camasunary, where we could make out some of the guys who must have come round from the camp. George and I decided to cut a more direct line towards them. This was a mistake, however, and we were soon coming out on top of various rocky outcrops which were difficult to bypass.

Difficulties over, we arrived on flatter ground, met Mark, Malcolm and Martin, and then took the coastal path round the bottom of Sgurr na

135

Stri towards the 'Bad Step.' This turned out to be not too bad at all, and round the corner on the grass just past the memorial hut, we found our little encampment. My tent was already up, so I could settle in right away and put on some clothes. At quarter to eight. it was getting cool, and our campsite was in the shade of the surrounding mountains. To my surprise, the guys produced some disposable barbecues and spread them with a carnivore's delight of various meats. They had also brought along cans of lager, and even I was allowed a couple. Now this was the life; beers and barbecue with a view of the world.

Polishing off our grub, there was another surprise when Dave Rogers of Westerlands rounded the corner, having come over Blaven himself on the way in. He was going to be joining us for part of the ridge tomorrow. Both of us being veterans of the West Highland Way race, he told me how he had ran it in twenty-two hours and forty-two minutes two weeks ago, taking a fantastic five hours off his previous time. Poor John Donnelly, though, who had joined me on the Crianlarich hills a few weeks ago, had got to within seven miles of the end and had to retire due to extreme nausea and vomiting, such are the joys of this race. I crawled into my tent at quarter to twelve. It had been such a pleasurable day for me, where everything had gone perfectly – I almost felt guilty for daring to hope that tomorrow would be the same.

Day 35 – Sunday 2 July

Stirring groggily at around six, there was no rush to get up, for I knew that I had relatively little to prepare. The others would have their large rucksacks, ropes, harnesses and so on. I did finally drag myself from my sleeping bag to get a coffee and, surveying the campsite, it looked like a bomb site with kit strewn everywhere. It was hard to believe that all this was going to disappear, and it didn't help when I dismantled my own tent and added it to the pile. What I didn't know was that Mark and Malcolm had arranged for the boatman from Elgol to come back and collect our gear for us; all we had to do was take the essentials and pack the rest to leave at the little landing point for him – what a great service! There was a bit of brightness but still no wind, so the midges were out in force as we tidied up the site to leave it spick and span.

Heading off at ten to eight, with a pleasant walk along the side of Loch Coruisk, we then parted company with Jim, who was going to take Martin up the classic Dubhs ridge scramble. The rest of us started climbing south west, where I quickly drifted to the back of the group. The initial grassy slopes soon gave way to rocks and boulders in An Garbh-choire, and still I couldn't keep pace with the others, who were not even walking particularly fast. Struggling on upwards, it took ages before I reached the Bealach a Garbh-choire, where the guys had already dumped their bags and were waiting for me. Then we just had to wander south south-east along the ridge for the slight climb to our first Munro, Sgurr nan Eag. I noted the time, eleven o'clock, as I was curious to see how long it would take until our final Munro.

Hazy cloud above the tops blocked out the sun, giving a comfortable temperature and clear views along the ridge, so weather-wise it looked like we were getting it just about perfect. Back to the bealach, over Sgurr Dubh na Da Bheinn and up to our second Munro, Sgurr Dubh Mor, we had perfect timing, as Jim and Martin were just arriving. Jim recounted how, not long after leaving us that morning, Martin had needed to go to the loo. Jim had continued round a corner to wait for him. Twenty minutes passed, Jim worrying that Martin was having a bad reaction to last night's barbecue. Just as Jim was about to go look for him, Martin came round the corner with his trouser pockets hanging out like a pair of floppy elephant ears. All was explained when Martin said he had gone to the water's edge to wash his hands, and was leaning forward when he over balanced and fell in head first. Managing to retrieve himself, he then had to wring out all his sodden clothes and was now trying to dry off.

Retracing to the main ridge, Jim and Martin headed to the tricky Thearlaich-Dubh gap while the rest of us continued to Sgurr Alasdair. Continuing on, I was looking forward to another section of the ridge with a name that I'd heard before – Collie's Ledge. Like yesterday evening's Bad Step, it was relatively disappointing from an adrenaline-seeker's point of view. Still, what the ledge did offer was a fantastic vantage point overlooking the top of Coire Lagan to Sgurr Dearg and the Inaccessible Pinnacle.

From the top of Sgurr Mhic Choinnich, we scrambled down the ridge to start on the eroded path up the side of An Stac. One or two folk coming down the path said a cheery 'Well done' to me, so I could only guess that June and Tricky, who had climbed up from the Glen Brittle side, must have been saying things. Trailing after the guys, I arrived at the side of the Pinnacle at about ten to three. June and Tricky were already on top. I was pleased for June, as she had been slightly apprehensive beforehand about climbing the In Pinn.

Heading to the start of the east ridge, George promptly flew up, while I tried hard to hang onto his heels. It was a big contrast to my last visit with Ian and Iain, when we had the accompaniment of wind and rain.

A light breeze and dry holds saw George and I to the top in a few minutes, with the summit a fairly busy place: the two of us, June and Tricky, and another couple of guys who were waiting to abseil off. Being *in situ*, Tricky asked the guys if we could use their rope. They kindly agreed and stepped aside, allowing George to whizz down with the camera to film everyone. Tricky then double-checked that I'd done up my harness correctly, and I followed at a slow walking pace down the face. We were all joking and having a laugh, when I realised that the other two chaps were still waiting patiently up top. I felt guilty that our little group had jumped the queue, and it was only later that Tricky told me the two guys were in fact Rod and Lindsay Munro, in whose shop in Aberfeldy I had bought my fell shoes two weeks before. I didn't get to say it at the time, but thanks again guys for letting us overtake and use your rope so that we could save time – much appreciated!

The whole process had taken over half an hour, so we were all keen to get going again, especially for June and Tricky, who had arrived up here at eight thirty. The six of us continued on, Sgurr a'Ghreadaidh and Sgurr a'Mhadaidh passing without any problems, and at last I felt my energy was starting to pick up – it had only taken nine hours. Fortunately, the boost came just in time, as I was told that the most difficult section of the whole ridge now lay ahead, between here and our next Munro, almost two miles distant. There were a few steep ups and downs, one in particular being a short vertical wall of about fifteen to twenty feet that called for proper rock-climbing skills and not just scrambling technique. I was a bit nervy heading up this but managed it. Peering back over the edge at Mark, a non-climber like myself, he looked like he was distinctly not enjoying it.

A few more tricky undulations led over Bidean Drum nan Ramh and An Caisteal, where Malcolm took us through what he called the wormhole (Belly Ledge) just to spice things up a little, before we came to Sgurr na Bhairnich. On this top we found the four litres of water that

138

John Mitchell had carried up this morning, so we took a quick rest and topped up our supplies. By now the sun had managed to break through to lighten the evening and, once over Bruach na Frithe, we turned right and descended east to the Bealach nan Lice beneath the Bhasteir Tooth. This was wonderfully lit up by the sun's rays and, proudly guarding Am Bhasteir, the sentinel looked awe-inspiring. The guys spoke briefly about climbing, but I certainly wasn't enthused, and in any event the plan was thwarted when two of our climbers, Malcolm and Jim, decided to head down. They wanted to get to the Sligachan Hotel for a few pints before closing time!

Jim and Malcolm, beer goggles firmly fixed on a far-away Slig, headed off. Mark, George, Martin and I continued across the screes to come out at the Bealach a'Bhasteir. The guys dropped their rucksacks and I even left the bumbag, taking just my small camera, before we headed back up the east ridge to the summit of Am Bhasteir. The golden glow from Sgurr nan Gillean was enticing us onward, so we returned to the bealach, where I collected my bumbag. Planning to return via this spot, the guys left most of the gear. The west ridge went okay until we got to a chimney, which Mark and I found fairly difficult, but once over that we had no problems all the way up to the summit. It was our last Munro on the ridge, so I looked at my watch: five to ten. It had taken us eleven hours, top to top, but the time was less important than the fact that we had done it.

And what a view to finish with. North and north-east, I witnessed my first evening temperature inversion, where a sea of low grey cloud filled the glens with only the hills jutting through. In contrast, out to the north-west, the twist of Loch Harport drew the eye to Loch Bracadale and the distant MacLeod's Tables, where the sun sank through hazy clouds. An atmosphere of euphoria prevailed, with the four of us just happy to be there. It wasn't difficult to smile for our summit photo but, at ten o'clock, it was time to get moving again. Mark and I definitely didn't fancy going back down the west ridge and reverse climbing the chimney, so we left the more proficient George and Martin to go for the gear and headed for the south-east ridge. Exiting Coire Riabhach, the pace of our jogging seemed to gather momentum with almost every stride, until we were running at full tilt. With gravity on my side, I could keep up with Mark.

After a whole day of slow walking, fast running was an invigorating sensation through the twilight, down along the boggy road to the hotel.

My watch read ten past eleven, so it had taken us an hour and ten minutes from the top of Sgurr nan Gillean, and almost fifteen and a half hours from camp to camp. With the van parked at the side of the hotel, we said hello to Mum and June to let them know we were down. More importantly, could we still get a pint? We wandered into the bar, but it was not to be; they weren't serving anymore, and folk were drinking up and heading out.

Drat, just too late! But, with the forward planning of a NASA scientist, Jim had hung onto a couple of our empty two litre water bottles, and had got them filled with finest Red Cuillin ale at the bar. Mark and I would be getting a pint after all. At the campsite, I later managed to clean up with a late-night shower, and then returned to the motorhome, where I found that Mum had made a monster pot of spaghetti bolognese. After midnight, all the guys were invited in, Jim poured the beer, and whilst wolfing down huge platefuls of nosh, we were already reminiscing about the wonderful day we had just experienced. A knock at the door saw the late arrival of George and Martin, who had taken a while to come off Gillean, before a long walk out with all the gear in the darkness. They were followed a short while later by Tricky, who had headed out earlier with extra supplies in case anyone was flagging. They needn't have worried about missing the banquet, however, for there was still heaps of food and some beer to wash it all down.

The guys retired to their tents and Mum worked on my legs for a few minutes; it had been a long day for me, but even longer for her and June, as they had been up since half past five. Finally to bed at quarter to two, my thoughts drifted to how everyone had worked together today to make it such a success. It wasn't just that I'd achieved a long-term goal in completing the whole traverse; the effort others had put in to make it a reality was what made it so special. Having chopped and changed my plans to get to Skye on time, I wasn't quite sure if it meant I'd dropped more days from the schedule. But I did know that one hundred and ninety-six Munros were in the bag, after thirty-five days. This meant that, to scrape under the fifty day mark, I would need to complete the remaining eighty-eight hills in fourteen days. Having averaged only thirty-nine Munros per week for the last five weeks, I would need to raise this to forty-four to bring home the bacon. With fatigue and exhaustion increasing daily, it was going to be a tall order. I could only try.

Week 6

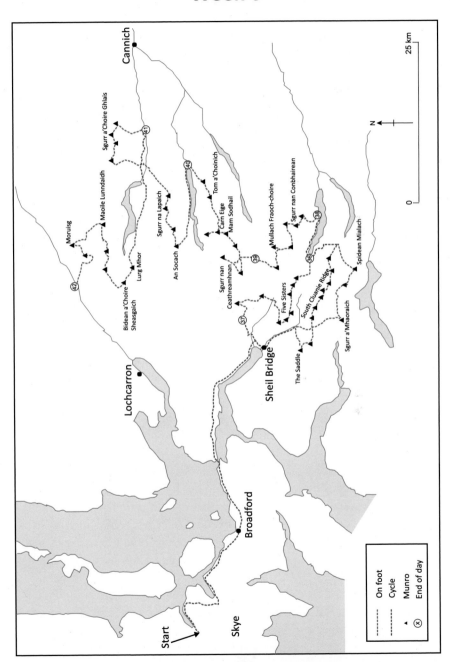

Week 6 – Big Days on Big Ridges

Days 36-42

Day 36 – Monday 3 July

I awoke at seven with the previous Friday night's question answered: the score line read Charlie two, Skye nil. It was a great way to start week six, and the sun was even shining. All the guys packed away their tents and gear, and when everyone was ready, I got June to do what she did best: get the video-cam out and film the team. With a clear sky, we had that classic backdrop of Gillean, Basteir and Frithe, resplendent in the distance, whilst we lined up in the foreground. Resembling a police identity parade of naughty little school boys who had been up to something mischievous, the cheeky grins on our faces said it all, and it has remained one of my fondest memories of the run.

George and Martin were the first to go as, their holidays over, they were now faced with the unenviable and mammoth drive all the way back to Germany. A few of the others left, and then it was our turn to do likewise. I set off on the bike at eleven, and Tricky joined Mum and June in the motorhome, as he would be helping out for the next few days. With the sun shining down, and tempered with a cool breeze, it was soothing just to turn the pedals and watch the splendid red Cuillin hills drift by. At Broadford, we pulled in for a short break, buying some provisions from the shop. Getting ready to leave, we noticed a guy hitch-hiking, heading east. I told him that there was room in the van if he didn't mind travelling at my bike pace, and he didn't mind this, so John from Canada joined us on the slow bus to Shiel Bridge. First, though, there was a bit of a climb over the Skye bridge, and then a whizz down the other side to Kyle of

Lochalsh and on eastwards. Luckily the breeze was soon pushing me down the side of Loch Duich and into my finishing spot a few miles up the glen, beneath Faochag.

I had enjoyed the forty-five miles of scenic cycling and, although it was now mid-afternoon, I still wasn't in a time-conscious mood. Donald Smith from Westies appeared, after having dumped a food and fluid parcel halfway along the South Cluanie ridge. This wasn't necessary for the ridge alone, but a much bigger day had originally been planned where it would have been vital. Donald had been working to the original plan. Manny arrived, and decided he would join me for the first hill. Saying goodbye to Donald, the pair of us set off at ten to four up the path towards the Bealach Duibh Leac. It was hot and sweaty work climbing over this high intervening pass, before a declining traverse took us to the small Loch Bealach Coire Sgoireadail. The jokes for the camcorder were now over, as we were faced with a steep climbing traverse south south-east through rocky outcrops that flanked Sgurr Thionail. This proved another toilsome task, which we managed with weakening legs, Manny was often well ahead, and I trailed him up the final climb to our hard-won summit of Sgurr a' Mhaoraich.

We descended east and then dropped off the ridge and down into Coire a'Chaorainn, aiming for a path indicated on the map beside a stream. When we got there it was fairly non-existent - just boggy mulch. On the last stretch into Glen Quoich, we entered a beautiful little wooded area with blossoming rhododendrons and flowers, where the sylvan setting was rounded off perfectly by a cascading waterfall. Stumbling upon little gems like this was always an added bonus on the run. Approaching a bridge over the River Quoich, we could see a body stretched out slap-bang in the middle of the wooden planks, apparently having a snooze. Manny and I tried to sneak up and frighten Tricky, but the git heard us first and got up. Wrapped in full waterproofs, as this side of the hill had long been in shadow, he was trying to keep warm.

Manny headed off for his lift, while Tricky and I headed by Alltbeithe, with the south Cluanie hills lit up before us in the evening sunshine. Round to our right, we joined a path that zigzagged up the steep slopes of Sron na Breun Leitir and, although labouring, we gained height fast to come out near the 845 metre top, then along the ridge and up to the summit of Gleouraich. We hung about just long enough to snap a quick photo and get a mouthful of food, before heading over the next little top and getting a good run down to the bealach before the climb up to Spidean Mialach. Again, we didn't hang about, as at ten past ten, the light was going. We then ran down the north north-east ridge, which was not too bad on the upper reaches, but became rockier lower down, with outcrops to be negotiated, only easing on the last stretch to the glen. Crossing the River Loyne, we got onto the opposite path and climbed east north-east in the twilight behind Creag Liathtais, then dropped round towards the old road. By this point we were struggling to make out the features of the path. Concentrating hard, we weren't sure if we could discern two figures in the distance, but the late evening air was pierced by a shout of 'Westeeez!' and we knew Manny was close by.

We arrived to find that he and June had cycled with the mountain bikes up the old road from Cluanie, and had been there only five minutes, so they had timed it to perfection and saved themselves a wait in the chilly air. Thankful for the bikes, Tricky and I cycled over the high point of the road and then had a good run down the other side. Speeding on, I almost cut myself in half on a vehicle barrier. It just loomed out of the darkness and I came to a screeching halt – close one! We got back to the van for eleven forty-five, with June and Manny trotting in at midnight. I didn't mind another post-midnight dinner, and we had a laugh when Mum passed Tricky a home-made pizza. He eagerly laid into it, only realising half-way through that the unique taste and texture was due to the greaseproof paper she had forgotten to remove from the base. Teflon Tricky was, of course, far too polite to make any comments about Mum's cooking, but June and I certainly were not.

Day 37 - Tuesday 4 July

The two late nights had now caught up with me and, despite a lie-in until half past seven, I was still tired getting up. Manny appeared at about nine o'clock and we set off from the Cluanie Inn on the mountain bikes, up the old road, passing Tricky and June who were walking in to retrieve the bikes once we had ditched them at the junction. Starting to pick up now, the pair of us climbed quite strongly, my enthusiasm buoyed by the fact that Creag a'Mhaim would be Munro number two hundred. We arrived at five past eleven and, despite the misty air, I was sporting a grin like a Cheshire cat. This was a really important psychological point for me, as

144

I felt things were finally turning my way, and now we were on the long countdown from eighty-four – Game on!

We continued, over Druim Shionnach, Aonach air Chrith, and then onto Maol Chinn-dearg, where we met another couple of guys who were walking west to east. Noting our running gear, they asked if we were the intended recipients of the parcel that they had seen on the top of Sgurr an Doire Leathain, our next hill. Confirming this, they said that mice must have got into it because part of the parcel was shredded. Feck! Soon enough we were at the next Munro to see for ourselves. The thick yellow plastic bag Donald had wrapped everything in had a large area missing on one side. It was quickly apparent that this was the work of crows rather than mice, as the whole summit area was covered in dozens of small pieces of yellow plastic; all that was left were wrappers containing a few crumbs of malted loaf, and two bottles of juice.

Arriving at our seventh Munro of Creag nan Damh about ten past two, I was fairly pleased that my double-century legs had managed top to top in just over three hours. Ten minutes later, we were down at the Bealach Duibh Leac to meet Tricky. Manny then headed down and I continued with Tricky over the intervening Corbett to a broad pass sitting below the steep face of Sgurr na Sgine. Moving to our right to avoid the immediate crags, we still had a steep and loose climb to gain the north-east ridge, before turning left and up to the summit. We headed along the ridge and then dropped to the wide Bealach Coire Mhalagain. Aiming west of Sgurr na Forcan, we climbed to the ridge and continued up to the summit cairn of the Saddle, where I took a few minutes breather to enjoy the view and stuff my face with some caramel logs. I jogged along to the trig point before dropping south on grassy slopes back towards the bealach.

Homeward bound, we followed the line of a wall cutting below the Forcan Ridge, over the top of Meallan Odhar and onto the stalker's path. Here we had a steady jog back down to the road and the motorhome for quarter to six. It was then that I noticed a figure running down the path at full speed. Tricky evntually recognised Nick Lancaster, the warden at Ratagan Youth Hostel which was a few miles down the road. When Tricky told him what we were up to, Nick was kind enough to offer the use of the hostel's laundry facilities.

I then had an easy cycle down the glen. Continuing along the A87, I turned off into Strath Croe and followed the little road towards Dorusduain, finishing in the car park. I then hitched a lift in the motorhome, back to the campsite near Shiel Bridge. The sun was out, and I hoped that its rays would brighten my next task, one that had been at the back of my mind for the last while. Now into the seventh week of my 'holiday,' I realised I was quite literally running out of time, as I was due back at work on Monday 17th July. If I wasn't allowed the extra time, I would take it anyway, and worry about the consequences when I returned to Glasgow.

With slight trepidation, I phoned Hugh Rennie, the manager at my Royal Mail delivery office. Hugh sounded genuinely cheery to be speaking to me and asked how the run was going. Explaining the situation, that I was potentially still on course to beat the record, but that it might overrun into a ninth week away from work, he immediately said not to worry, I could have the extra week, and he wished me well with the rest of the trip. Good old Hugh; I couldn't believe it had gone so smoothly, and I walked back to the van with a weight lifted from my shoulders.

Day 38 – Wednesday 5 July

We all drove round to the road end before Dorusduain, where I'd finished the previous night. Leaving at half past nine with Lesley Gorman, I jogged up the path in Gleann Choinneachain. This soon gave way to a steady walk where, as Lesley would join me for the second Munro, we said goodbye, and I dropped down over the stream and started climbing. Entering the mist at about the seven hundred metre level, I continued to the summit of lowly A' Ghlas-bheinn, took a compass bearing, and ran off down the south south-east ridge, trying to go as fast as possible and aware that Lesley was waiting at the Bealach an Sgairne. Meeting her there, we had a steep climb up Meall a' Bhealaich, all the way to the summit of Beinn Fhada.

We had a short rest and a quick snack before jogging south to where, like a roller coaster about to plunge, we were faced with the very steep drop down into Gleann Lichd. With aching knees and tired quadriceps, I found it difficult to walk fast, never mind jog, and was struggling on the incline. three thousand feet of discomfort only eased when we got to the path and crossed a bridge to where Manny was waiting patiently. Taking a late lunch, I enjoyed twenty minutes rest before we continued, Lesley heading out the of glen in the company of another walker who had appeared.

146

Manny and I had an easy path for all of half a kilometre before we turned west for the very steep slopes that would lead us up to the Five Sisters of Kintail. Sgurr Fhuaran made me suffer the whole way, every step taking a mountain of willpower, creeping ever higher. Even super-fit Manny was finding it hard. The 910 metre top didn't allow much respite, before a final struggle along the ridge, where I wandered in a daze to drop at the misty summit cairn. 'I'm absolutely jiggered,' were words which understated how I felt but were all my brain could muster. Sitting on the rocks for a minute to catch our breath, we were aware that we had a meeting with Tricky further on.

Sgurr Fhuaran's little sisters passed only marginally more easily, and we slowed on the incline to Sgurr na Carnach and the longer drag round to Sgurr na Ciste Duibhe. Over the Peak of the Spaniards, we then had a long, steady descent to the Bealach an Lapain, dropping just below the cloud to meet a thoroughly wrapped-up Tricky Dicky for the third stage. Like Manny, he had underestimated how long it would take me to get here. There was also a negligible breeze at the pass, so the poor guy had been plagued by midges for the last three hours. We left Manny at half six and headed onto Saileag.

My food stop must have been worthwhile, as I was climbing slightly faster out to Sgurr a'Bhealaich Dheirg, and marginally faster again to Aonach Meadhoin. Perhaps Mark Rigby's flippant comment on Skye, that I only started getting going after five o'clock, had some truth in it after all. Descending the south south-east ridge, the pair of us had a steady run all the way down to a stream, which we followed to come out on the road. At half past eight, the slight problem was that although this was the prearranged meeting point, there was no motorhome here, or anywhere in sight. Not knowing which direction the van would be coming from, our committee meeting of two decided that Tricky would stay here, in case it appeared from the Glen Shiel side, while I would head east along the A87, my intended route, where I could intercept the van if it appeared from that direction.

Off I jogged, but not for long, as tarmac was the last thing my legs needed after more than eleven thousand feet of climbing. I settled for a walk, with glances over my shoulder for the non-existent van. About a mile and a half later at the Cluanie Inn, the motorhome arrived with Tricky safely onboard. Cycling shoes on, an easy five mile spin along the loch side was a good way to wind-down the legs, and I pulled into the old road lay-by at Lundie. It was now half past nine, so I had been on the go for twelve hours, but the tag team had worked well in getting me through it all, and it was pleasing to have another eight Munros in the bag.

There were quite a few calls to make for tying up various bits and bobs, but the main duty was to get in touch with webmaster, Mark McColl. Mark was heading off to Cyprus for a couple of weeks, on Sunday, which meant that we needed someone else to update the site. We decided my friend, Mark Pacitti, in Melbourne, who just happened to be an IT consultant, would take charge of the site, starting next Monday.

After all the chopping and changing of hills and routes in the last week, today was the first time in nine days that the plan I was following came back into line with what was down on paper. Unfortunately, it didn't make for good reading, as today had been number twenty-eight in the original schedule, but was actually my thirty-eighth. A week last Monday I had been running seven behind and now I was ten, three days just disappearing into the ether of Knoydart and Skye. Like a baseball bat to the head, it hit home how all my built-in spare days and leeway had now gone, and that I couldn't drop any more. Even if I made it now, it would be breaking the record by a day, rather than dipping below the fifty-day barrier, which was what I really wanted. Looking forward to the big ridge days ahead, I knew that if I could just hold to plan for the next nine days, there was one final trump card I could play.

Day 39 – Thursday 6 July

With today's six Munros involving only about fifteen miles and seven thousand five-hundred feet of ascent, there was no rush to get away this morning. I finally got round to packing everything for the support team to carry into Alltbeithe Youth Hostel for tonight's sleepover. Tricky was chomping at the bit, and we got going at half ten, climbing the stalker's path with the sun on our backs, and getting up to the summit of Carn Ghluasaid just over an hour later. Another little jog and walk over the intervening top brought us to a big sweeping ridge up and round to the summit of Sgurr nan Conbhairean. It was nearly half past twelve and we decided to have lunch, enjoying great views, the sun's rays through broken cloud casting shadows on the surrounding hills. Running down to the next col, we dumped the rucksacks before the easy little pull up to

148

Sail Chaorainn.

Collecting the rucksacks, we traversed south-west into the corrie, followed by another traverse out the other side to come to the Bealach Choire a' Chait, where Lesley was waiting. At this point, I had to say goodbye to Tricky after almost a week, as he was now heading to Skye to supervise a group of seventeen-year old girls doing their Duke of Edinburgh Award. Lesley and I had a steady walk up to the summit of A' Chralaig, with its monster cairn. The ridge northwards made for pleasant jogging, and it didn't take long until we were enjoying the little scramble up to the summit of Mullach Fraoch-choire. Back to the col, we then dropped quite steeply down long grassy slopes into Coire Odhar, meeting a path cutting through the glen. Saying goodbye to Lesley as she turned to head south for the return to Cluanie, I then stared up at Ciste Dhubh and its nearly two thousand feet of climb.

Meanwhile, at the big roadside lay-by on the A87, Tricky had returned to the motorhome safely. A short while later, Dave and Muffy Calder arrived, bringing Isabel Coombs from Westies with them. They had all kindly volunteered to be the pack mules for this stage, getting all the gear into Alltbeithe Youth Hostel for the overnighter, and Manny would be joining them as well.

I had been having a steady plod up the slopes of Ciste Dhubh, at one point coming over an undulation to be confronted by a huge herd of several hundred deer, which scattered on seeing the stranger with the big white hat. Further up, as the ridge narrowed, I turned and could make out the tiny figures of the back-up team as they crossed the high point of the pass. I couldn't resist cupping my hands and bellowing 'Westies!' in their direction, unsure if they would hear it in the breeze. It was slightly startling when the shout of 'Westies!' came right back at me, distinctly louder than anything they could possibly muster. I looked around, but there was no-one else to see. Five minutes later 'Westies!' rang out again, even louder. Eh? What was going on? Was the ghost of Westies Past haunting this hill? There was no-one to be seen in any direction, but a figure gradually appeared from behind a small ridge a few hundred metres further south. This must be the answer.

Waiting five minutes for the figure to arrive, my query was answered when I recognised 'Nagasaki', that is, Westerlands member, Chris Osmond. It was a welcome surprise to see Chris and I asked what the heck he was doing up here. The story was that, heading to Skye for the Glamaig hill race two days hence, he was driving past the lay-by on the A87 and had recognised Manny, pulling over to say hello. Manny told Chris what was happening, so for a final training run before the race, he decided to take a quick jaunt up Ciste Dhubh and intercept me on route. By chance I had waited at the top, and it was a bonus to enjoy this meeting.

Enjoying the run down the north north-east ridge, I was buoyed up with the thought of seeing the others, who could not have been far in front of me, and the final walk along a path by the sparkling river was a fitting end to a good day. Dave, Muffy and Isabel came out just as I approached the hostel for quarter to seven and we talked in the sunshine with the surrounding glen making a beautiful setting. Isabel and Muffy put on a great dinner with garlic bread for starters, followed by curry and salad, then a variety of cakes for dessert, all washed down with a couple of refreshing lagers. I felt like a king at a banquet, and the good news was that there was plenty left over for breakfast. The hostel warden, Dorothy - a bit of a character - kept us entertained with stories, before it was time to turn in at quarter to eleven, Manny rounding off the evening with *The Waltons* 'good night' routine.

Day 40 – Friday 7 July

Sleeping all night in a room with Dave was not a problem, but it was an altogether different story with Manny. It was obvious that Manny's infamous guts had been at work during the night, leaving a unique sort of garlic and curry *eau de toilette* hanging in the air. Allowing the room to freshen, we headed for the kitchen and enjoyed a hearty breakfast, then promptly felt sick when Manny surpassed even himself. He mixed last night's rice and curry leftovers into his bowl of muesli, topping it all off with custard, then spooned all of the sloppy mixture down his throat, uttering, 'It's all going the same place anyway.' Stepping outside at five to nine, the pair of us said goodbye to Dave, Muffy, and Isabel.

Yesterday's good weather was now replaced with a blanket of grey cloud and, following the path behind the hostel, Manny and I climbed up into increasingly damp and windy conditions. With the next group of hills lying along two ridges either side of a deep glen, it was rather awkward to combine them, but my original plan was to try a clockwise route, which seemed the most efficient. Manny disagreed and suggested the other way, so I just went with that instead. Changing into my heavyweight jacket and stuffing some snacks into pockets, we left the rucksacks at the col and headed west up the ridge.

Sgurr nan Ceathreamhnan came easily enough. It's a favourite big hill of mine and usually a great viewpoint, but not today in the mist. We followed the long north-east ridge, with an intermediary top en route, to Mullach na Dheiragain, where the dreich weather urged a quick about-turn, munching biscuits as we ran. Once over the other top again, we had to try and judge where to drop down into the corrie, but getting it just about spot on, we were soon past the wee loch, and a steep little climb took us back to our rucksacks at the col.

We had hardly started again before we were standing on our next summit of An Socach. Over a little top and down to the Bealach Coire Ghaidheil, we picked up a path that wound round the side of Mam Sodhail's outliers on a climbing traverse, then faced the last pull up to the summit itself. Dropping to the next col, at least we could pass Carn Eige by traversing its western flank and continuing down to the Bealach Beag, where the rucksacks could come off again. Less weight didn't really seem to improve my climbing, and the legs were weakening by the time we got to Beinn Fhionnlaidh. Collecting the sacks again, I really dragged my heels on the three hundred and fifty metre climb up to Carn Eige.

Heading eastwards, the next Munro wasn't easy, as it lay almost three miles along the ridge, and there were several tops to climb en route. With energy levels waning, it took a while, but we made it out to Tom a'Choinich, which just left one hill to go. I was relieved to get to Toll Creagach and Manny snapped a little photo as I guzzled my bottle of Irn-Bru. We then set off down the north-east ridge. We knew what to expect on this upper section, as Manny had ran it as part of his own three week jolly two years ago, so the heather slopes didn't bother us too much. The problem was that, cutting to the left of Creag a Bhaca and dropping north north-east, the heather was getting worse, making for very tough going, and Manny and I were turning the air blue with our cursing. Knackered legs taking a beating, we decided to cut our losses and head straight for the shoreline; although it would be a slightly longer route to home, it was surely a much easier one.

151

Wrong! Far from being easier, this part of the Loch Mullardoch shoreline was a jumble of rocks and boulders, some of huge proportions, that we now had to find a way over, under, or round. Low on food as well, the pair of us stumbled along any which way we could, but at least we didn't totally lose our sense of humour. On seeing an enormous rock, precariously perched on the side of some others, I talked Manny into going underneath it so that it looked as if he was about to get obliterated, like Wile E. Coyote in a Road Runner cartoon. The photo reminds me of a moment of fun, but belies how we truly felt at that time, that single mile of shoreline sapping what little energy we had left. Arriving at the dam, it was a small mercy that we weren't forced to go the long way round, but could drop below the giant wall, over the outflow and up the other side to where the motorhome was waiting.

Half past eight meant it had been eleven and a half hours in the wind and drizzle. As strong as he is, Manny was a bit wasted, probably because of his wet clothes. Mum had decided to empty all the spare gear out of the shower cubicle so that it could be occupied. Having been the rule of the trip that it was for storage space only, this was the perfect time to make an exception, and I enjoyed a refreshing shower. Lesley, who was away with the boys to visit her sister for the night, had left Manny a change of clothes in the van. As he was getting changed, Jim Hall turned up. Mum made us dinner and, relaxing afterwards with some bottles of beer that Jim produced, Manny and I were starting to recover.

My fortieth day at an end, if things had gone to plan, it would have been my last day and filled with celebration. It was not annoying or distressing, it was just a plain and simple fact. I'd given it my best shot and this is was the result. The main thing was that the big days were still getting bagged, and no matter how much they sometimes hurt, that was all that mattered.

Day 41 – Saturday 8 July

With the guys present, I was a bit quicker getting ready and stepping outside. Manny had the video-cam and promptly zoomed in on what he called my 'crispy bacon' ears. My embarrassment didn't last long, as Jim appeared and Manny swung the camera onto him. Decked out like the Scarlet Pimpernel, Jim was wearing red leggings and a bright red jacket. He explained that he had recently been to a photography competition where a speaker had told the audience to always have some red in a photograph – fair enough, but I think Jim was taking this a wee bit too far.

Jim and I left at twenty to nine and headed up the wee road to the dam wall, and the north shore of the loch. Starting on the path, we noticed a group of walkers getting into a boat, and a short while later, we heard the tell-tale buzz of an engine. The boat overtook us, heading west. This seemed to spur Jim on, and I tried to stick to his heels as best I could, all the way down the loch-side. After a quick breather, we headed up the path into Coire Mhaim and onto the south-east ridge, where we were soon in the mist. Jim spied the group of walkers and, like the Red Baron going in for the kill, he upped the pace again, which left me puffing and panting. Further up, as the angle eased, we followed the ridge to the summit of An Socach, where at last I could enjoy a five minute rest and some food.

The weather was similar to yesterday, damp mist blown in the wind, but at least there wasn't the same drizzly rain; the cropped grassy ridges made for pleasant going. An Riabhachan came and went, followed by the steep thousand feet to Sgurr na Lapaich, down to the broad col and up to Munro number four, Carn nan Gobhar. It was here that I said goodbye to Jim, as he was heading back down to the Mullardoch dam to collect his car, whilst I took a compass bearing for the little point of Carn nam Fiacal. Descending rougher slopes here made for slow going, which wasn't helped by tired legs, but it meant I could keep a better eye on the compass. Over the little top, I dropped out the mist and down heather slopes to meet the track that passed near Inchvuilt. Out on the road in Glen Strathfarrar, I found the van sitting a few hundred metres to the west.

It was now four o'clock, my slow time for the section reflecting how drained I felt, and at the van, I could immediately tell Manny was anxious about my late arrival. He had promised to help me with the next four hills, but he knew Lesley and the boys would be appearing in the next couple of hours to collect him. My plan had been to cycle down the glen and to do the hills from east to west, but Manny said we should just start from this end and get on with it. I did need a rest, however, to recharge the batteries, so I changed into fresh gear, while Mum heated a tin of spaghetti and tomato sauce. I bunged this on two rolls and wolfed it down. Manny's eagerness helped get me out of the door by half past four, but straightaway I realised the thirty minute break had made no difference at all. Climbing the initial track beside the Allt Toll a' Mhuic, every step was a triumph of the will against gravity. Manny was always several yards in front and continually geeing me on. I don't think he appreciated how much the earlier nineteen miles and two thousand metres of climb had taken out of me, but at that moment he was basically flogging a dead horse.

My climb from hell ended as we got onto the ridge and turned east to the summit of Sgurr Fhuar-thuill. Here, there was palpable relief for Manny, as I finally managed to break into a jog down the far side. The top that had to be climbed on the way to the next Munro rubbed salt in my wounds, but at least we didn't have to go all the way to the summit, traversing the south side to save a few metres. Another slow ascent took me to Sgurr a' Choire Ghlais, a jog to the next col, then up to our third Munro, Carn nan Gobhar. Another jog and one final climb saw us to our last hill of the day, Sgurr na Ruaidhe. The cloud level having risen slightly, we were soon out of the mist and just getting into our stride when we heard a shout out to our left. Looking over, we saw Dave Rogers, who had come up to meet us and, since he was already about three quarters way up the hill, continued for the top. Manny and I ran on down, the smoother slope here making for fast going.

Arriving at the track end beside the road for twenty to nine, the motorhome was parked up, and Dave soon joined us inside. I was half expecting a visit from James Phimister, who had kindly given permission for me to remain in the glen overnight, but he did not make an appearance. Looking out as the last of the light faded, the quiet stillness of the glen was soothing after all the rush and exhaustion of today.

Day 42 – Sunday 9 July

Up at quarter to seven, and a casual glance out of the window revealed low cloud and light rain, which wasn't inspiring for today's big trek through remote land. With no chance of a rendezvous today, spare clothes and much grub were required. Dave brought along his big old canvas rucksack and loaded all my stuff into it. This was good as it meant I could leave my rucksack and take only the bumbag. I started on the bike, the glen giving me a gentle warm-up as I manoeuvred to avoid the worst of the puddles. I was soon over the wall of the Monar Dam, where I had a brief flashback to the documentary of the 1992 record, with Rory and Andrew cycling to this exact spot.

Turning the motorhome around by the power station so that Mum could get back out onto the small road, Dave and I said goodbye to her and set off just after half past nine, into dreich surroundings. Climbing north-west over the pass between two small hills, we then traversed the boggy slopes on the south side of Loch Monar, passing some wire bird traps en-route to Pait Lodge. We were soon into the mist for a long walk up the ridge of Meall Mor, then a little scramble onto the summit of Lurg Mhor. On the way to Bidein a' Choire Sheasgaich, the rain was starting to get heavier.

My original plan had been to head north from the summit, following the textbook route which involved climbing over an intervening Corbett, Beinn Tharsuinn, on the way to the next Munro. Dave, however, reckoned it was easier to traverse round the bottom. Agreeing on this, we headed south-west down the ridge before turning right and dropping into Coire Seasgach. Working our way through little rocky outcrops, the heavy rain meant that the slopes were saturated, and we jumped over little streams in a vain bid to keep our feet even remotely dry. Peering out from my hood, the sheets of rain reminded me of my wet and lonesome day at the start of week three, but at least I had Dave for company this time. Following the path that wound round the western flank of Tharsuinn, we saw two figures in the distance coming towards us, which was surprising as this spot was way off the beaten track. It was only when the couple got close up that we recognised the pair as Mark Rigby and Jenny Rae. Fantastic!

Having been up for yesterday's Glamaig hill race on Skye, Mark and Jen had decided to come out here to do their usual long Sunday run, hoping to intercept me at the same time. It was a total fluke that, in all this wilderness, they had managed to do so. Another bonus was that Jen produced a plastic tub with more of her tasty home baking, which I ate most of. They told us that Archie Cameron and Ronnie Gallagher from the club were also out on the hill somewhere, looking for us. Time getting on, we said goodbye and squelched our separate ways. I felt quite strong on the climb up the west ridge of Sgurr Choinnich, then along the level top, which we shared with some high-altitude sheep who didn't seem to mind the inclement weather as they cropped the grass.

Dropping down to the next bealach, it didn't take long to get to Sgurr a'Chaorachain. Approaching the summit, Dave and I laughed when we spotted a bright yellow banana skin, spread out in the shape of a perfect W and held in place with small rocks. I just had to get a photo of the Westies' symbol, alerting us that Archie and Ronnie had passed through. It was a pity not to see them, but I appreciated that they had made the effort on such a dismal day. Dave and I started talking about tough long distance challenges and he mentioned a couple of events that he still wanted to do. When I said that I wouldn't mind trying a twenty-four hour track event just to see what it was like, he baulked at the idea, the antithesis of what he loved about ultra-endurance and the outdoors.

Any sense of our toughness was dispelled on the climb up the steep slopes from Drochaid Mhuilich to the shoulder of Carn nam Fiaclan. Like a shock from a defibrillator, the painful work seemed to jump start my mind, bringing home just how tired I was, and how far Dave and I still had to go today. Wandering over this top and then round to the summit plateau of Maoile Lunndaidh, we noted that the old Gaels had certainly named this mountain correctly - 'Bare hill of the wet place.' Descending west north-west to the glen, it was early evening and the track out of the glen looked extremely appealing. Like a spoilt child, I just didn't want to do this anymore. Letting my internal spat spill briefly over, I even muttered that I could leave the last two hills and pick them up tomorrow, but Dave was having none of it. He walked off and told me to get on with it, and there really wasn't anything I could say to that.

Deep down I knew he was right. It may only have been two hills, but I couldn't afford to drop them and mess up the schedule again. Resigning myself to this, we started on the steep zigzags of the stalker's path by Glenuaig Lodge, and my mind became contemplative. I remembered walking here in April 1997, thinking of Mum and how she was another reason to try for the Munro record. I knew that if she came along, she would love the whole adventure, so it wouldn't just be for me, but for her as well. Sometimes in life there is only a certain window of opportunity to do things in. It's so easy to leave it or procrastinate, but time slips by, life moves on, and the situation won't present itself again. At least I hadn't let that happen this time.

The need to seize the day had been hammered home to me a few months later, in the summer of 1997. I had taken part in the Lochaber marathon in April, and for over half the race, had run with an English guy called Richie. Richie kept me entertained with his stories and was a bit of a character; this man from deepest Brighton had come all the way up to

156

Fort William to run his first ever marathon in a proper heavyweight kilt, and the crowds loved it. My brother had taken photographs of the run so, afterwards, I got Richie's address so I could send him some copies when we got the film developed. Colin took a few months to finish his roll of film, but it was duly developed and I posted some photos down to the kilt man at the end of July. I also told him to get in touch if he was ever coming up for some races in Scotland again. The following week, a letter came back from Richie's mother; he had committed suicide at the end of June. I was absolutely stunned, and couldn't believe that this guy, who had been so full of life, would leave a girlfriend and child and just end it all – how had it come to that? But it had come to that, and life was changed forever for those around him.

With my body on autopilot and legs pushing ever upwards, my mind was free to realise that here I was, three years later, at this exact same spot. I had made it reality. I had taken the opportunity while it was there, and brought Mum along on the trip. Despite her heavy workload, she was positively thriving on the experience, and that was what I had hoped for.

The path petered out as the angle eased, and we climbed the gentler slopes of Moruisg to its summit. In the gloom it was no place to hang about. I took a quick compass bearing and ran off, closely followed by Dave. Over the 854 metre point and down to the col, we got stuck into our last little climb with what remaining energy we had. At the summit of Sgurr nan Ceannaichean, I could tell Dave was starting to feel tired as well now, the large rucksack finally taking its toll.

The shortest route off the top would have been west and north, but we opted for a longer but safer route on the stalker's path to the south-west. After a while, we dropped below cloud level and down to the track, which was streaming with water. By now it was well after ten o'clock as we sploshed our way along, using the last remnants of blurred grey light, and although the track was flat here, I couldn't even muster a jog. Getting out onto the main road, by Craig, the motorhome was in place and we got to its door at quarter past eleven. The rain was still falling, and hadn't let up for the whole of the thirteen hours and forty minutes we were out. Dave's car was difficult to see in the darkness but we could certainly hear where it was. Poor Mary had been sitting for hours with their two young daughters, Helen and Ruth, the latter's cries making it evident that she was none too pleased with having to wait this long for her daddy.

Meanwhile, Drew Turnbull from Westerlands had arrived earlier in the evening, and was parked on the other side of the road and currently trying to get some sleep. I didn't bother annoying him. I was glad of that when June me told that Drew had pulled up beside the motorhome earlier, all smiles and laughs as usual, until she asked him what had happened to the front of his car. Mentioning that he had hit a sheep further up the glen, Drew had obviously not checked the damage at the time. Getting out to take a closer look, his jaw dropped on seeing the dented bumper, twisted bonnet and broken headlight. Apparently all he could say was, 'Oh no, Margaret is going to kill me when I get home.'

June had arrived back herself, after two days away, and drove up in the family's Nissan van to draw up the great Campbell master plan for the forthcoming week. The main predicament was that, with the schedule over-running, the lease for the motorhome was coming to an end, and it was due to be returned to Glasgow for the coming Wednesday – not exactly ideal when I knew I would still be going until the following weekend. Fortunately, as a second vehicle, my family have always preferred owning a van for its practicality, and now this would hopefully solve the problem. In fact, it would be two vans that were needed for all the gear, so June's little Suzuki (one of Mum and Dad's cast-offs) was also coming up later in the week. But I would worry about organising all that when the time came.

Whilst eating, June told me that Steven Fallon, whom Mark and Jen had also bumped into this afternoon, had come by the motorhome after his walk to see if I was about. Steven had already clocked up a fantastic seven rounds of the Munros, and was nearing his eighth, but his main aim was to try and catch up with another gentleman by the name of Stewart Logan who had completed ten rounds.

Midnight munching and massage over, I finally got to bed at one o'clock and took time to reflect on the end of another week. Richard Speirs, along with Manny and Lesley, had helped me over several big days, and this had resulted in collecting forty-nine Munros for my toil, ten hills more than I'd averaged during the previous weeks. Now sitting on two hundred and forty-five and with only thirty-nine to go, under fifty was still on the cards and there was everything to play for in the week ahead. Dave Rogers' contribution today had been particularly vital. He had helped me hold it together for the last two hills in depressing conditions, which meant that we had thankfully stuck to the schedule.

At the back of my mind, I was also planning for a finish next Saturday, which would tie in nicely for anyone wanting to come up for the finale. In the far north, it would allow folk to stay over and head home on the Sunday. But I was not getting my hopes up too much, for I knew that physically, I was very near the edge, if not going over it. At the start of the week, a strange type of sore that I'd never seen before, about the size of a penny, had developed on the back of my left hand; during the rest of the week, another few had come up on my hands and fingers. These were only mildly irritating and, if I didn't scratch them, were not a problem. But they were a sure sign that my body was starting to break down from the constant onslaught, and it was now a race against time to see if I could get to the end before going into total meltdown. If only I could hold together it for one more week, just one more week, please. A little prayer was sent skywards to that effect.

Week 7

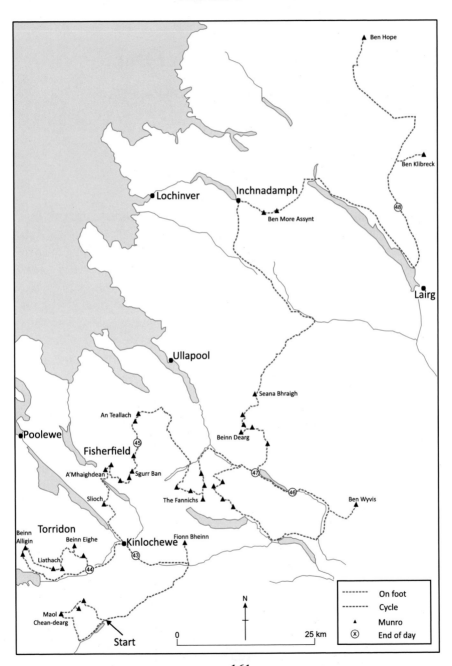

Week 7 – Running for Home

Days 43-49

Day 43 – Monday 10 July

Up at seven thirty, my grogginess lifted gradually over breakfast. This day had originally been planned as a monster trek through the Achnashellach and Torridon Munros, only about twenty-six map miles in distance but with over seventeen thousand feet of climb. Stuff that for a game of soldiers! After my lacklustre performance a few weeks ago in the Cairngorms, I knew it just wasn't on. Now I needed to split it without losing any time; how did I not see this when writing the plan? The very easy day tomorrow, with just a single Munro, could be added to the first three hills of today, and then I'd do the Torridon six tomorrow, giving me two medium-sized days.

I had the pleasure of an easy six mile cycle down the glen to warm up the legs, but again the weather wasn't looking too great. It was overcast and cloudy on the hills, with a light rain falling. Drew and I started on the path by Coulags at quarter past ten, the initial fast walk breaking into sporadic jogging on the easier angle by Clach nan Con-fionn. Turning west on a steeper path to the bealach, we climbed into the mist. From the summit of Maol Chean-dearg, we managed to find a route east, down through rough stony ground, to eventually come out just above Loch Coire Fionnaraich.

Treating ourselves to a five minute breather and some biscuits, the little respite was needed before the steep five hundred and fifty metre pull up the other side to the ridge, where we turned south-east for the climb to Sgorr Ruadh. Retracing our steps along the ridge, we dropped north-east to the bealach then worked our way up and round to the lowly summit of Beinn Liath Mhor, our third Munro. Drew and I jogged east along the summit ridge, dropping to the col before the middle top, then made a steeper descent south, to meet the path in Coire Làir. The sun was breaking through as we continued jogging and, having never been in this coire before, it looked a fantastic and impressive setting. The rest of the path down by the river made for pleasant going and we soon emerged by the train station, and out onto the main road for five o'clock.

Gordon Robinson had appeared again, having promised to meet me somewhere in this area, but with the ever-evolving schedule, things were slightly adrift. He would join me now for Fionn Bheinn once I got the cycle out of the way, so I grabbed some snacks and started on the bike for the gradual climb up Glen Carron to Achnasheen. Getting there and pulling into the little parking area beside the station, Drew told me that, rather than stay another day, he wanted to get back down the road with his damaged car, so he had swapped with Gordon for tomorrow, and he would now join me for Fionn Bheinn instead.

Although the cycle was only been about twelve miles long, it had been tiring, so I took a longer rest with several mugs of tea. Drew and I got going at seven o'clock. The break seemed to have done the trick, as we climbed quite strongly on grassy slopes by the stream, and then continued in a straight line all the way to the summit. With the sun now shining below cloud level, we still had to wrap up in our jackets from the wind, but for a few minutes we took in the panorama northwards to the Fannich hills. Reversing our route, we broke into the fastest run of the day over smooth slopes, saturated from all the recent rain. Although this made for softer going, further down it was more slippy and, with my knees and left ankle playing up, I could only manage a slow jog, while Drew moved a few hundred yards ahead. He waited for me as we got to the road, and at nine o'clock, I was quite pleased with our time of two hours.

The day wasn't over yet, however, so we said goodbye to Drew and I got on the bike again for the trundle westwards along the A832. The few miles of lonely road beside Loch a' Chroisg were atmospheric, grey clouds broken with rays of sun glinting off the water. The road then started climbing as it turned towards a distant Kinlochewe. I knew that I should have been cycling at least as far as there, if not further on towards Torridon, but once cresting the top of the pass, I decided to call it a day. I was also aware that there were a few phone calls that had to be made and, at ten to ten, I didn't want to leave it much later than that. The fact that there was a big transmitter mast back down the road also meant that at least we were guaranteed phone reception in this lonely spot. At bedtime, I thought about how I had enjoyed my day in the hills with Drew, his easier pace being more amenable to my fatigued state.

Day 44 – Tuesday 11 July

Having finished on the bike last night, and then starting with a cycle first thing this morning, I hadn't bothered to untie the cover or put the bike on the rear carrier overnight. Happily munching away and listening to a heavy five-minute shower bounce off the roof, muggins now remembered his trusty steed was still sitting outside, with no poly bag over the saddle for protection. Too late, the soft foam-like material was saturated, and even trying to press dry it with a towel didn't remove all the water. I just had to grit teeth and get on with it.

At least the road was all downhill in Glen Docherty to give me a gentle warm-up, and I took advantage of the public loo in Kinlochewe before heading past the little outdoor shop round the corner. This wasn't your usual shop venue, but more like an enlarged garden shed, crammed with gear, but unfortunately it didn't open until later. There was a telephone number to call, however. Ten minutes later we were inside and, after a brief perusal, I splashed out with the old visa card for the first time on the trip. Continuing on the ten miles from Kinlochewe to Torridon, where we collected Gordon who had been patiently waiting, I then had a further three miles with a stiff climb before getting to the car park below Beinn Alligin. I decided to put on my lightweight boots for the rough ground I would encounter today, and to give my left ankle, still aching from yesterday, a bit more support.

Away at quarter past eleven, a steady walk led to a steeper incline in Coir' nan Laogh, where the upper reaches saw us climb into mist and light drizzle. After the first summit, Tom na Gruagaich, we pressed on down to the col, then round by the top of the Eag Dubh. The sheer drop from here looked frightening in the swirling cloud, but we were soon onto the summit of Sgurr Mhor. Having originally planned to climb over the Horns of Alligin, we arrived at the col before them, and Gordon suggested it would be possible to descend the steep slopes to the south and save us the extra climb. I agreed to give it a go, but it proved to be quite difficult, working our way through rocky outcrops on steep grass, but we managed it and continued south-east all the way down to the Abhainn Coire Mhic Nobuil.

Crossing the river, the weather was starting to brighten slightly and, getting warmer, I was sweating on the long slog south-east, finally getting over the crest of the ridge at about the seven hundred metre level. From here, the ridge eastwards was hardly a ridge at all, but just a whaleback of ground, steadily rising for a thousand feet over a mile to Mullach an Rathain. I took advantage of this for an easier slow walk to the summit from where, after a short break, we continued down to the col before Am Fasarinen. We automatically opted for the path that bypassed the pinnacles on their southern side, to avoid an airy scramble, and I remembered how the SMC guidebook said that this should not be regarded as an easy option.

This fact had been brought sharply into focus on my first visit here, in November 1996. Iain, Ian, and I had set off on a bright wintery morning but, as we climbed higher on Liathach, the clouds gathered and the showers turned to sleety snow above two thousand feet, adding to an already thick snow base. Heading east to west on that occasion, we took the path beneath the pinnacles, which promptly faded as it cut across very steep snow slopes, disappearing altogether in several places.

Just to spice things up even further, yours truly had on this occasion forgotten to bring the most important piece of kit – my ice axe. This was a serious slip of the mind and slipping was certainly on my mind as, teetering on precipitous slopes, there was no chance of self-arrest without one. Our solution was that Big Iain would stay right behind me with his axe whilst Ian gingerly moved forward to try to find the path, then pass his axe back to me for the particularly dodgy bits. This all went on in slow motion, but we did eventually come out at the far side. Completing the other Munro and getting back down to the roadside as darkness fell, it was certainly the closest I have ever come to needing nappies in the hills.

The Grey One had made its point that day and, with this in mind, Gordon and I set off. It was so much easier now that I could actually see the path. After a simple crossing of the pinnacles, it was up to Spidean a' Choire Leith for Munro number four. After some food came the part I was slightly worried about; would we be able to find a way off Liathach on its north side? The Harvey's Torridon map indicated that a north-westerly direction from the summit might be promising. We headed down that way and, although twisting and turning to avoid rocky outcrops, the slope and terrain eventually eased as we neared the south side of Lochan a' Choire Dhuibh.

Starting to feel tired, we crossed the lower path and climbed to a higher one above the lochan, legs noticeably heavier and beginning to drag. The more worrying point was that a slight ache had developed during the descent, in the *vastus medialis* muscle beside my left knee, was now becoming painful and gradually increasing. Passing a few walkers on their way out, we eased our way round the base of Sail Mhor as the path inclined to Coire Mhic Fhearchair and its dark loch. We started on a steeper climb to the col in the south-east corner of the corrie, where every step upwards on my left leg was painful, the muscle complaining at having to fight gravity. Dumping the rucksack and turning north at the col, the gentler angle made things easier, but it was still a slow walk to gain the summit of Ruadh-stac Mor.

Returning to the col, there was another little climb to the main ridge, then down to the next col before the final drag of the day. We were both relieved when we finally gained the summit cairn of Spidean Coire nan Clach. Returning past the trig point, we cut down to our left and round into Coire an Laoigh. Even descent was causing much discomfort now, and I grimaced with each step. Nearing the bottom, we could see the motorhome and what looked like June outside, filming our last fifty yards to the van. It was ten minutes to ten and I was knackered, but we still had to get Gordon back along to Torridon to pick up his car.

June told us the good news that, during the day, she and Mum had gone to Torridon Youth Hostel to ask if they could use the laundry facilities. Not only had the warden, Neil Hinchliff, said yes, but he also gave a donation to the Dreams Come True charity, and said that all of us could have free use of the facilities for the night. As we were getting ready to leave, Dave Calder arrived, having just driven straight up after work in Glasgow, ready for his stint tomorrow. Dave followed us along to Torridon, and Gordon collected his car. Before leaving, as it was now after ten, Gordon thought it prudent to call his wife, just to say he was off the hill and on his way home. Lending Gordon the mobile phone, I soon wished I hadn't, for even standing several yards away, the vociferous emanations from the phone could be heard. June and I were half expecting smoke to start billowing from his ear with the bashing it was getting, and poor Gordon couldn't get a word in edgeways to explain. He returned the phone and set off on his long drive to Nairn, looking thoroughly dejected. I felt guilty, because it had been my slow progress today that had caused him to be so late.

After a quick scrub, we all enjoyed a bit of late dinner, Mum telling me that she had managed to move some of the gear I would need in the next few days from the motorhome into the van. With the muscular tension removed, the area just beside my left knee was feeling okay, but I took extra ibuprofen and hoped the problem wouldn't return tomorrow. There was a seriously big day planned for Fisherfield.

Day 45 – Wednesday 12 July

The alarm sounded at six o'clock, and I managed to spring into action by ten to seven for the drive back along the glen, to last night's finishing spot near Loch Bharranch. From there, I started on the bike into a cold, bright morning, along to Kinlochewe, then down to the road end car park by Incheril. Having arranged a week's holiday up at Gruinard Bay with her friend Shelagh King and daughters, Christine Menhennet from the club had kindly offered to help with this big day, and she was already waiting in her car when we rolled in.

Christine and Dave talked whilst I packed my rucksack, had some breakfast, and then checked that all my essential gear had been moved into the van from the motorhome. Big Iain had loaned us a roof box to put on the van but, even with that, it was going to be a tight squeeze. The Campbell master plan was now being rolled out, and the whole thing now looked as though it was going to be a bit of a logistical nightmare. The motorhome would go back to Glasgow for tonight, then tomorrow Dad, Mum and June would head down to Manchester to see Colin graduate from the University of Salford, return to Glasgow, then finally they would all head to the far north-west again on Friday – a busy forty-eight hours! In the meantime, Big Iain would finish his work in Airdrie at ten this evening, and drive up overnight in June's Suzuki van to lend a hand from tomorrow morning, and provide some extra carrying capacity.

Saying cheerio to Mum and June and wishing them good luck for their journey up and down Britain, we told Dave we'd see him later, and Christine and I got going at twenty to nine. Following the path by the river, I managed to jog a bit, enjoying the scenery and chatting to Chris, then we turned and started climbing north-east and north into Coire na Sleaghaich. Allowing a brief stop for the fantastic view from the summit trig on Slioch, we took in the other summit cairn before managing to work our way down the north-east slopes, and then north to come out on the shoreline of Lochan Fada. Following this north-west under the rugged cliffs of Beinn Lair, we rounded the head of the lochan and crossed the inflow for a steep little climb east north-east to gain the long, grassy slopes of A' Mhaighdean. A steady walk took us to the summit, but it was a shame that the cloud level had now lowered so there wasn't much to see from here, this being one of the remotest Munros with the finest of views.

Managing a steady jog to the col before Ruadh Stac Mor, we worked our way up the scree to come out at the summit trig, before reversing to the col and traversing south over Stac a' Chaorruinn. Despite taking ibuprofen every couple of hours, at this point I noticed yesterday's muscle ache above my left knee starting to get sore again, rather ominous after only three Munros and with such a long way still to go. From the broad col, more grassy slopes took us to the ridge of Beinn Tarsuinn, which we gradually worked our way along, taking a long break at the summit. Continuing on over the rough boulders of Mullach Coire Mhic Fhearchair, then onto Sgurr Ban, the whole thing really knocked the stuffing out of me, and my knee was almost as painful as last night.

As if that wasn't enough, having worn lighter fell shoes today with the aim of saving weight and travelling faster, the angular edges of the quartzite stones were stabbing on the soles of my feet, and I was desperate to get back onto softer ground. Hobbling down to the col above Loch a' Bhrisidh, then up the ridge to Beinn a' Chlaidheimh, I realised it was getting late. Descending north off our seventh Munro, we ran into rocky outcrops and crags, partially hidden from above. The plan had been to get to Shenavall bothy by about five or six o'clock, where Dave was waiting with extra provisions for us, then continue over An Teallach and out to Corrie Hallie, thereby completing a grand sweep of the Fisherfield Munros. I had long given up hope that Dave would have waited this late, as he was due back in Glasgow for work the next morning, but I just hoped he had left our goody bag, as Christine and I were low on supplies.

As it turned out, he had indeed left our goody bag – all the way back in Torridon youth hostel.

Wading across the Abhainn Srath na Sealga, which thankfully wasn't too deep, and walking the last few hundred metres, we could see Dave standing outside the bothy. At half past nine, I was really surprised he was still here, but it was great to see him, and he told us how his day had gone. Leaving us at Kinlochewe, he had meandered round the coast road, taking in little villages en route, and only when arriving at Corrie Hallie had he realised the supply bag was back at the hostel. This necessitated a flying visit to the Safeway store in Ullapool to recoup supplies, before dashing back and hoofing it into the bothy. Worrying that he might be late for us he had arrived after three o'clock, so by now had been waiting over six hours. This was his third stint at helping, however, so Dave was a veteran of all this back-up malarkey, and had brought a book with him. Between admiring the scenery and reading, he had managed to while away the hours.

His obvious question was whether we going to continue but, like me, he already knew the answer. My left knee was certainly not fine, and to round it off, the top third of An Teallach was enveloped in dark menacing cloud; if the Forge was getting fired up, I didn't want to take a hammering.

Only one choice was left, an impromptu overnighter in the bothy. On that note, and with the sky almost dark, Dave set off at half past ten for his run back to the car, and Chris and I settled in for the night. Unfortunately there wasn't much to settle into. Eating some of the chocolate Dave had brought in, we had to ration it, because we still faced a tough climb tomorrow morning before getting out. A couple who were through in the back room of the bothy offered us the use of their stove, a couple of teabags and even milk, but no energy-raising sugar.

Christine, a more experienced bothy-goer than me, went scouting about to see if there was anything else that could be put to use. In one of the corners, she managed to find a moth-ridden old sweater that was full of holes and said that we could use that. For what? Generous to the end, Christine passed me my bed for the night and found a bit of old plastic sheeting for herself, but of course I'd been saving the best till last. From the bottom of my rucksack, I retrieved my orange plastic survival bag, which unfolded to cover quite a large area. Spreading it on the floor to save our jackets from getting dirty, and tucking the old pullover underneath it

169

for a bit of cushioning, Chris and I put on every bit of spare clothing we had, and with our rucksacks as pillows, lay down on the cold floor.

I was annoyed that I hadn't completed today, and dropping more time at this late stage of the journey was exasperating, but I couldn't physically do anything about it. Another fairly large blister was developing on the top of my right cheek; along with my sizzled ears and blistered hands, it was becoming evident to others that I really was starting to fall apart. Not wanting to mess up tomorrow's planned schedule, it meant a very early start to complete An Teallach first, so I set my watch alarm. I didn't expect I'd need it, though.

Day 46 – Thursday 13th July

Beep beep beep at four o'clock, but I had been correct in my assumption that I wouldn't need it. The hard bothy floor, combined with the cold, had meant a night of restless dozing and frequent waking. Stepping outside just after half past four, we were met by an eerie gloominess. A gusting breeze drove light rain which leaked from a blanket of thick cloud, shrouding the hills to half their height. Trudging towards Loch na Sealga in the dim light, I had one of those moments where you think, 'What the fuck am I doing here?' Christine was no doubt thinking the same. Wandering minds were quickly brought back to the here and now as we swung to our right, however. The rough, heathery slopes got steeper as we climbed higher into Coir a' Ghamhne, where we were thankful for a newly-built deer fence that we used to help pull ourselves upwards in several places.

This early morning workout felt brutal to a tired body and mind, but we kept soldiering on up increasingly stony ground to come out at the col, where we ate the last of our meagre rations. Climbing south-east, wet and windy conditions greeted the pair of us at the summit of Sgurr Fiona, and we scuttled off north north-east down to the col. Thankfully, there wasn't too much of a climb up the other side, and it didn't take long until we were on top of Bidein a' Ghlas Thuill. With a lighter shade of grey for backdrop, I managed to balance the camera on top of the trig pillar without it blowing off, and the resulting photo shows two very weathered, tired, drookit faces sporting big, cheesy grins. Dropping north to the next col, we turned right and descended into the corrie of Glas

170

Tholl, continuing across wet ground east north-east, by the waterfalls and all the way down to the A832.

We then had to walk back up the road to Corrie Hallie and, rounding a bend, we could see the white Nissan van where June and Mum had left it yesterday. The wee yellow Suzuki van was also *in situ*, which meant that, as Dave had been driving down one side of A9 during the night, Iain had been coming up the other way. Support like this was helping the Munro Run 2000 bandwagon roll on in these final days. On the same note, we also met Elspeth Scott from Westerlands who, after arriving late yesterday evening, had been snoozing in her car when Dave had loomed out the darkness and explained the situation. Of course, Big Iain had arrived during the night and just crashed out in the back of the van.

It was half past nine, and before I had a chance to think, Christine and Elsie suggested that we all go down to the Dundonnell Hotel and discuss the next part of the plan over breakfast. Iain and I readily agreed. Elsie and Chris ordered, and we all took a comfy seat; five minutes later, we had a platter of bacon sandwiches and large pots of coffee and tea on the table. Christine had been a vegetarian for over a decade (and still is) but, after little to eat during our five hours on the hill this morning, and almost nothing for dinner last night, that went out the window. We were ravenous, and quickly demolished all the sarnies. So what to do? That's right, order another platter of bacon butties. These tasted lip-smackingly good, and they were all washed down with lovely fresh-brewed coffee – I felt ready to take on the world again.

Well, not quite the world, but the range of hills known as the Fannaichs. This had been put down on paper as another big sweep, from the two western outlying Munros to the seven on the main ridge itself, but An Teallach this morning had put a spanner in the works. The women considered the plan, and Elsie suggested that, as with Monday and Tuesday, I could split today's lot with tomorrow and still not lose any further time. This would involve doing the five most western Fannaichs this afternoon and lumping the eastern four with Ben Wyvis tomorrow. That was a great idea, and the only viable option I could see at the moment, but it effectively scuppered any chance of the Saturday finish.

Returning to Corrie Hallie after over an hour of rest, the legs should have recharged. Although the cycle I now faced was only around seven and a half miles, it involved a climb of nine hundred and fifty feet. I took it easy on the bike, especially with a full stomach, and gradually wound my way up the A832, and through the wooded gorge of the Dundonnell River. The abysmal weather of early morning having abated somewhat, the light showers were now permeated with brief periods of sunlight, which illuminated the waterfalls on the river and took my mind off the climb. This changed when leaving the gorge and climbing out onto the Fain, where I struggled into a headwind on the appropriately named Destitution Road.

Reaching the track end, I pulled in behind the van and started packing my rucksack for the hill. Iain was going to run Christine back round to Kinlochewe to collect her car, so Elsie and I set off at midday on the track down to Loch a' Bhraoin. Passing the boat house and over the bridge, we turned west south-west, managing a jog here and there, before turning south south-west and climbing directly to the ridge of Sron na Goibhre, which went up to the summit of A' Chailleach. About halfway up the next hill, Toman Coinnich, I was keeping right for the traverse, skirting well below the summit, and Elsie told me that she was also doing the Munro Tops. She therefore headed off to the left to take in the summit, while I continued with an easy jog down to the next col. Elsie quickly caught up, and together we climbed to the summit of Sgurr Breac, from where we took a bearing and dropped below the cloud to the pass at five hundred and fifty metres.

From here it was a straightforward walk just south of due east to gain the main ridge and drop the rucksack, before a little pull up to the top of Sgurr nan Each. Returning, I was by now feeling jaded again on the bigger climb from the col to the summit of Sgurr nan Clach Geala. Another bearing took us to the two following cols for the last little climb of the day, to the summit of Meall a' Chrasgaidh. Once that was over, we aimed northwards for a path indicated on the map. What the map didn't show were some craggy outcrops here, making for a rough descent, but as the angle eased, there was still no sign of a path. Further down, we picked up a bit of a line and followed it all the way to the bridge over the Abhainn Cuileig on the A832, where Big Iain was waiting with the van.

It was now half past six, and Elsie was heading down to book herself a room in the Aultguish Inn. Iain followed me in the van for the upcoming cycle. I turned onto the A835 and climbed up the road towards Loch Droma, the cranks steadily revolving. I switched to autopilot, and my mind got back to thinking about the Saturday finish. For some reason I couldn't let go of it, probably because I wanted a good soirée following the finish. Yet for all intents and purposes, that idea was dead in the water – how would I be able to squeeze the remaining fifteen Munros, and a vast tract of land to be covered, into the next forty-eight hours? The trump card I had been waiting to play would help me get home in under fifty days, but the Saturday finish was probably beyond me.

The 'trump card' had been gleaned from the Johnston and Gibson documentary, where they had compressed their last two days into one huge day in a bid to save time as they pushed for the finish. Seeing as my last two days were going to be the same as theirs, it left me with the same option. As I was still tracking ten days behind on my forty day schedule, combining the last two in the same way would bring me in a day early. But why couldn't I try and go one stage further by combining my last three days in one last gasp, head back, chest out, *Chariots of Fire* style lunge for the tape? That was the secret plan I had been harbouring, but I knew even that wouldn't produce the goods for Saturday afternoon.

Churning through scenarios, what if I tried to do my single outlier of Ben Wyvis tonight? That would leave me the four hills with Elsie tomorrow morning, in addition to then continuing on for the mega trek; surely far too much. Admittedly, the left quadricep and knee problem had miraculously been non-evident today, but I would almost certainly go up in a mushroom cloud somewhere in the wilds of Sutherland, if I attempted fourteen Munros spread over at least one hundred and twenty miles in one zigzagging all-or-nothing dash to the top of Scotland. Expletives rang out as I swore at myself for letting this situation arise; my dream of a Saturday finish seemed to be drifting away with the wind.

Feeling slightly blue, I should have kept cycling the extra few miles to the Wyvis path end but, while freewheeling down from the Glascarnoch dam wall, Aultguish Inn appeared like an oasis in the desert. At quarter to eight, fifteen hours after starting, I crumbled mentally, and stopped the bike. Iain pulled the van in and I told him that we'd take advantage of the bunkhouse here to get a good sleep and to treat ourselves to a meal. The facilities meant that I enjoyed the luxury of a bath, then fresh clothes, before heading to the Inn where we ordered dinner. Even a simple bar menu was much appreciated after no dinner the previous night and, with the meal finished, Iain and I relaxed over a pint. Whilst chatting, I noticed a man come in at the far end of the lounge, and looking about, he made a beeline towards us.

It was only when the man got closer that I realised this was the guy from my Munro videotape, Andrew Johnston himself. Having only made brief contact by email before the run started, I was thrilled to be meeting the other half of the record-holding duo. How had he known I'd be here? Unbeknown to me, Mark Rigby had added Andrew's email address to the Westerlands circulation list, so he had been receiving all the progress updates, and knew my approximate location. Having arranged to meet up with Rory for a round of golf in Tain on Friday, he had driven up a day early and had climbed two of the eastern Fannaichs this afternoon. Obviously I should have been on one of them, but because of my change of plan, he hadn't found me. Stopping for a shandy before heading to Tain, he had seen the van and now here he was – great!

Andrew turned out to be quite a character and, over several pints, kept Iain and I laughing with his stories, banter and recollections of the 1992 run. By sheer coincidence, it turned out that today, 13th July, was exactly eight years since he and Rory had achieved the record, so we toasted the anniversary as well. By closing time, Andrew was in no position to drive back, so he booked himself into the bunkhouse. Despite having been up since four o'clock, I was still in socialising mode, and threw caution to the wind, seeing as I only had a few days to go. Scrummaging about in the back of the van, I managed to find some of my emergency beer stash, and a bottle of whisky just happened to be located as well.

Talking about life in general, the late hour finally got to Iain and he dozed off, while Andrew and I continued talking. After a while, the conversation turned and, although I had been vaguely aware that Andrew's wife, Kate, had been seriously ill with cancer, he now told me that she had died only two weeks previously. As I sat in utter silence, he described how back in May, knowing the end was near, they had gone on one last holiday, to visit California and the Cascade Mountains, then returned for their final weeks together. I was amazed that Andrew felt comfortable enough to talk about this, and at his strength of character when he candidly described her actual moment of dying – heaven only knew what he must have been going through these last few weeks. The fact that his wife, at thirty-two, had been only two years older than I was, was sobering to say the least, and it again brought home the preciousness of time and the importance of this once-in-a-lifetime event.

We spoke of other things, but the whisky must have amplified our voices, as an employee, who we hadn't realised was staying in one of the rooms further down the corridor, came up and knocked on the door. Andrew answered and just managed to get a quick apology in before the verbal onslaught hit him full on. The girl was absolutely livid because it was after two o'clock in the morning; saying sorry wasn't good enough, and she stormed off. Oops! Andrew slinked back to his room and I switched off the lights. After being awake for over twenty-two hours, I was asleep almost instantaneously.

Day 47 – Friday 14 July

Not surprisingly, I slept through my early alarm and suddenly woke just after seven o'clock, the old internal body clock trying to jump start me into action. Damn! Wake Iain up! Then I realised I was still tipsy, as I swayed about the room trying to get dressed – bollocks! Knocking on Andrew's room door, we managed to wake him, and I helped Iain with packing the gear back into the van. Grabbing a quick snack and some juice, I set off on the bike for the five mile cycle down the road, dwelling on how rough my head felt – bloody whisky, always the same. At Garbat, I pulled in and got ready for the hill while Andrew arrived and told us of his latest experiences. When he had got back to his room last night, the poor old dog had peed on the floor without an evening walk. Andrew had the enjoyment of cleaning that up before getting to bed. Just to make matters worse, the employee we'd upset must have told her story to the proprietor, as the owner had apparently said that Iain and I were welcome back but that our friend was banned from the premises. Despite Andrew's embarrassment, I couldn't stop laughing when I heard that one. Poor old Andrew, getting barred from a highfalutin' establishment would have been fair enough, but the Aultguish Inn?

It was twenty past eight when we started on the path up through the forestry trees, Andrew and I managing to jog the odd section, but slowing down when we hit the steeper slopes towards An Cabar. Getting to the broad ridge, what had been a breeze lower down was now a strong headwind, and we struggled with a slow jog all the way to the summit of Ben Wyvis. With cloud blowing over the top, there were no views, so we just took a couple of minutes to catch our breath, then, with the wind at our backs, reversed our route at a much faster pace. All the while, Andrew was still keeping me entertained

Our van contained Mum's all-in-one folding picnic table, and Iain had this out waiting for us. The double burner stove was also in action, a pan sizzling away on top. Andrew and I tucked in and enjoyed a mug of coffee, while the breeze kept the midges away – bliss. Elsie had been busy on the phone while we were up the hill, and had managed to get permission for us to use the private road from Grudie power station towards Fannich Lodge, thereby giving much easier access for our afternoon hills. This was good news, so I readied myself for another cycle. Thanking Andrew for his help, he mentioned that he and Rory would try and get north to meet up with me at some point on Sunday. It had been a laugh having Andrew about, and I looked forward to seeing him and Rory in a couple of days' time.

It was an easy few miles to Gorstan and then along the A832, before we came to a sign for Fannich Estate. A steep little climb up the private road brought me to a gate, where Elsie jumped out of the van and let me through, and I continued up the single track road, struggling into a headwind. At the bridge over the Allt a' Choin Idhir, the meeting point of several tracks, I changed to hill shoes, checked the rucksack, and set off with Elsie at one o'clock, jogging along the top of a giant water pipe before taking to the slopes.

I hadn't seen An Coileachan from this side before, and it was much more impressive than from the north west, the rugged walls of Garbh Choire Mor crowned with a nice little peak at either end. Feeling fine now, despite last night's overindulgence, Elsie and I climbed quite strongly all the way to An Eigin. From the misty summit, we continued with a jog into the strong headwind, down to the next bealach. Elsie bagged her Munro top, while I skirted to the left, the broad ridge giving easy progress to our second Munro, Meall Gorm, and a final walk to Sgurr Mor. I collected my rucksack and we headed out for a mile to our last hill, Beinn Liath Mhor Fannaich, then worked our way down to meet the track end by the Allt a' Mhadaidh. Following this to Loch Droma, we crossed the dam to the main road beside Lochdrum, where we met Iain with the van, just after half past five.

Before I could finish for the day, there was a little cycle to complete, down to tomorrow's starting point. It was good to be finished before six and, while Iain and Elsie talked on the drive back to Aultguish, I lay on cushions in the back, staring at the roof. The movement of the van on the road was relaxing, encouraging me to close my eyes, and my mind drifted off. I came to realise that the penultimate day had just been completed. Although tomorrow's trek would go through the night and into a second day, it would just feel like one big outing, so today really was my last 'normal' hill day. This stirred conflicting emotions; on the one hand, there was excitement at the possibility of the big run in – I might just do this thing after all. On the other, it meant the adventure was coming to an end. This hadn't registered with me until now. Being so focused every day on the here and now, every minute, every hour, one hill at a time, I had not contemplated it all coming to a sudden end. And yet it had to, and very soon at that.

Back at the inn, Iain and I enjoyed a quick thirst-quenching shandy, and feeling tired, I had to go for a lie down, dozing on my bed for an hour. In the meantime, Elsie had collected her husband, Peter Baxter, another member of Westerlands. They were followed not long after by Mum, Dad and June, who all booked themselves into the bunkhouse. It was great to see them, and they told me that the big drive up and down the UK had been fine. Mum and June had managed to unpack all the gear from the motorhome on Wednesday evening, and returned the van to the hire company. The three of them had then watched Colin graduate in Manchester yesterday, before returning to Glasgow, which only left the drive up here today – easy! I treated myself to another bath and a shave before we all headed into the lounge for some pub grub. Jim Hall was sitting pouring over maps, having arrived a while earlier.

Following the meal, Jim asked me which route I intended for leaving the Beinn Dearg hills tomorrow. This was to return from Seana Bhraigh back out to the A835 at Inverlael, before cycling north. He suggested it would be better to drop northwards to the track in Strath Mulzie, using a mountain bike out to Oykel Bridge, and then cycle north on the A837 to Ledmore, saving me from the extra climb and distance involved on the A835. If this would save more effort in the long run, and there was a decent track for bike, it seemed like a good idea. The problem was that my mountain bike had gone back with the motorhome on Wednesday. The new route looked good, however, so we'd go with that and hopefully pick up a mountain bike tomorrow, somehow.

Heading back to the bunkhouse, I made a few phone calls informing friends of the outline for Sunday. Gary Tompsett and his girlfriend, Caitlin Evans, were late arrivals at the bunkhouse, so it was a quick hello, then lights out after eleven. After two nights with very little sleep, it was great to get to bed at a reasonable hour, and there was an air of excitement. This was the real deal – family and friends gathering to help me through one super-sized day. Having overcome so much in the last few weeks, could I make this final hurdle? It was still all too easy to take a tumble and break a leg, but never mind, I was relishing the thought of the challenge.

Days 48 & 49 – Saturday 15 and Sunday 16 July

Enjoying a fairly solid sleep until ten to seven, I was up and readying myself because a photographer from the *Sunday Mail* was due to arrive, for a piece they were going to use the next day. The sun was shining, but I felt like a bit of a ponce running up and down the side of the road, smiling for the camera as cars went by. I then had to speak to the journalist on the phone, to answer a few questions, so that was another fifteen minutes lost. It was arranged that Gary and Caitlin would go to Ullapool to try and hire a mountain bike, and I asked Mum to pick me up some cans of Red Bull for my nocturnal stint.

Back up at the top of Loch Glascarnoch, the early brightness had disappeared behind a blanket of grey cloud, and it was cold. I had to wear full leggings, windproof jacket, hat and gloves. Pete, Elsie, and Jim were joining me for this stage and, with thoughts in my head of 'Let the games begin,' we started off just before nine o'clock. A nice easy walk warmed us up nicely and we managed to cross the Abhainn a' Gharbhrain without any problems, before taking to the slopes of Am Faochagach, where a straightforward walk took us up into wispy cloud and the summit. Elsie returned to the A835 to collect her car, but the three of us jogged down to Loch Prille. After crossing the outflow, we had the odd glimpse of sun as we climbed up rocky shelves to Cona' Mheall. The cloud lifted to just above the tops as we got to the summit.

This was ideal weather for me, cool and clear, but the legs were starting to feel tired over the boulders to Beinn Dearg. I was glad of a wee five minute rest at the summit, then we dropped back down beside the huge dry stone dyke, passing several other walkers, which felt a bit strange after seeing almost no-one on the hills all week. The three of us were soon on our own again as Meall nan Ceapraichean came and went, and then on our fifth Munro of Eididh nan Clach Geala, it was time for Jim to depart and head back to his car. Pete and I continued over rough, undulating ground with a jog down to the edge of the Cadha Dearg, then followed the line above the high crags. Gentle slopes soon took us to the summit of Seana Bhraigh, and with my only previous visit here having been shrouded in mist, I was in for a surprise. There before us, away in the distance to the north west, were the jewels of Coigach and Assynt: Ben More Coigach itself, Beinn an Eoin, Stac Pollaidh, Cul Beag, Cul Mor, Suilven, Canisp – who needs Munros when you've got beauties like these?

With the cloud layer now breaking up, the sun was shining a bit more, but it was still chilly in the wind and we kept our jackets on. That changed when we descended north and north north-east to the track end in Strath Mulzie, where it was much more sheltered and warm. Big Gary was already in place and had managed to hire a mountain bike in Ullapool. Leaving him and Pete to jog, I set off down the track where, after a few miles, I met Caitlin sitting sunning herself and enjoying the tranquillity of the strath. A brief stop and I was on my way again, passing the lodge, then Gary's car, and over Duag Bridge. Then I made a mistake. A few hundred metres on, a track branched off to the left and, with a quick glance at the map, it looked like there would be less climbing on this than on the main path. Heading down the slope, this turned out to be much rougher than the main track and quickly deteriorated into nothing but vegetation, making progress difficult – pants! I turned about and pushed the bike back up the rough incline to the better track – more energy wasted.

The track again split further on and had a few more junctions, but remained of good quality. The sound of a car confirmed that the other three had caught up and, letting them past, it wasn't long until I pedalled up to the end of the little road beside Oykel Bridge. Several vehicles parked at the side of the road indicated others had arrived, namely Donald Smith and my good friend, Stuart Burns, who I'd known since our first year at secondary school. Stuart and I had been well-matched hill walking contemporaries in our early years, during adventure training on Arran and on the odd walking trip since leaving school. The demands of marriage and fatherhood meant that he didn't get out to the hills much now, but it was good to see that he had come up for the last Munros.

Although it was now late afternoon, the sun was out in full force and it felt very warm; it was a peaceful spot beside the river, and no-one was in a rush to get away. Elsie had the OS maps out on the bonnet of the car and was proposing another alteration for the upcoming stage. Again, my plan had been to come out from the next two Munros back to the A837 at Inchnadamph, and cycle all the way round via Lairg to head northwards. Elsie suggested I could go cross-country to meet a track that would take me over to the top of Loch Shin to meet the A838, cutting down considerably on my cycling distance. With that agreed, I first had to get myself to Inchnadamph, so the road bike was rolled out again. Gary, having brought his own road bike along, was going to join me.

Setting off at the back of six, the road was slowly climbing for the first few miles and, legs feeling drained, I found it hard work to keep up with Gary. Dropping down towards Ledmore, we were pushing into a strong north-west headwind, but I crouched low over the handlebars behind him to ease the effort. Past Ledmore and continuing north, Canisp cast a shadow over the A837 where, out of the sun's rays, the drop in temperature was pronounced, and my cycling top was not offering much resistance to the chill wind. I felt cold by the time we arrived at Inchnadamph. With the evening and night shift ahead, I lingered over preparations as the others got ready, Pete and I both opting for walking boots for this rougher section. Mum made us cups of tea whilst I tucked into some lasagne for dinner, and then, at quarter past eight, Pete, Elsie, Donald and I started on the track by the hotel and into Gleann Dubh.

The walk up the glen was pleasant at this time of evening, the slope to the col harder work, but it was good to have the other three for company and, once we got onto the main ridge, a steady walk took us to the summit of Conival. Tonight was a full moon and, while it started to rise out to the south east, it held our attention on the walk to Ben More Assynt, slowly creeping upwards through deep turquoise skies. Getting to the summit at quarter past eleven, there was still a slight glow behind the bank of clouds to the west, but it was much gloomier where Pete and I were now heading. He and Elsie swapped some kit and then we said goodbye to her and Donald, who were both heading back to Inchnadamph. We then took a compass bearing and started down the north-east ridge.

With the last vestiges of light, the upper portion of the ridge wasn't too difficult, but as we gradually descended east north-east and east, the ground became more challenging underfoot, and we couldn't see properly. The moon had by now disappeared behind some cloud, and the light from our head torches didn't seem to be helping much over the rutted heather, so we proceeded cautiously, eventually arriving at the River Cassley. The water wasn't too wide here, so we crossed to the other bank and followed the approximate line of the river east south-east, all the while looking out for any light from the track end before the power station. It was only getting much closer that we finally saw a pair of headlights, perpendicular to our approach, and after a few more minutes, we were at the wee yellow van with Dad in the driver's seat. The good news was the van was in the right position, the not so good news was that Jim Hall, who had come along with the van, was now out there somewhere in the darkness looking for Pete and myself – bloody great!

My tired brain dawdled for a bit but the answer was quite simple: keep moving. Jim would hopefully come back to the van soon, and then they would catch me up on the track over the hill. Pete and I set off on the track, which turned out to be a small tarmac road, so this helped with progress, but that was a relative term by this stage. My legs felt very heavy indeed and, with mental and physical fatigue setting in, I inched my way up the hill, Pete walking patiently alongside. The van did catch us so we let them past, on up to the high point of the road where they waited. Catching up in turn, I got on the bike and set off down the far side.

Impatient to meet up with the other van at the main road, I pedalled as fast as my head torch would allow in the darkness. Immediately, I was aware of my poor hands. It had been cold when walking, but now, whizzing down over a thousand feet in three miles, the wind-chill effect was freezing them. I kept pushing on through the cold night air, round the top of Loch Shin and eventually to the little collection of houses by the main road. It was two o'clock in the morning when I prised my numb hands and sclerosed frame from the bike, with Mum opening the side door of the van to let me crawl inside and find a sleeping bag. Shivering, I lay for over twenty minutes as the pain engulfed my hands when the blood and warmth returned to them. I could hardly believe that this had all happened in the short space of six miles. Sure, I've suffered it on many cycling stints in the winter, even when wearing gloves, but I just didn't expect this on a summer's night.

It was so tempting to lie there in the warmth and accept the sleep that my brain needed, but I managed to fight the urge, and got up to find that Mum had a pot of soup warmed and waiting. To say this hit the mark would be an understatement, as my central heating switched back on inside and I came to life again. The reason the cold had affected me so badly in the first place was probably that I hadn't eaten enough on the last stage over from Inchnadamph. Whilst getting ready, Jim told me that, when he and the others had arrived earlier, the vehicle barrier had been locked. They had managed to persuade the gatekeeper to open it and let the wee van through, which had been a great help. Thanks, gatekeeper!

With the other supporters having gone on ahead to try and snatch a couple of hours' sleep, Gary was left to accompany me on this longer cycle. We wheeled out onto the A838 at about ten to three. Perhaps as a result of focusing on the small circle of light from my headtorch gliding along the tarmac, or perhaps the slow rhythm of turning the cranks, I was struggling to stay awake after only a couple of miles. Gary must have sensed this, probably because I wasn't saying very much, so he compensated by talking more. In fact, he seemed to be talking a whole lot more about everything, which was good because, before this weekend, I had only met Gary once, so this was giving me an idea of what he was all about.

I struggled to keep my eyes open and focus on the road. Gary continued rabbiting on, but the game he was playing to keep me awake was failing. Had Gary just said he'd seen a large owl sitting on the fence, watching us as we drifted past? I looked out to the land at the side of the road and saw sheep, I think, but was it sheep? The very first hints of grey light were not enough to let me decide. I slowly moved my head and looked again. Yes, it's sheep, staring back at us. But hold on, they are moving about, and fast, and, well, sheep shouldn't be yellow, and why are they moving about so quickly all over the place? I blinked, rubbed my half-shut eyes one at a time, and refocused. No, no, it's definitely not sheep. But I can still see yellow blobs moving about in my vision, with other colours flashing in and out. What a strange place to exist in, neither dreaming nor fully conscious, as colours moved about in transitory hallucinations before me – my own little parallel plane of existence. The road along Loch Shin felt like the longest fifteen cycling miles of my life.

Turning left at the junction of the A838 and A836, the vehicles were waiting for us, so I took the opportunity to fetch a pair of windproof trousers before we set off again. The short break in routine didn't help with the fatigue, however, and very quickly my brain was shutting off and my eyes starting to close. Like the nodding toy dogs in car windscreens, my head started bobbing as my mind slipped into little micro-sleeps. Although the legs kept turning, with my upper body weight over the handlebars, each little shutdown meant my arms fractionally gave way; I was jolted back to life when my brain realised what was happening and locked the muscles again. Admitting defeat, I mumbled to Gary that I would need to stop the next time we met the van.

Thankfully, we didn't have far to go, as the family convoy had pulled over near to Rhian Bridge. I told them what was happening. As they were all looking tired themselves, it was probably a good idea for us all to get a nap. Crawling into the back of June's wee van, I got a sleeping bag and managed to stretch out on the carpet. At ten to five, I figured about ninety minutes would be enough to take the edge off the tiredness, so I set the alarm and closed my eyes. But the sleep I had been craving didn't materialise straightaway. Although I knew sleep was the only answer to my shattered condition, there seemed to be an underlying zing in my body, like a tiny current of electricity, which wouldn't switch off. Damn! Nothing to do but just lie there and get some rest, but after a while sleep did come.

In what seemed like an instant, the alarm sounded and I awoke. It was like a horrible hangover. I stirred to a groggy headache and nausea. At half past six it was now bright, but I felt extremely cold in the crisp morning air and had to put on more layers. Mum made a mug of coffee for us all. I didn't hang about long and got going up the road again, looking a right sight for sore eyes. Decked out in full leggings, windproof trousers, a thermal top, fleece jacket and Buffalo mountain shirt on top of that, with hat and mitts to round it off. Scott of the Antarctic had probably ventured forth with less gear.

The road headed into a forestry plantation, climbing gently, and I slowly warmed up and came to life. Leaving the forest, the Crask Inn appeared, and there in the parking area were cars belonging to Jim, Donald, and Pete and Elsie. I peered into each through condensation-laden windows, and it looked like they were all sleeping peacefully, so it was with some guilt that I gently tapped on the glass to wake them. A long day and night with little sleep had ensured they were almost as dishevelled-looking as I was, so I left them to it, and continued the three miles to finish in Strath Vagastie.

Sunshine now filling the strath, it had the makings of a good day. Mum got the stove out again, and it wasn't long until I was enjoying bacon rolls and more coffee, while changing into my hill gear. As the others got ready, Big Iain and Stuart turned up after the luxury of a night in a B&B, and Christine arrived to complement the team. Calories on the inside plus sun's rays on the outside meant my body had dispelled the overnight chills and, at twenty to nine, Jim, Pete, Elsie, Christine, Stuart, June and I set off for the penultimate Munro.

Crossing the bridge over the river, we all tried to keep quiet as we passed Gary and Caitlin's tent, the backdrop of Ben Klibreck giving it a lovely outlook, and continued on with an easy walk to the south end of Loch nan Uan. The steep slopes east soon had us working much harder, but at least we were in the shade before coming out onto the ridge. Turning north, we were on the top for ten to eleven. To get a group photograph, I set the camera on the trig pillar and, to liven things up a bit, Pete thought it would be a good idea if they all held shoulders and did a high-kicking can-can whilst I lay at their feet. The resulting photo doesn't look so much like a dance, more like a mob trying to kick the proverbial out of me, which was probably true after everything I had put them through.

Frivolities over, we dropped north-east to the col before Meall Meadhonach, and steeply north north-west. Elsie hung back with June, whose road running shoes didn't stick too well on the steep heather, and once over the Klibreck Burn, Stuart, Pete, and I were a bit quicker walking to the little track-end by the farm. Here we met Dave and Muffy, and then headed back out to the side of the A836, which now resembled a mini car park. One vehicle belonged to Brian and Louise Bonnyman, who had given a lift to Manny and my brother, Colin. Spotting Donald as well, I realised I had forgotten about him. I asked where he had got to and he told me that, heading down the strath for a mile to find a parking place this morning, he had presumed we would follow him. Cooking himself breakfast and waiting a while, he soon saw our group on the skyline and realised there had been a mix up. After that he had come straight down here instead, missing out on the penultimate hill.

At one o'clock, the sun was blazing down, so for my last cycle of the whole journey, it was a pleasure to put on the sun hat and glasses and start with Gary again. Even this barren wilderness looked good with the sun shining. I gazed over it, a grin on my face, knowing that this was the last ground I was covering before the last hill. A fast descent took us down into Strath More and northwards to the parking area for Ben Hope. Getting ready, Mum told me that Andrew Johnston had phoned her late last night to ask of our position, so perhaps he and Rory would make an appearance at some point.

I had asked Mum to bring up my kilt, as this was a good time to roll it out at the end of a big Scottish run. Changing into that, the others gradually left in various little groups until it was just Jim Hall, myself and the family left at the car park. Feeling in a boisterous mood, despite all the meticulous planning that had taken place over the previous weeks, I now found myself without a beer. Jim saved the day by sifting through his personal stash to produce two bottles of Waggledance – great! Mum was worried about Shaw in the van, but we assured her that the front and rear windscreens had been blacked out, the windows were rolled down, and he had a big bowl of water. She and Dad set off. I filled up my large cycling bottle with beer, then Colin and I headed up. June and her beloved video camera started last, along with Jim Hall.

It was just after half past two when we got going on the initial slopes. I was talking to Colin and taking it easy, sipping my beer and enjoying the heat; only twelve hours previously, I had been suffering painfully cold hands in the darkness, but it felt a world away now. June and Jim caught us up and Jim asked about the number of days I was on now, which seemed obvious; it was the last day of my seventh week, so it was day forty-nine. I would be finishing on forty-nine days and however many hours. But 'No,' said Jim, for although this was my forty-ninth day, I was actually on forty-eight days and so many hours. Eh? How could it be forty-eight when I was on my forty-ninth day? Jim explained and it took a while for the penny to drop in my tired head. Then I remembered, back before the trip began, how I had explained this to myself when calculating the days and hours (see Appendix). Fantastic; so not only was I breaking my target of the fifty-day barrier, but I was throwing an extra day into the bargain.

Like someone who had just found a tenner in an old jacket pocket, I was thrilled with this news, and then a further realisation dawned on me.

185

Until now I'd have been happy to finish at any old time when I got to the top, but way back on Mull I had started at exactly quarter past four in the morning. If I got to the summit for quarter past four in the afternoon, that would give me an exact half-day of twelve hours – a time that was nicely rounded off and simple to remember. This clinical precision very much appealed to me but, glancing at my watch, it was already quarter past three and we were still beside the stream and hadn't even cleared the line of crags. Heck, for me to climb from here to the summit in an hour would require a right good move on, so with Jim saying that he would hang back to walk with Mum and make sure she was okay, I downed the last of my beer and upped the tempo.

Colin came with me and we climbed quickly, passing Dad and getting to the escarpment to veer left for the long slopes ahead. Iain and Stuart were complaining of cramp problems, sweating in the heat. Leaving them, we soon caught up with some of the others. Manny decided to have a laugh and complement the sun with a moon of his own – not a pretty sight at any time of day. Climbing at my fastest rate of the whole trip, before I knew it, the line of the slope suddenly sank and I could see across the summit plateau. Too quick, for once; it was only five past four, so I reversed and dropped back several metres, with the folk at the trig wondering what I was playing at.

Colin, Pete, and some of the others passed me again as I counted down the minutes on my watch, thinking back to seven weeks earlier on Mull. On the evening before the run started, I had spoken to the camcorder about giving it my best shot and seeing what happened. Having experienced the beautiful sunrise on that first Munro and the nervous anticipation of what lay ahead for the next two hundred and eighty-three, the numbers were now reversed and here I was, two hundred and eighty-three hills behind me and the last one just a few metres away. Four thirteen arrived, so I stood up and shouldered the rucksack for the very last time, fastened the belt, and started on the last little jog. A minute later, I crested the edge of the plateau, immediately embarrassed that all these people were shouting and clapping for me as I ran towards the trig pillar. Almost there, another glance at the watch and a few quick strides over the rocks, I slapped the pillar at exactly quarter past four, to give a finishing time of forty-eight days and twelve hours. A laugh, a smile, folk cheering, shaking hands, and it was all good fun and jokes.

Someone shouted that there was something for me in the rocks behind the pillar, but suspecting a Westies joke, I didn't fall for it. They kept insisting, so I looked on the far side and there, wedged in the rocks, was a rectangular box wrapped in plastic. It took a while, but I managed to peel it open; written along one side of the box, it said, 'Please leave for Charlie Campbell Munros Run 2000.' On the other side was, 'Congratulations Charlie from Andrew and Rory.' Opening the box revealed a bottle of Macallan malt whisky. I felt honoured that the record holders had made the effort to come up here and leave this for me; beating their time was something I still couldn't take in. Christine also presented a cake that Shelagh's daughters, Sarah and Louise, had made, decorated with a tartan band, a real thistle and a little cardboard model of a runner holding a Westies flag. This looked fantastic placed on top of the trig pillar and flanked by two bottles of champagne; it made a great photo, as the deep blue lochs sparkled with Ben Loyal in the background.

A few minutes later, Stuart and Iain arrived, with Mum, Dad, June, and Jim not too far behind, so it was hugs all round for the family, and more champagne from the heavy rucksack Iain had been carrying. As if I hadn't run enough miles, Manny took it on himself to chase me about the summit spraying the bottle everywhere, promptly drenching my top and kilt. Drying out, we took several varied photographs of the sponsored items: training shoes, socks, shirt, beer, Irn-Bru, and of course, Tunnock's Teacakes. That done, the man who had been patiently waiting during all the shenanigans stood forward and it was good to have a few calming minutes chatting with Dave Hewitt. Dave was the only journalist who had been interested in writing an article before the run started, and now he wanted to do a follow up piece for his own publication, *The Angry Corrie*, as well as, he hoped, some of the London broadsheets. Dave asked what might be regarded as the usual questions for this type of event, but the one I remember most was about the weather, and how many good days I had experienced. Taking time to think, I answered that it was probably only four or five (see Appendix), in contrast to the perfect weather we were all enjoying today.

If I was feeling strange leaving the top it was because, in a way, I didn't really want to go, for it meant that, both literally and metaphorically, the party was over. Taking a quick look back at the empty plateau, it had been fun playing king of the castle in a Warhol-esque way, and now the 'fame' was at an end. Passing folk on the descent, we caught up with most of the others by the bottom of the path, which enabled me to say cheerio before people headed for the long drive south. Seeing them away, Iain, Colin and I set off in the opposite direction for Tongue, where Jim, Christine and Donald had gone on ahead to get themselves a meal at the Tongue Hotel. By the time we got to the hotel, the other three were finishing off their dinner and it turned out that we were too late, meals no longer being served. We did manage to get a bowl of soup, then went over to the campsite and put up the tent while it was still light. I also managed to get a wash, removing a unique combination of salty sweat and champagne, and making myself a bit more presentable.

On the walk back to the hotel, the sunset was beautiful, 'iridescent Turkish Delight,' as Christine called it. We met the others in the public bar, which was a bit gloomy, but at least it was still serving beer. A pool table meant we enjoyed a few games with our drinks, along with several packets of crisps and peanuts for dinner, but whether it was the dim lighting, or my body catching up with me, I started to feel extremely tired, eyelids as heavy as lead. Telling the guys I had to go, we got back to the campsite for half past eleven. Donald produced a carryout and was all ready for a bit of a late soirée, but I had to tell him I just couldn't keep awake. Iain and Colin shared the tent, allowing me the luxury of the folding foam bed in the back of the van, which I gladly crawled onto. And so the bacchanalian celebrations I had always envisioned hadn't materialised, and all because of me – I physically couldn't do it. In the scheme of things it didn't matter, because the whole day had been such a thoroughly enjoyable occasion, with family and friends making it special. On that thought, sleep quickly took me away.

Part III: The Countdown

T minus 7 days and counting – Monday 17 July

To say I slept soundly would be an understatement, but I awoke after eight o'clock still feeling extremely tired and groggy. Colin, Iain, Donald, and I headed back up to the hotel and, this time, we were not too late for food. Compared to the breakfasts in the motorhome over the last two months, this seemed a rather stately and formal affair; Colin had grilled haddock in milk, I opted for the continental breakfast. That over, we headed outside, where Colin and Iain took what little gear they had in the van and put it in Donald's car for their journey home. Waving them off at the back of ten, I said goodbye to Jim and Christine at the same time, then I took the van and headed west, not thinking about where I was going, for in this land, it was an automatic choice for me.

Playing a haunting music tape, I drove slowly over the Moine. Gazing southwards and seeing my last Munro, the emotion hit me. In the previous years, in my mind's eye, I had always pictured myself running to the top of Ben Hope in a new record time and being overcome with emotion, and yet yesterday, maintaining composure had been second nature. Now, as I got out the van on my own to take one last self-timed photograph, I had to fight back the tears. I had achieved my dream. The charity name was correct indeed – Dreams Come True. Sitting for five minutes to let it sink in, I then continued on the slow, scenic drive round Loch Eriboll and onto an old favourite of mine, the Sango Sands campsite in Durness.

I first visited the campsite on that school trip way back in 1984 and I have always loved its situation, perched high over the beautiful sands of Sango Bay, with views to the distant Orkney Isles on a clear day. Finding a good pitch for the van, I bought some papers to read over lunch and catch up with what was happening in the big, bad world. But still feeling extremely lethargic, I had to go for a lie down at one thirty. Not wanting to totally ruin my sleeping pattern, I forced myself up at five o'clock and, as the van was a bit of a mess, tidied up what would be my home for the next few days. After a shower, with the sun shining and views to inspire, it was time to write up my diary of the weekend's events. Also with several bottles of whisky on board, given by various folk the previous day, I cracked one open to enjoy a wee dram whilst musing and writing. With mobile phone reception being poor here, I just read for the remainder of the evening, turning in at ten after a restful and relaxing day.

190

T minus 6 days – Tuesday 18 July

I didn't rise until a quarter to ten. It had been a disturbed night's sleep, waking every hour or two covered in sweat, so the first thing I did was get showered and then pack up the gear. Wanting to make myself a coffee on the stove, I realised I had forgotten to retrieve my billycan from the other van on Sunday. Fortunately, the village shop had a neat little camping pot with a folding handle. Having missed the company of Mark and Jen for the final day, I saw some postcards and took the opportunity to send one to say thanks for all their help. I drove down the A838 for a few miles. Finding a pleasant spot overlooking the Kyle of Durness, I finally had my coffee and some breakfast, before another relaxing slow drive, listening to music and enjoying the scenery. Passing Inchnadamph brought a smile to my face and it felt strange, as though I had been there just the night before and not three days previously.

Arriving at the Broomfield campsite in Ullapool, another favourite of mine, it was rather busy for the time of day, but I managed to get a pitch on the shorefront overlooking Loch Broom. A beautiful evening, it was pleasant just to sit in the front of the van overlooking the loch and have another few whiskies whilst phone calls came in. Phoning Andrew Johnston, there was no answer, but I managed to get Rory at home and say thanks for the surprise bottle of whisky at the top of Ben Hope, as well as the food parcel he had left on Cairngorm. The latter had given me an all-important psychological lift all those weeks ago.

All the people I had spoken to over the past two days had commented that I must be feeling extremely pleased with myself, but I had mixed emotions. It was not an anti-climax, because I could still appreciate what I had done and give myself a wee pat on the back, but my overriding feeling was one of 'so what?' or 'big deal'. All these years of striving and, now that it was done and dusted, it didn't feel like anything: this could have been just any old evening on any old camping holiday. So had my challenge been ill-conceived? Perhaps, perhaps not, but it is challenges that keep us all going: getting through another day, putting bread on the table, being the best charity worker, making your first million in business. Mine just happened to be to traverse all the Munros, under my own steam and in the quickest time, and now that it had been done, I didn't like the hollow feeling that came my way. Tiredness winning again, I had to leave my diary and thoughts and go to bed at quarter to nine.

T minus 5 days – Wednesday 19 July

Getting up at ten o'clock, the night had been better than the previous one but, again, I had awoken a few times covered in sweat. My body was obviously taking a while to adjust back to normality. Ready to go after midday, I drove up to the Safeway store for some shopping, and had a quick look to see if any newspapers had mentioned anything – several of them had run the story. Leaving with bags of groceries and a wad of papers under my arm, back at the van I was curious to see what had been written. The *Daily Express* had done a good half-page article and photograph, with the broadsheet *Herald* devoting a quarter-page and a different photo, but when it comes to sensationalism, you just cannot beat *The Sun*. There, in a little three-inch column, it mentioned how an adventurous postie had smashed the world record for bagging all of Scotland's Munros. World record! So the Munros had just gone global! I chuckled to myself at that one, but the best bit was that they had stuck me only a few inches away from a half-page spread of a semi-naked woman – now I knew I had arrived.

Leaving Ullapool about one, I took the coastal road round by my bacon buttie haven at Dundonnell, and on by Gruinard, Poolewe and Gairloch, before stopping at Loch Maree to admire Slioch. I was surprised at how much even a few hours of slow driving was taking out of me, and after some food at this spot, I had to grab an hour's snooze. On the road again by six o'clock, at Kinlochewe I took a right and headed along to Torridon Youth Hostel, hoping to say thanks to Neil Hinchliff for the accommodation last week (leaving early on the Wednesday morning, I hadn't managed to do so at the time). At the hostel, Neil wasn't in, so I left a message and then drove over to the Strathcarron Hotel, where I read my paper and enjoyed a shandy. A few miles down the road, as it climbs through the forest high above Stromeferry, I managed to find myself a quiet parking spot with good views over the loch, and settled in for the night with the obligatory music, whisky and diary.

T minus 4 days – Thursday 20 July

I was up at ten o'clock with breakfast and coffee, then started the drive down to Fort William for lunch. By Ballachulish, and feeling tired again, I took the wee road from Glencoe village towards the Clachaig to find a quiet spot for a snooze. I was woken by a phone call from a researcher at BBC Radio Scotland, wanting to know if I would do a few minutes on the Fred MacAulay morning show next week. Gulp! I was familiar with the incisive repartee that Fred and his studio guests bandied about, so I was hesitant. I knew I'd get slaughtered but, stuff it, I'm up for a laugh, so I agreed. Into the Clachaig, I went through my Munro schedule for an hour, writing in the alterations that had been made during the run. Driving to Bridge of Orchy and still feeling knackered, I had another rest, finally getting to Glasgow at quarter past eight to see my folks again. A few friends phoned to say well done. Bath and bed.

T minus 3 days – Friday 21 July

It was another sleep-in until ten, but at least my body didn't have the night sweats anymore – perhaps sleeping in my own bed again was helping. I spent the whole day sorting gear and clothing. I checked my e-mails for the first time since Glen Clova, five weeks ago. There were fifty-two of them, so that took up my evening, and it was nice to read so many kind words of congratulation. I managed to make it through the whole day without needing a sleep, so I must have been recovering.

T minus 2 days – Saturday 22nd July

Up at ten again, I phoned several folk, but most of them were not in, so I left messages. I managed to speak to a few others that had helped me, and said thanks. I then spent most of the day sorting the other half of my gear. I put on my lottery numbers for tonight – boy, did I need them to come up now, to pay all the bills. Saturday night meant a wee drink and a relaxing evening of reading. A late finish, with bed after one o'clock, meant I was already slipping back into old habits.

T minus 1 day – Sunday 23rd July

Ten o'clock rising had been the order of the week, and so it was again. I wrote letters and thank you cards to people who had sent donations for the charity. I had just about answered all the e-mails by now. I got to bed nice and early, at ten o'clock. The three days up north and the easy remainder of the week had been therapeutic. But I couldn't sleep. I lay there worrying about what it would be like to go back to work tomorrow.

Time – Monday 24 July

Alarm at quarter to five. I felt tired. Pint of coffee. Jeez, this was just like the Munro run all over again. I removed nine weeks of dust from my postman's uniform. Down to the sorting office for twenty to six, I walked through the doors ... and I was launched straight back into the banality of everyday life. I knew the adventure was well and truly over.

Photographic Memories

Mum

Tunnock's Time - with Boyd

Munro #1 with June

Sound of Mull

12:50 a.m. finish in Glen Tilt

The Drumochter Four

Barber Colin

The Cuillin Boys

SYHA Alltbeithe

The long run for home

Enjoying the final view

Calling Oz, with family

The Party's Over

Postscript

With one week of complete rest following the end of the run, I felt my body had at least partially recovered, particularly from the mental tiredness of the final weekend. Physically, I knew it would need much more than that. Starting back on my postal round would be exercise enough, so I took another two weeks with no formal training whatsoever. Then from the second week of August, some gentle sessions were reintroduced; any sort of jogging or running felt heavy and sluggish, as though there was nothing in the tank. This continued throughout September, with comments like 'slow', 'tight legs', 'hard work' and 'aching knees' in my training diary. With my already large appetite in overdrive after the event, the weight was steadily piling on which didn't help with the sore knee scenario. By the end of October, things started to get a bit better and, come January 2001, I was back into full-blown training again, feeling none the worse for wear. So it took me approximately six months to recover fully from the event.

On the publicity front, it was fantastic to receive so many cards, notes, e-mails and expressions of congratulations from relatives, friends and others I didn't even know – it was the icing on the cake, as far as I was concerned. In August, Paul Currie of John Smith & Son books, which had an outlet in the large Tiso Outdoor shop in Glasgow, asked me if I would be up for doing a slide show and presentation there. Immediately, the butterflies started in my stomach; I had spoken in front of small, informal groups before, but never on this scale. We arranged a date in November, and I gave myself a rudimentary crash course in the use of Microsoft Powerpoint. I then had a couple of months to sift through several hundred photographs. I selected about one hundred and sixty to highlight the tale, scanned them all into the PC, and then started thinking about how I to condense a seven-week story into under two hours. When the day finally arrived, the room kept filling and filling. Gulp! We lost count at about ninety, one of the largest crowds ever for the venue, but I went for it, and despite a slight technical glitch half-way through, the whole thing went well. It had been great to see so many people were genuinely interested in hearing about the record-breaking run.

The best acknowledgement of all, however, came in December. In what had been a very successful year for British hill running, the Fell Runners Association chose for me as the winner of their Long Distance Award. With Mum, Dad, June, Colin, and friends, Iain and Peter, we travelled down to Shap Wells Hotel in Cumbria for the annual dinner, where I was presented with the award. It felt great to be recognised in front of my fellow runners. Seeing my name on the silver platter, alongside some of the greats of British hill running, was an honour and a privilege. That night rounded off a very special year for me. I'll certainly never forget my Millennial Munros.

Second Postscript – July 2016

Be careful what you wish for. Sixteen years ago, I jogged the final few yards to the top of Ben Hope to a new Munro record. Hopefully you've enjoyed reading about it in this book. That's a very special day in my memory, and I wish I could go onto say that it led to more successful years with even greater achievements. Alas, it was not to be.

Once fully recovered and still with fire in my belly, I tried a few other multi-day challenges in 2001 and 2003. For one reason or another, they didn't pan out, mainly due to fitness problems and injury. The years between 2004 and 2007 were fine for general training, with the odd race and hill walk here and there, but two years of driving taxis all day had started my decline. Having purchased a flat, what I initially thought would be a little painting and decorating turned into a major renovation job, with just about every spare minute, evening and weekend, spent working at the place. Even with the huge amount of help I received from my family, especially my brother, it was two years before the place was finally ready and I could move in, in April 2009.

By this point, the damage had also set in. During all the work, and to alleviate the boredom of DIY, it had been the custom to have a few cans each night, and so the weight went on and my fitness plunged. Sitting at a desk job all day didn't help. I turned forty at the end of 2009, an age I just didn't want to be, and there followed a few years of feeling low, and really low. Joining a gym again with a friend, and getting some strength back with the weights, didn't help my mindset, and beyond that, all I could manage was the occasional jog. This didn't help on the cardiovascular front, as I couldn't drop the fat or get any endurance back. The last time I managed to climb a Munro was back in 2012. They are essentially just a dream now, and any hillwalking these days is reduced to a slow drag up the track to Loch Humphrey in the Kilpatricks. I still get some wilderness kicks, however, with a group of friends, where we head to various bothies all over Scotland, to enjoy a haggis, a few whiskies and some new vistas.

On a personal level, there must definitely be some sort of obsessive, compulsive, addictive side to my psyche, and exercising, the hills, and the Munros were a great positive habit to have. As I've said, beware. Do not let your good habits turn bad, and if you ever hit your highest high, don't let yourself crash and burn the way I have done. It's the little decisions you make (or don't make) every day that cause the cumulative damage. When you've had a crap day at work, or whatever, don't fall in front of the TV and crack open the booze, at least until you've put on the trainers, or jumped on a bike, or dived in a pool, or just enjoyed a steady wee walk for a while. That's where I went wrong, turning myself into a twenty-stone Munro in the process.

Iggy Pop sings about a lust for life. Well, that used to be me. But now it's gone, and to where, I don't know. Perhaps a remote mountain top, or somewhere else, but I'll keep trying to find it again while there's still some time ...

Appendix

Statistics

The 284 Munros were climbed in an exact time of 48 days, 12 hours, beating the previous record (51 days, 9 hours and 22 minutes) by 2 days, 21 hours and 22 minutes. This involved:

Total Distance	893 miles/1437 km on foot
	764 miles/1229 km on bike
	2.33 miles/3.75 km of swimming
Total Ascent	411,717 feet/125,491 metres
Daily average	18½ miles with 8500 feet of ascent
Highest Mileage	Day 29 – 30½ miles
Greatest Ascent	Day 32 – 14,300 feet
Most Munros in week	54 (Days 18 to 24)

Munros per day	Occurrence (days)
0	1
1	1
2	2
3	6
4	7
5	5
6	7
7	7
8	7
9	1
10	3
11	2

284 Munros in 48½ days gave an average of 5.85 Munros per day. Subtracting the one day of enforced rest (due to injury), giving 47½ days on the hills, the average moves to 5.98, giving a revised average of six Munros a day.

Timing each day was taken from when I first started exercising in the morning to when I finished exercising for the day, which included all rest breaks, food stops, transitions from bike to run and the like. Times have been rounded up or down to the nearest ¼ hour.

Shortest day	Day 30 – 6 hours 0 minutes
Longest day	Day 12 – 16 hours 0 minutes
Average day out	11¾ hours
Latest Finish	Day 19 – 12.50 a.m.

Distances

All measurements were taken from Ordnance Survey Landranger maps, 1:50,000 scale. All distances were measured using a trundle wheel map measurer, with the appropriate scale. My daily measured distances have erred on the conservative side, therefore the overall total distance is probably slightly short. Flat map miles are short of what happens in reality in any case, because they do not take account of vertical displacement. Hugh Symonds, in his book, reckons 5–10% could probably be added to map mountain distances.

The amount of climb and ascent was measured simply by counting contours and summit heights or spot heights. However, as the contour lines on these maps are only every ten metres, there are obviously tops you cross, or cols you drop into, that fall between contour lines and don't have spot heights. How do you measure these? To get round this problem, I split the difference between two contour line heights which, funnily enough, always gave five metres. This same scenario was used for all the bumps, mounds and tops I climbed that didn't have spot heights. Over a huge run like the Munros, this would average itself out, so that I ended up with a figure about as accurate as you can get.

Of course, by today's standards this all seems a bit Neanderthal. Back in 1997 and 1998, when I was working on the schedule, we didn't have all the modern gadgets and software – digital mapping on a PC would have made this task so much easier.

Time

So why, on my final day climbing Ben Hope, was I was confused about the total number of days I was on? Tiredness aside, I had figured this out in my own simplistic terms before the journey began, but promptly forgot it in the interim. As we all know, by definition, a day is a 24 hour period, but most of us just use it to signify the period between early morning to late evening, when we are usually up and about. At Ben Hope, on the 7th day of the 7th week, I thought my time was going to be 49 days and so many hours, forgetting that the 'real' 49th day would only commence when the 24 hour period was over, which for me would have been at 4.14 a.m. the following morning, having originally started my run at 4.15 a.m. Thus, my running time ended at 48½ days when I hit the summit trig at 4.15 p.m. that afternoon.

Weather

When Dave Hewitt asked me on the summit of Ben Hope how many good-weather days I had enjoyed, I answered and genuinely thought that it was only about four or five. Perhaps a few drinks had skewed the thought process slightly. Thinking on it now, I had answered in terms of what would be regarded as 'perfect' weather days – sunshine, warmth, little or no cloud, little or no wind, and good air quality giving great views. That is what we often hope for when hill walking, and my final day had been a fine example. Counting back, I had indeed enjoyed just four 'perfect' weather days, but there were certainly many more days where the weather could simply be described as 'good.' There were also many days of mixed weather – misty cloud cover, wind and showers, damp and dreich – but the torrential days were the ones that had the biggest psychological impact. I can now fully understand why the British talk so much about the weather. Here's the breakdown:

Heavy/torrential rain with high/gale force wind	6
Mixed (showers, wind, damp, misty, odd bright spell)	14
Fair (dry, breezy, overcast, some mist or cloud)	6
Good (longer bright spells, broken cloud, warm)	15
Perfect (sun, warm/hot, little cloud, clear views)	4
50/50 days*	4

*These were days when the weather changed, quite distinctly, from one type to another at some point during the day, as opposed to variably mixed. A good example of this is Day 13 on the Crianlarich hills, where we had enjoyed fair weather until later afternoon and then got set upon with torrential rain and gale force winds in the evening.

Clear summits: a few folk who have written up their completion of a continuous Munro round have included this statistic in their book, so I have done so for comparison. The brief list below shows that even Martin Moran, during his winter round, enjoyed more clear summits than I did.

Martin Moran   1984/85   172 views from 277 peaks (62.1%)

Hugh Symonds   1990   185 views from 277 peaks (66.8%)

Charlie Campbell 2000   139 views from 284 peaks(48.9%)

Support and Hill company

Of the 49 days of the trip, one was an enforced rest due to my ankle/ shin injury, so I had 48 days in the hills. I was on my own in the hills for 16 days, exactly one third, and had company for either part or all of that day's Munros on 32 days. The days on my own were spread over the first 33 days of the journey. I had hill company for the last 16 days in a row, which was great for the big run into the finish. Of the 284 Munros, I climbed 119 peaks by myself and had company for the other 165.

Having pacers or helpers on the hill can be a bit of a double-edged sword: you need people for the psychological boost and for the social interaction they provide but, in terms of a schedule, you are committed to meeting them at certain dates, times, and places. This has the drawback that, if the schedule gets knocked off for whatever reason, folk need to be contacted and things rearranged. And, although hill pacers are there to give you assistance, you can't help feeling guilty for being slow and constantly holding them back.

The summit group on Ben Hope consisted of – Mum, Dad, June, Colin, Iain Barr, Stuart Burns, Manuel Gorman, Dave Calder and son, James, Muffy Calder, Jim Hall, Donald Smith, Christine Menhennet, Elspeth Scott, Peter Baxter, Gary Tompsett, Caitlin Evans, Brian and Louise Bonnyman, and Dave Hewitt.

Route

As mentioned back in Part I, knowing that my journey was starting on Mull and finishing on Ben Hope, I simply sat down with loads of maps and built up what I thought was the most logical, time-saving route through all the Munros. As it turned out, it was very similar to that used by Gibson and Johnston back in 1992; I didn't know this beforehand, but a map of their route, shown during the documentary film, proved it to be so. Their route itself was probably a refinement of the first continuous round in 1974, by Hamish Brown, which had started in Mull and finished on Ben Hope. I believe that this route, either south to north or vice versa, is the quickest line through the Munros and will be used by future record-breakers.

Small route changes were made during the run by myself, with some fine-tuning suggestions made by others, especially during the last two days.

Diet, Food, and Health

Diet is always a personal matter and what suits one person's taste buds would be anathema to another's, so I'm not going to make any recommendations. Having always had a hearty appetite, I'll eat most foods, but I noticed a distinct change in my palate during the run, starting almost immediately. Whereas at home, I'll try and be relatively strict and eat only wholesome, nutritious food, what would be deemed healthier choices became unappetising to me very quickly. I started craving more fatty-tasting foods. This wasn't a conscious decision, but I think it was my body's way of getting the extra calories it needed.

Breakfast – Although fry-ups had never been part of my plan for breakfasts, they almost became the daily menu. I rotated between sausages, bacon, black pudding, potato scones and tomatoes. Having always loved bread, I would usually stick my plateful of items onto three or four bread rolls and slap on some tomato or brown sauce, and the same thing if it was an omelette or scrambled eggs for breakfast.

Hill food – I always carried bread rolls, which I never tire of. The filling was usually cheese, ham, chicken, turkey, beef, etc., with perhaps a dash of Branston pickle or sauce on top. The other savoury snack I carried every day was a few bags of plain, old 'Ready Salted' crisps. To satisfy the sweet tooth, I relied on the supply of Tunnock's biscuits and also the toffees from McCowan's. The amount carried was adjusted depending on how long I was going to be away from the van, using a ratio of one roll and one biscuit per hour as a rough guide. My biggest days, where I was out on the hill and away from the van for up to 12 hours, meant that I usually carried the following, all washed down with at least 5 to 6 litres of water and a couple of small bottles of Irn-Bru:

10 to 12 rolls with a variety of fillings

2 x four pack of Tunnock's Caramel Wafers/Logs

4 packets salted crisps

Bag of toffees or other sweets

Small selection of chocolate, or salted peanuts etc.

Dinner – As with the breakfast menu, I craved the opposite of the usual guidelines for an everyday healthy diet. Bulking up, low-calorie vegetables were off my menu and higher calorie dishes were the order of the day. Mum rattled up what she knew were old favourites of mine: macaroni cheese, cheese & tomato pizzas, spaghetti bolognese, chilli con carne, steak pie, and her speciality, a macaroni and mince pie with a toasted bread and potato crisp topping, which I just can't get enough of.

Bedtime snack – A large glass of milk, and a sachet of Nestlé Build-up to give even more calories, vitamins, and minerals. Dairy Crest had sent vouchers, which I received about half-way through the run, enabling us to get a load of 500 ml bottles of Frijj milkshake. I also used these as a bedtime snack.

The eating plan must have been spot on because I started the run at 13 stone 0 lbs, and finished at 13 stone 0 lbs. My legs certainly put on a bit of muscle and size so, as expected, I must have lost some muscle from the upper body. There was no visible or perceived change in body fat levels.

Health – I generally keep in good health all year round, with only the odd minor malady like a cold or sore throat. In January 2000, I did get a chesty cold bug, which took me about two weeks to shift properly and, at the end of March, I got an aching stomach bug which knocked me out of training for a week. Despite a sore throat for a week at the beginning of May, I had a good rest and felt fine and fit going into the run. My biggest fear was that I would pick up a bug during the journey, which would have

205

spelt disaster. I wouldn't be able to rest to let it clear, and yet forcing on with extreme exercise whilst carrying a virus can be fatal. Thankfully, I remained free from any bad bacteria or virus during the run and wasn't faced with that dilemna.

I take a multi-vitamin and mineral tablet as part of my everyday diet, and during the run I increased this to ensure the body wasn't depleted of anything essential while it was going through the mill. Even this wasn't enough to stop a few sores developing on the backs of my hands, and one on my face, during the last two weeks of the run. Having not seen anything like them before or since, what were these? A bit of detective work on the internet brought me to Erythema multiforme minor, with exactly the 'bulls-eye' target-shaped blisters I had developed. But why? I had experienced the odd cold sore in the past, from the Herpes simplex virus, and this was the most likely culprit. Another potential cause are medications like NSAIDs, and what had I been taking for 6½ weeks to try and keep the injuries at bay? 1.5 to 2 grams of ibuprofen every day. One of these, or more likely the double whammy of both, combined with a run-down body, must have kick started these sores. Fortunately, they resolved themselves and disappeared within two weeks of the trip ending.

Pre-Munro Run 2000 training

As previously mentioned, I undertook a great deal of training in the months before the journey. But on the Munro run, and looking back now at my training diary, I feel I didn't do enough miles. Much of my workload was cross-training, because the journey involved several disciplines and not simply running. Additionally, I've always found that, when I try to do two running sessions a day in training, I very quickly become drained and lacklustre. If I substitute some other discipline for one of the sessions, I'm okay.

Below are some excerpts of typical weeks from my training diary, to give an idea of what I was doing:

January

11 – Easy 2 mile run (wheezy – recovering from a cold)

12 – Easy 4¼ mile run (still wheezy but cold better)

13 – Slowish 7½ mile run (shit – feel heavy and drained)

14 – Weights, 15 sets, whole body
    – Rowing machine, 30 mins
15 – Hill run, 8 miles with 4500ft climb
16 – Rest (slightly sore legs)
17 – Hill run, 8 miles with 1450 ft climb;
    – Fartlek group run, 5 miles, various reps

February

21 – Hill run, 8 miles with 1800ft climb
    – Running intervals, 5 x 1 km
22 – Rest (tired)
23 – Weights, 6 sets, upper body
    – Easy treadmill run, 10 km
    – Swim, 1600 metres
    – Group run, 4¼ miles
24 – Steady run, 10¾ miles
25 – Steady treadmill run, 5 miles
    – Swim, 800 metres
26 – Race, 7½ miles cross-country
27 – Weights, 10 sets legs, 8 sets upper body
    – Steady run, 26½ miles on West Highland Way

March

19 – Hillwalk, 11 miles with 8200 ft climb
20 – Weights, 9 sets upper body
    – Running intervals, 4 x 1 km (weak legs)
    – Exercise bike, 30 mins, very easy
21 – Exercise bike, 30 mins, various speed reps
    – Swim, 200 metres (just not into it)
    – Steady run, 11¼ miles
22 – Cycling, 26½ miles, hilly route on mountain bike
    – Steady group run, 7¼ miles
23 – Cycling, 19 miles, hilly route on mountain bike

- Treadmill run with strides, 5 miles
24 - Swim, 1000 metres
25 - Rest
26 - Race, half marathon PB, 82 m 38 s
- 3 hour hill run

April
4 - Weights, 11 sets upper body
- Swim, 1200 metres
- Cycling, 19 miles, hilly route on mountain bike
- Steady run – 7½ miles (weak legs)
5 - Cycling, 9 miles
- Hill run, 7½ miles with 3300ft climb (knackered)
- Cycling, 9 miles
6 - Cycling, 51 miles on racing bike
- Steady run, 8 miles (weak legs)
7 - Swim, easy 800 metres
8 - Rest
9 - Hillwalk/jog, 19 miles with 12,150ft of climb
10 - Running intervals, 3 x 1mile (stiff legs)

It must be remembered that this training was done on top of my early morning postal round, which consisted on average of two hours every morning, Monday to Saturday, with a heavy mail bag. This meant that I never really got a true rest day, unless I did no training on a Sunday. That was rarely the case, as a free day meant trying to get in some big hills. This probably helped with the Munro run, where no rest days were scheduled, and only one occurred with the injury.

Sponsors

Several sponsors helped out in different ways, but special thanks have to go to Boyd Tunnock, who not only provided all the Caramel Wafers, Caramel Logs and Teacakes we could eat for the whole journey, but also gave a financial donation towards my costs.

Many thanks also to the following:

Saucony	– Training shoes
Páramo	– Jacket and clothing
Sealskinz	– Waterproof socks
Baxters	– Fine soups
Michelob	– Fine beers
A.G. Barr	– Irn-Bru
McCowan's	– Toffees
Nestlé	– Build-up instant drinks and soups
Dairy Crest	– Frijj milkshakes

Charity

'Bringing joy to terminally and seriously ill children'

Mission Statement, Dreams Come True

As mentioned earlier, I chose to raise funds for the charity Dreams Come True because I liked what they did. I also liked the name. Check out their website to see all the good work they do making the dreams of seriously ill children come true. Donations from the Munro run totalled £3145 for the charity, and as a knock-on effect, I raised a further £321 for them running the Honolulu marathon. These amounts are small compared with big business sponsorship, but they were raised from family and friends, and I was quite happy with the total. I am sure that a few children have benefited as a result.

Motivation

For all that the Munro run was a hugely physical task, the mental aspect was tougher. Much of the time I was in good spirits, especially when new faces were coming and going, but I was also quite crabbit on more than one occasion. I have always known that when tired, I can be curt, and if there is one thing that distinguished the Munro run, it was the state of tiredness and lethargy it constantly left me in. Needless to say, there must have been a few times when Mum and the rest of the back-up crew felt like throttling me. Thanks to their ever-patient good nature, we got by fine.

Out on the hill, most days felt good and some were just magical – the best thing since sliced bread – but one or two did feel like hell on earth. Thankfully, these were few and far between. Sometimes there were variable days, where emotionally I was as up and down as the terrain I was crossing. Again, tiredness and physical duress didn't help, a sort of reverse or inverse psychosomatic relationship was at work, and it was during those times that I used the little motivational cards I carried with me. One of these cards had the following poem, a personal favourite of mine, which helped to keep me keeping on when the going got really tough:

Don't Quit

When things go wrong as they sometimes will;
When the road you're trudging seems all uphill;
When the funds are low, and the debts are high;
And you want to smile, but have to sigh;
When care is pressing you down a bit –
Rest if you must, but don't you quit.
Success is failure turned inside out;
The silver tint of the clouds of doubt;
And you can never tell how close you are;
It may be near when it seems afar.
So, stick to the fight when you're hardest hit –
It's when things go wrong that you mustn't quit.
Anonymous

Belief and Philosophy

It might come as a bit of a surprise, or even a shock, but I do try to be a Christian, with the emphasis very much on trying. Although I don't regularly attend Church anymore, I do still read my Bible, say my prayers, and try to keep life in perspective. I think that's also why I love doing the Wordsworth *Lonely as a Cloud* bit, wandering over the hills and using nature as the great stimulator to ponder on life. As to be expected with a record attempt, there wasn't much time for slow contemplation during the Munro run, but God had certainly come to mind. Not 'God get me out of here!' but more along the lines of how, even with the superb endurance I had at the time, did I make it through some of these big days? It reminds me of the poem *Footprints in the Sand*, for although my physical body was going through the motions, there were times when a divine hand must have been giving me a gentle lift. Thank you, Lord.

'Why, you do not even know what will happen tomorrow. What is your life? You are a mist that appears for a little while and then vanishes.' – James 4:14

The more I go on in this life and the older I get, the more I realise the full implications of the words of the Apostle. How precious time really is; I've seen friends go long before their time. I remember years ago, having decided to have a go at the Munro record, I got bogged down in all the nitty-gritty planning details, I was procrastinating and considering ditching the whole thing. What kept me going was the old deathbed scenario. Imagining lying there and coming out with a string of 'what ifs' and 'if onlys' – surely there can be nothing worse or more crushing to the human spirit than looking back on a life of regrets. Whatever plan or dream gives you inspiration, make it live and make it happen – *carpe diem*!

Miscellaneous

'Don't fret if you find your body cannot run. Just remember to feel the ground beneath your feet – every stone and tussock. Become part of the earth.' –Satish Kumar

This quote, used at the start of Part II, was taken from Damon Rodwell's little book, *The Pixie Run*, where Damon recounts his 23 day run over the South West Coast Path. During his run, Damon was raising funds for Intermediate Technology (now Practical Action), and in relation to this he met up with a director of Schumacher College in Devon. Satish Kumar imparted the above words of wisdom to Damon, and although Damon used several other quotes in his book, this was the one that stuck most in my mind. I have quoted it because it was so apt for the Munro run: there were indeed times when my body would just not run, and I certainly did feel every stone and tussock under my feet, as I was getting ground into the earth.

One question I've often been asked is - 'What was the best day?' That's a fairly difficult question to answer because different days stand out for a variety of reasons; good company, good weather, a big day going to plan, favourite hills and so on. However, if I had to narrow it down to a single day, I would say day 35 was best, the day I completed the Cuillin ridge. Not only had things been set up well the day before, with the successful Kylerhea swim and an enjoyable evening barbecue, but everything on the day itself fell into place. Completing the full ridge and 11 Munros, the good weather, having a laugh with the guys, and the midnight meal with a beer to round things off nicely – perfect! So many people had worked together, in all their different ways, to make that day a success. As such, it was a microcosm of the whole journey. Then, and now, I summed up the Munro run as a 'people thing', and it was the help, the friendship, and the camaraderie, all along the way, that made it special. That's my enduring memory of the summer of 2000.

On the evening I met Andrew Johnston at Aultguish, he told me I would probably feel nothing for a few months after the event, and he was exactly right. I was back at work and jumping through the hoops and it just felt null and void. And just as he had predicted, over the course of six months to a year, the achievement was gradually to sink in, and a small inner contentment developed. Yes, I had failed my original forty-day target, but I had still taken just shy of three days off the old record, dipping below fifty days while also cramming in an extra seven peaks, due to the 1997 SMC review. As the first person to shun ferry, sail boat and kayak, to swim the island sections* and give a 100% self-propelled continuous round, I hope I've left my own little mark in this arena.

*At time of printing, this has still not been repeated.

Hill Running Records

Since the Munro run in 2000, Stephen Pyke ran, cycled and kayaked between the Munros, and on the 3rd of June 2010, smashed the record with a fantastic 39 days 9 hours and 6 minutes. This was a tremendous effort and I was well chuffed for Spyke, and also for myself, as it showed that my forty day plan back in 2000 had not been outwith the realms of possibility. At some point the record will come down again; the Munros in a Month, as Andrew Dempster quoted in his book, must surely be the Holy Grail of ultra-distance hill running in Great Britain, if not the world.

But will anyone be bothered to take the time, money and effort to even make an attempt? We will see.

There is a great section on all sorts of Scottish hill running records at the Scottish Hill Runners website, and Martin Stone keeps a register of Long Distance Individual Fell records and a news summary in the FRA member magazine.

Bibliography

Bennet, D.J. & Anderson, R.A. (eds) (2013): *The Munros. Scottish Mountaineering Club Hillwalkers' Guide.* Scottish Mountaineering Trust.

Brown, H. (2010): *Hamish's Mountain Walk.* Sandstone Press.

Caldwell, C. (1991): *Climb Every Mountain.* Sphere Books.

Dempster, A. (1995): *The Munro Phenomenon.* Mainstream Publishing.

McNeish, C. (1998): *The Munro Almanac.* Neil Wilson Publishing.

Moran, M. (1986): *The Munros in Winter: 277 Summits in 83 Days.* David and Charles.

Rodwell, D. (1996): *The Pixie Run - Running the 610-mile South West Way*

Symonds, H. (2004): *Running High: The First Continuous Traverse of the 303 Mountains of Britain & Ireland.* Hayloft Publishing.

Acknowledgements

Where does one start to thank so many people, who helped in so many different ways to make the run and the record a success? Without making another large list, I'd like to say a heartfelt thank you to everyone mentioned in this book, and sincere apologies if I've missed anyone.

Thanks too to everyone at Ringwood Publishing who have played a part in ensuring my book has made it into publication. Special thanks are due to my editors, Phil Dunshea, John Donnelly and Isobel Freeman, for all their hard work, and to David Webster for the maps and the layout of the book. Thanks too to Eilidh Muldoon for her brilliant cover design.

Also, to the man himself, Sir Hugh T. Munro, whose original list started this crazy, fun-filled pursuit. If he were here today, I would doff my cap to the man whose tables have inspired generations to take to the Scottish hills, giving countless hours of pleasure. There may already be one 'Beautiful Game' in Scotland but, as far as I'm concerned, climbing Munros is the other Beautiful Game – how privileged we are in this little country of ours.

Finally, a massive thanks to Westerlands CCC and Tunnocks for their very much appreciated support in helping get the book published and publicised.

Some other books from Ringwood Publishing

All titles are available from the Ringwood website
(including first edition signed copies)
and from usual outlets.

Also available as e-books

www.ringwoodpublishing.com

mail@ringwoodpublishing.com

Ronnie (A Dog Owner's Guide to Fulfilment)

Susan Campbell

When Susan and Colin Campbell settled down to married life without children, they instinctively felt it was the right time for them to adopt a dog.

Ronnie, a big-hearted lurcher-cross, bounced into their lives and transformed them in unimagined ways; healing past wounds, introducing them to new friends, and pointing them in the direction of life changing opportunities.

This book is the candid, funny and moving story of how one stress busting, four-legged intervention, with a VERY waggy tail, changed everything.

'Ronnie' tells the heart-warming story about how a dog, the power of positive thought and perseverance can completely change your life for the better. Ronnie, a rescue dog from the Dogs Trust, changes the lives of Susan and Colin Campbell for ever. Showing that a dog is never simply a pet, Ronnie not only becomes part of the family, he shapes the careers, and future, of Susan and Colin and shows us that even the most daft of dogs have the power to make the most difficult times in life easier to bear.

Susan, a full-time Life Coach, demonstrates in this engaging book how the interconnection between her professional skills and knowledge, and the lessons being learned from caring for Ronnie, combine to produce lessons of wide relevance. Emotional, uplifting and enlightening, 'Ronnie' captures the special place that animals have in our lives and shows that it is never too late to change your life for the better.

"A joyous must-read for all dog lovers; a moving and inspiring lesson for all those seeking the motivation to change or improve their life."

Or in the words of Phil Cunningham *"If only the whole world had a Ronnie"*

ISBN: 978-1-901514-29-2   £9.99

Jinx Dogs Burns Now Flu

Alex Gordon

Ale Alex Gordon, after almost half-a-century in the Scottish newspaper industry as a Sports Sub-Editor and Editor, spills the beans in a frank and candid manner. Much is revealed within the pages of this book that was previously kept out of the public domain. And you'll see why!

Jinx Dogs Burns Now Flu is a rollicking, often hilarious, trip through the crazy world of Scottish newspapers. It's a journey that takes the reader behind the headlines of the biggest, most sensational stories of our national press. It also introduces the fascinating if madcap characters whose job was to bring you your daily news. Prepare to be bewildered by their antics as they chase front and back page exclusives. You'll be amazed and amused by the tales that did NOT make it into print. Until now, as Jinx Dogs Burns Now Flu brings many sensational stories into print for the first time!

Other stories here throw an entirely new light on what actually happened around many of Scotland's most famous sports stars; stories that will cause quite a few reputations to be reassessed.

ISBN: 978-1-901514-28-5   £9.99

A Subtle Sadness

Sandy Jamieson

A Subtle Sadness is a rigorous exploration of Scottish Identity and the impact on it of the key Scottish obsessions of politics, football, religion, sex and alcohol. It focuses on the family and personal history of Frank Hunter, a sad Scotsman with a self-destruct streak enormous even by normal West of Scotland male standards.

A Subtle Sadness is also the story of a 100 year fight for Scottish Home Rule, from 1890 to 1990, as told by Mary Ewing, a wise but bitter old woman, his guide to his Protestant roots and his political inheritance. It also covers the emotional and political impact of Scotland's quest for the World Cup, with 5 consecutive qualifications in the crucial years from 1973 to 1989.

A Subtle Sadness covers a century of Scottish social, political and football highlights, with disasters and triumphs aplenty, including the impact of Thatcherism on Scotland's industrial base.

ISBN: 978-1-901514-04-9   £9.99

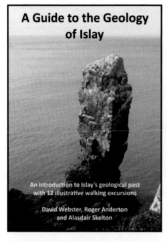

A Guide to the Geology of Islay

A Guide to the Geology of Islay

David Webster, Roger Anderton and Alasdair Skelton

This guide describes 12 varied excursions on Islay that tell the fascinating story of Islay's geological past from 2 billion-year old gneiss to the Ice Age.

The geology of each walk is described at an introductory level with maps and photographs and the book also contains an introduction to geology section.

For those with some geological background there is a section describing Islay's geological framework in more detail with some key references for further reading.

The walks range from leisurely rambles to more demanding longer excursions.

"A geological wonderland" Scotland Outdoors.

" ... will lead us into the unknown and enable us to return, informed and enthused" Scottish Islands Explorer.

" ... explained very clearly with excellent use of maps, diagrams and full-colour photographs" Down to Earth.

ISBN: 978-1-901514-16-2   £14.99

The Activist

Alec Connon

Unfulfilled by student life, Thomas Durant and two friends decide to cycle the length of Britain during their summer holidays, dressed as superheroes. The experience of their short trip is enough to whet Thomas's appetite for further travel and set in motion his decision to drop out of uni and see the world for himself.

Influenced by a burgeoning interest in marine conservation, what begins as a typical gap year develops into over decade's worth of involvement and participation in animal rights activism. The story follows Thomas, from his first tentative steps into the life of an activist in Vancouver, to his battles with the Japanese whaling fleet in the Southern Ocean.

"The enthralling tale presents the plight of the natural world – and its relationship with the human race – with an intimacy that is unlike anything I've ever seen in a novel." Peter Mountford, Washington State Book Aware Winner.

ISBN:978-1-901514-25-4   £9.99